ASSET PRICES AND THE REAL ECONOMY

STUDIES IN BANKING AND INTERNATIONAL FINANCE

General Editor: Geoffrey E. Wood

Roy Batchelor and Geoffrey E. Wood (*editors*)
EXCHANGE RATE POLICY

Forrest Capie and Geoffrey E. Wood (*editors*)
FINANCIAL CRISES AND THE WORLD BANKING SYSTEM

Brian Griffiths and Geoffrey E. Wood (*editors*)
MONETARISM IN THE UNITED KINGDOM
MONETARY TARGETS

Donald R. Hodgman and Geoffrey E. Wood (*editors*)
MACROECONOMIC POLICY AND ECONOMIC
INTERDEPENDENCE

Zannis Res and Simu Motamen (*editors*)
INTERNATIONAL DEBT AND GENERAL BANKING IN THE 1990s

Asset Prices and the Real Economy

Edited by

Forrest Capie
Professor of Economic History
City University
London

and

Geoffrey E. Wood
Professor of Economics
City University
London

in association with
Centre for Banking and International Finance
City University
London

First published in Great Britain 1997 by
MACMILLAN PRESS LTD
Houndmills, Basingstoke, Hampshire RG21 6XS
and London
Companies and representatives
throughout the world

A catalogue record for this book is available
from the British Library.

ISBN 0–333–62892–6

First published in the United States of America 1997 by
ST. MARTIN'S PRESS, INC.,
Scholarly and Reference Division,
175 Fifth Avenue,
New York, N.Y. 10010

ISBN 0–312–12983–1

Library of Congress Cataloging-in-Publication Data
Asset prices and the real economy / edited by Forrest Capie and
Geoffrey E. Wood.
p.   cm.— (Studies in banking and international finance)
Includes bibliographical references and index.
ISBN 0–312–12983–1
1. Securities—Prices.   2. Negotiable instruments—Prices.
3. Real property—Prices.   II. Capie, Forrest.   II. Wood, Geoffrey
Edward.   III. Series.
HG4521.A77   1996
332.63'222—dc20   96–7693
                                                                        CIP

10   9   8   7   6   5   4   3   2   1
06   05   04   03   02   01   00   99   98   97
Printed in Great Britain by
The Ipswich Book Company Ltd
Ipswich, Suffolk

Contents

Notes on the Contributors

Andrew Bain is Visiting Professor in the Department of Political Economy at the University of Glasgow, a board member of Scottish Enterprise, and a member of the Secretary of State for Scotland's Panel of Economic Consultants. He was previously Group Economic Adviser to the Midland Bank and has been a member of the Wilson Committee on the City, the Monopolies Commission, and the Advisory Council on Science and Technology.

Roger Bootle is Chief Economist of the Midland Bank and Chief Economist and Director of Research at HSBC Markets, part of the HSBC Group, where he is also an Executive Director of HSBC Greenwell, the leading gilt-edged market maker. He is the joint author of the book *Theory of Money*, and author of *Index-Linked Gilts* and of many articles. He is a Visiting Professor at Manchester Business School and a well-known broadcaster on radio and television.

Alan Budd has been Chief Economic Adviser to HM Treasury and head of the Government Economic Service since 1991. He was previously Economic Adviser to Barclays Bank. Before that he was Professor of Economics and Director of the Centre for Economic Forecasting at the London Business School. He has been Visiting Professor at Carnegie-Mellon University, Pittsburgh and at the University of New South Wales, Sydney.

Charles W. Calomiris is Professor of Economics at Columbia University. Professor Calomiris is also a faculty research fellow at the National Bureau of Economic Research and an adjunct scholar at the American Enterprise Institute. He currently serves as a consultant for the World Bank and the St Louis and New York Federal Reserve Banks, and has been a visiting scholar at the Federal Reserve Board and the Federal Reserve Bank of Chicago.

Forrest Capie is Professor of Economic History in the Department of Banking and Finance at City University Business School in London. He has also taught at the Universities of Warwick and Leeds. He is Editor of the *Economic History Review*.

Nick Crafts has been Professor of Economic History at London School of Economics since 1995. Previous appointments include Fellow in Economics, University College, Oxford (1977–86), Professor of Economic History, University of Leeds (1987–8) and Professor of Economic History, University of Warwick (1988–95).

Alan Davies became the Chief Economist of Barclays Bank in August 1991. Since graduating from Southampton University, his career has been with Barclays. After a period of five years working in a variety of banking areas, he joined the Economics Department, eventually becoming Head of the Department.

Leigh Drake is Senior Lecturer in the Economics Department at Loughborough University and is Deputy Director of the Loughborough University Banking Centre. His research interests are in the areas of monetary economics and financial institutions and markets. He is author of the book *The Building Society Industry in Transition* (Macmillan, 1989) and has published numerous papers in academic journals.

Barry Eichengreen is John L. Simpson Professor of Economics and Professor of Political Science at the University of California, Berkeley, Research Associate of the National Bureau of Economic Research, and Research Fellow of the Center for Economic Policy Research.

Patrick Foley has been Chief Economic Adviser to Lloyds Bank since 1991. In 1994 he also took a responsibility for the Bank's group strategic planning. He has written numerous articles for Lloyds Bank publications and for outside journals and has contributed to a number of books an issues including the economics of the professions, the state of the economy; inflation and exchange rate economics. He is editor and principal contributor to *Lloyds Bank Economic Bulletin*.

Richard S. Grossman is Associate Professor of Economics of Wesleyan University, Middletown, Connecticut.

Lars Jonung is Professor of Economics at the Stockholm School of Economics, Stockholm, Sweden. His main research interest is monetary economics and the evolution of stabilisation policies. His research has dealt with monetary history, central bank behaviour, inflationary expectations and Swedish economic thought, in particular the work of Knut Wicksell. Jonung served as Chief Economic Adviser to the Prime Minister of Sweden (1992–4).

Kagehide Kaku is currently Director of the Bank Supervision Department of the Bank of Japan. He has worked in several different departments of the Bank since joining is in 1965.

Mervyn King joined the LSE as Professor of Economics in October 1984 after teaching at Cambridge and Birmingham Universities, and spells as Visiting Professor at Harvard and MIT. He is the author of books and articles on corporate taxation and finance, and reform of the British tax system. In 1990 Professor King became a non-executive director of the Bank of England. During the autumn of 1990 he was Visiting Professor of Economics at Harvard University and Senior Olin Fellow at the National Bureau of Economic Research. On 1 March 1991 he became Chief Economist and Executive Director at the Bank of England. Mervyn King is a Fellow of the British Academy and a member of Academia Europaea and a past President of the European Economic Association.

David Llewellyn is Professor of Money and Banking at Loughborough University and Chairman of Loughborough University Banking Centre. He is also a Public Interest Director of the Personal Investment Authority (London), and a member of the International Advisory Board of the Italian Bankers Association. He has been a Visiting Scholar at central banks in Scandinavia.

Allan Meltzer is University Professor of Political Economy and Public Policy at Carnegie Mellon University. He has been a Visiting Professor at Harvard, University of Chicago, University of Rochester, City University, London and others. He has acted as a consultant as a consultant to the President's Council of Economic Advisers, the US Treasury Department, the Board of Governors of the Federal Reserve System, to foreign governments and central banks, and the President's Economic Policy Advisory Board. Currently, he is Honorary Adviser to the Institute for Monetary and Economic Studies of the Bank of Japan and a Visiting Scholar at the American Enterprise Institute.

Terence C. Mills is Professor of Economics at Loughborough University, having previously held professional appointments at City University Business School and the University of Hull. He is the author of two books on time series econometrics and over seventy articles in journals and books.

Athanasios Orphanides is an economist in the Monetary Affairs Division at the Board of Governors of the Federal Reserve System. He did his undergraduate work in economics and mathematics at the Massachusetts Institute of Technology and completed a PhD in economics at the same institution in 1990. While at the Board of Governors, Orphanides has also tought monetary economics at Georgetown University and the Johns Hopkins University.

Gordon Pepper, CBE, is a Professor in the Department of Banking and Finance at City University Business School. He has been a member of the committee on Industry and Finance, National Economic Development Council, and of the Economic and Social Research Council. Prior to joining City University he was Joint Senior Partner of W. Greenwell & Co. and subsequently chairman of Greenwell Montagu. Professor Pepper's publications include *Money, Credit and Inflation*, Research Monograph 44, IEA, 1990 and *Money, Credit and Asset Prices* (1994). In the 1970s he was editor of *Greenwells Monetary Bulletin* which became one of the most widely read monetary economic publications produced in the UK in the 1970s.

Anna J. Schwartz, a member of the research staff of the National Bureau of Economic Research, is a Distinguished Fellow of the American Economic Association. She is co-author with Milton Friedman of studies of monetary economics. A collection of her articles, *Money in Historical Perspective*, was published in 1987.

Steven A. Sharpe is an economist in the Division of Research and Statistics at the Federal Reserve Board, where he has been employed since 1986 after receiving a PhD in Economics at Stanford University. His current position is senior economist in the Capital Markets section, with responsibility for conducting research on a broad spectrum of issues in finance and economics.

Joakim Stymne was educated at the Stockholm School of Economics and Harvard University. His main research interests are in international economics, especially sovereign debt, and in issues concerning economic growth. In 1991–2 he advised the Polish government, and in 1992–4 he was economic adviser to the Swedish Prime Minister. He is currently chief economist with Alfred Berg, a Swedish investment bank.

John Whittaker is Principal Lecturer at Staffordshire University. He was previously Associate Professor of Economics at Cape Town University and has held visiting positions with the City University Business School and with the University of Nottingham. His research interest is monetary policy.

Geoffrey E. Wood is Professor of Economics at City University in London. He has also taught at the University of Warwick, and has been with the research staff of both the Bank of England and the Federal Reserve Bank of St Louis. He also acts as Economic Adviser to the Union Discount Company of London and is a Managing Trustee of the Institute of Economic Affairs.

Opening Remarks

Gordon Pepper

In macroeconomic as in microeconomic analysis, it is important to distinguish stocks from flows. The accounts of a company can be used to illustrate the difference: a balance sheet is about stocks; a trading account is about flows. The same distinction also occurs in national accounts. The Keynesian income–expenditure tradition is about the economics of flows, as in Monetarism with attention focused on changes in the rate of growth of the money supply rather than on its level. The city University Debt-Deflation Conference held in April 1994, by contrast, was about balance sheets; that is, it was about stock economics. This is a subject which, although not ignored, has received much less attention than flow economics.

Stocks affect flows. The strength of balance sheets affects expenditure decisions, but the concept of balance sheet strength needs defining. Precisely what is meant by over-extended balance sheets and over-indebtedness? Which ratios are the more important? Debt–income or debt–wealth, to give an example of two distinct types? Other factors are also relevant, for example the amount of debt that will need to be refinanced over the short term and the quality of banking relationships.

Various degrees of balance sheet influence can be identified. Starting with the smallest, any significant change in wealth and confidence has some effect on expenditure decisions. Major changes that are the result of credit cycles and financial bubbles have a greater effect. There are two cases here. The first is where symmetry exists between an upswing and a downswing of a cycle. The second is where there is asymmetry in which case the impact on expenditure decisions can be magnified. Asymmetry starts when a decline in the value of assets is so large that there are widespread examples of the value of collateral falling below the amount of a loan being secured. People then become afraid of financial difficulties and retrench. The next stage is people and companies being declared bankrupt. What follows is banks calling in loans because their capital has been depleted by bad debts, which causes further bankruptcies. The final stage of asymmetry is bank failures, and depositors losing their money.

Various intermediate stages can be discussed, for example banks

1

becoming risk adverse, asymmetry of information, general deterioration in credit-worthiness and collapse of loan demand because people have witnessed the bitter experience of others getting too deeply into debt.

The term 'debt-deflation' probably implies asymmetry but it and the other degrees of balance sheet influence need to be defined, as does balance sheet strength. One of my hopes of the conference was that they would be. Precision is needed.

Returning to a company's accounts, the strength of a balance sheet can alter quickly but there can also be trends that materialise over the long term. Balance sheet strength can alter quickly because of refinancing. This could happen for example, by an issue of ordinary shares to re-pay a bank loan, or because of a valuation change that affects wealth, such as the revaluation of property. In contrast, the cumulative effect of trading profits or losses over the years appears only slowly. The result of the latter can be a long-term trend that eventually becomes most significant. Quick changes and long-term trends can also occur in national accounts.

I am concerned about a possible long-term trend in national accounts which is continuing. There would appear to be three possibilities. The first is that the danger of debt-deflation has been peculiar to the cur-rent business cycle; that is, there is not a long-term trend. The second is that debt-deflation will rear its ugly head again in the future; a problem of roughly similar size has merely been postponed until after the end of the next boom or the one after. The third is that the underlying situation is becoming worse; that is, that there is an adverse long-term trend.

Anyone arguing that debt-deflation has been peculiar to the current cycle must explain why the cycle has been special. A word of caution is appropriate. Special explanations for events that are *a priori* unex-pected are easy to find with hindsight, and may be erroneous. General explanations are to be preferred. In the current circumstances an ex-planation that helps to explain deflation in the 1930s carries more cred-ibility than a special one that does not. Financial innovation is an example of a such a general explanation.

The following thoughts perturb me. The first is that there have been historical episodes in which over-indebtedness has been corrected quickly but in a most undesirable way. Hyper-inflation and financial crashes wipe out debt and wars can lead to repudiation of debt. We must be thankful that these have been avoided this time, but has debt been reduced sufficiently to restore economies to health?

The second thought is that the debt–income ratio tends to improve if the rate of growth of national income in nominal terms is greater than the level of nominal interest, whereas it deteriorates if interest rates are above the growth of national income. This is almost the same as saying that the debt–income ratio tends to improve if real rates of interest are below normal but it deteriorates if they are above normal. In the latter case the remorseless power of compound interest is stopping people from getting out of debt. It is worrying that real rates still remain historically high in many countries.

The third thought is that much of the recent decline in private sector debt has merely been transferred to the public sector without there being an overall reduction in debt. In effect, the debt has been nationalised. The most obvious example of this happening is the transfer of the debts of savings and loans organisations in the USA. Another very general example is large budget deficits, which have the same overall effect of transferring debt from the private to the public sector. Over-indebtedness may in due course reappear, but in a different guise.

The question that I most wished to hear answered at the conference was whether the danger of debt-deflation had indeed been peculiar to the current business cycle, whether the problem had merely been postponed until the next recession, or whether there was an adverse underlying trend.

City University Business School, April 1994

Introduction: Asset Prices and the Real Economy[1]

Forrest Capie and Geoffrey E. Wood

The recession which many countries experienced in the early 1990s had certain unusual aspects. Most notably, and common to all countries, was the behaviour of asset prices relative to the general price level. Before the recession, the prices of both real and financial assets had risen very substantially. This rise was reversed with great speed while the general price level, in contrast, slowed in its rate of increase but fell nowhere. Also much discussed was the fact that most economies entered the recession with an unusually high level of debt relative to income. When the recession came it was in some countries – such as Britain – long lasting, and in some – such as Sweden – unusually severe. In consequence reasons were sought to explain these (and other, noted below) special characteristics of the recession. As a result of the behaviour of asset prices attention turned to 'debt-deflation theories' associated in different forms with J.M. Keynes and Irving Fisher.

These theories, as their name makes clear, claim an important role for debt in causing or exacerbating recession; and they were originally promulgated when there was a recession in the UK, and a depression of extraordinary severity in the USA. Could they, perhaps, somehow modified, help explain the unusual characteristics of the recession of the 1990s? The chapters in this volume are derived from papers (and comments on them) given at a conference held to discuss these issues. In this Introduction we first discuss briefly the theories, their history and their historical context, and their current applicability. We then set out the main points of the Chapters in the volume. The Introduction concludes with a summary of the main general points to emerge from the conference discussions.

THE THEORIES

Interest in the effects of the behaviour of the general price level on the real economy may have been revived by James Tobin in 1975. In a paper published in that year he pointed out that while a once for all fall in the price level could stimulate the real economy (via the real balance effect), a *falling* price level, if it were expected to continue, would lead to a move into money and away from physical assets, raise the real rate of interest (as in Mundell, 1963), and lead to deferral of spending so long as prices were expected to continue to fall. This analysis did not have any particular role for debt in the process; but it did bring to the attention of economists in general what had for many years been a minority interest – the possibility that price flexibility might be destabilising.

This possibility had been discussed by Keynes in the *General Theory* (1936) and by Fisher in several places, but most notably in *Booms and Depressions* (1932) and 'The Debt-Deflation Theory of Great Depressions' (1933). The two, somewhat different, theories of these authors are the basis of the debate on the role of debt. We summarise them before turning to some modern theories, which by different but manifestly related routes also give debt an influence on economic activity.

Keynes's main objective when discussing price flexibility (Chapter 19 of the *General Theory*) was to show that a fall in the price level could not be counted on to restore economic activity to a non-depression level. Keynes argued that a fall in money wages and prices need not increase aggregate demand. However, it *could* increase aggregate demand through three channels:

> the reduction in money wages will have no lasting tendency to increase employment, except by virtue of its repercussions either on the propensity to consume for the community as a whole, or on the schedule of marginal efficiencies of capital, or on the rate of interest. (Keynes, 1936, p. 262)

Keynes also identified several ways by which a fall in (or falling) money wages might fail to stimulate demand. It could, he thought, redistribute income from workers and entrepreneurs to rentiers. This would increase the overall propensity to save. (There is further discussion of this channel in Chapter 5 by Mervyn King (pp. 197–227) and the comments on it (pp. 228–41).) In an open economy, while the fall in prices would stimulate demand for home goods (given a fixed exchange rate) this effect would be offset to some extent by the effect of the worsening terms of trade. There could be an intertemporal substitution effect; if wages were thought to be low relative to future wages, investment would rise. But, on the other hand, if wages were still falling, and expected to be still lower in the future, investment spending would await further wage falls. The fall would reduce money demand relative to money supply; but the resulting positive effect of interest rates on spending could readily be offset by uncertainty engendered by falling prices. If businessmen thought that wages *to them*, rather than wages in general, had fallen, they would employ more workers. But, against this, Keynes pointed out that if workers also had limited information (as seems a reasonable assumption), they would resist wage reductions in the belief that they applied to them only, rather than being part of a generally falling price level.

So far there appears no particular role for debt (although it should be noted that, as discussed in King (op. cit.), debt can explain the different savings behaviour of entrepreneurs and rentiers). The next channel has an explicit role for debt:

> the depressing influence on entrepreneurs of their greater burden of debt may partly offset any cheerful reactions from the reduction of wages. Indeed, if the fall of wages and prices goes too far, the embarrassment of those entrepreneurs who are heavily indebted may soon reach the point of insolvency – with severely adverse effects on investment. (Keynes, 1936, p. 253)

That last channel seems to be what many recent commentators had in mind. It was not, however, one which Keynes emphasised. He focused on an intertemporal substitution channel, and the effect of falling prices on real interest rates, which he summarised thus:

> the effect of an expectation that wages are going to lag by, say, 2 per cent in the coming year will be roughly equivalent to the effect of a rise of 2 per cent in the amount of interest payable for the same period.[2] (Keynes, 1936, p. 265)

Although debt plainly had a role, it was not key to explaining why deflation would not revive output. Further, it seems that Keynes was, in Chapter 19 of the *General Theory*, not aiming to produce a 'debt-deflation' theory of the business cycle. His concern was to argue that falling (or lower) prices could not be relied on to cure recessions. In contrast, Fisher argued that debt was of major importance in cyclical fluctuations.[3]

The Great Depression of 1929–32 in the USA was one of the most dramatic events in the economic history of the world. The scale of the

collapse in output and the failure of the financial system left economics
in some considerable disarray. A long list of explanations poured forth
at the time and soon after, and explanations have continued to do ever
since. Many of the early attempts at explanation contained essential
elements of what now goes to make up the most widely accepted view
– monetary policy failure related to the operation of the gold standard.
But an important strand in the explanation that appeared at the time
but was not picked up has been emerging in the last decade or so; the
role of financial markets and their relationship with the monetary sector
and the real economy.

The earliest contribution on this was made by Fisher. Fisher's name,
naturally enough, will keep cropping up in the chapters in this book,
and some explanations are also given as to why his ideas failed to
have greater impact at the time (such as King, pp. 221–3). As noted,
in his *Booms and Depressions*, Fisher developed what he called a debt-
deflation theory of great depressions. He stated that he believed his
views were essentially new. When he made a summary statement in
the article 'The Debt-Deflation Theory of Great Depressions', he claimed
that the novelty of his views had been confirmed by other authorities.

The essence of Fisher's theory was that in the normal path of economic
activity there were occasional disturbances which led to new opportunities
to invest (this would be the case particularly when there were spectacular
new inventions). These would lead to what Fisher called over-
indebtedness,[4] and subsequent attempts to liquidate debt led to falling
asset prices after which distress selling took over. In Fisher's model
this led to a fall in the general level of prices and then to a still greater
fall in the net worth of business. Bankruptcies followed, and so led on
to the fall in the real economy. Obviously a large number of complicated
inter-relationships existed among the variables. But debt and deflation
went a long way to explaining a great number of phenomena. Fisher
argued further that when over-indebtedness stood alone and did not
lead to a fall in prices the resulting cycle would be milder.

Fisher felt that his model had application to a number of previous
experiences in US history. But it was the great depression of the early
thirties in the USA that was for Fisher, 'an example of a debt-deflation depression of the most serious sort' (1933, 345). The scale of
debt in 1929 was, he claimed, the greatest ever known both in nominal and real terms. When liquidation took place it *reduced* the nominal debt by 20 per cent by March 1933, but the price fall at that point
had resulted in real debt *rising* by 40 per cent.

The downturn started, Fisher thought, with the economy in a state of over-indebtedness. Some event caused a change in confidence, which in turn caused distress selling; note, then, that the theory requires an exogenous shock to set the cycle off. Some bank loans are repaid, and in view of the climate new ones are not extended. The money supply therefore falls. (Fisher implicitly assumed the absence of offsetting central bank action.) This leads to a fall in prices, and reductions in net worth and in profits. There is a fall in output and unemployment, an increase in pessimism, hoarding of money, a fall in nominal interest rates, and a rise in real rates.

The combination of debt and deflation was, in Fisher's view, crucial, and he provided a vivid account of how debt and deflation produce recessions:

> The very effort of individuals to lessen their burden of debts increases it, because of the mass effect of the stampede to liquidate in swelling each dollar owed. [Fisher's phrase for a rise in the purchasing power of money.] Then we have the great paradox which, I submit, is the chief secret of most, if not all, great depressions: the more debtors pay, the more they owe. (1933, p. 344)

In other words, the process of paying off debt leads to a decline in the money stock and in prices. That last fall leads to a further rise in the burden of debt, and eventually even the best of risks is not safe. Hence once a shock is given to an indebted economy, a process which produces a severe recession inevitably follows. That would certainly seem to accord with at least casual observation of recent experience in Britain, Japan and Sweden (all of which countries are discussed in subsequent chapters). Before turning to a review of these chapters, however, a brief examination of modern extensions of the debt-deflation theories is useful.

In both Keynes and Fisher, the effect of falling prices on redistributing wealth from debtors to creditors was important. Recently-developed theories also have an important role for that redistribution. If information is 'asymmetric', in that insiders to a firm (its managers and financial advisers) have more information about the firm and its prospects that do 'outsiders' (the relatively uninformed equity and debt holders), then the insiders can supply funds at lower cost. Thus changes in the distribution of wealth will increase the cost of capital, if the distribution shifts from insiders to outsiders.

Bernanke (1983) extended this analysis in his study of the Great Depression. The destruction of financial intermediaries and the reduction in borrowers' net worth, both results of deflation, increased the marginal cost of funds by eroding the equity stakes of insiders and reducing (by their failures) access to well informed ('inside') banks. Financial collapse was not, then, just a symptom of the recession: once the process of collapse was under way, it served to make the recession deeper.

RECENT BACKGROUND

There was a long period of relatively steady growth around the world from the 1940s through to the 1970s. This probably contributed to Fisher's ideas being neglected. The experience of many OECD countries in the 1980s and 1990s brought a change.

There was in these later decades remarkably similar experience across countries: steady growth in output, but above all rapidly rising asset prices, there then followed a sharp reversal. Many of the explanatory factors are naturally common to many countries. It is interesting to note how often this applies in the modern world economy as fashions in ideas and practice spread rapidly. When the histories of these countries are studied in isolation there is a danger of attributing some result to a cause that looks specific to that country. But a little comparative history brings out how common the experience was, and shifts attention to other explanations. An example is the 'cheap money' policy followed in Britain in the late 1940s and reversed in the 1950s. This used to be told in terms of the Labour Government being replaced by a Conservative Government which had a stronger commitment to sound money. But with perspective and greater familiarity with the experience of others it has become clearer that the 'cheap money' was partly a function of excess liquid balances built up in wartime (this was true of many countries), and the reversal of policy came with the Korean war boom and world-wide rise in inflationary pressures (and again was common to many countries). Recent experience provides a sharp reminder of the usefulness of such comparisons, and it is to discussions of this recent experience that this Introduction now turns.

ORGANISATION OF THE VOLUME

The UK–Mervyn King

In his Chapter 5, Mervyn King draws attention to the unusual behaviour of consumption in the UK in the recession of the early 1990s. It fell much more, relative to income, than was usual in post-1945 recessions. This fall in consumption was not, however, unique in the experience of all twentieth-century recessions. It happened in other countries in this recent recession, and in the USA in the 1930s. Debt enters King's analysis because there was, in all these episodes where consumption fell abnormally, an abnormal prior rise in debt relative to income. King's chapter links those phenomena, by using a model with *two* 'representative agents'.

There are creditors and debtors; when the price level falls, the burden of debt increases as debts are fixed in nominal terms. Debtors therefore increase their savings. Creditors meanwhile do not reduce their savings by an offsetting amount so there is a fall in aggregate consumption. The model certainly corresponds to a wide range of 'real world' situations, when debtors borrow to buy assets whose price risk they bear entirely by themselves. The model does not explain why the recession started – there must be a shock of some sort to start the process off – but once started, it provides a mechanism by which it is prolonged, can explain why consumption falls abnormally when the initial level of debt is unusually high, and is consistent – a notable feature – with time series as well as cross-section data. It also shows how in some circumstances a single representative agent model is not a useful simplification, and that greater complexity is sometimes not only helpful but actually essential.

That model is rooted in the work of both Fisher and Keynes and, by extending them, gives an insight into one part of the cyclical process.

The UK–Llewellyn and Drake

British experience has similarities with Swedish (discussed below), but there are also differences. Llewellyn and Drake in Chapter 3 focus on the dramatic decline in bank lending after 1989, which followed several years of very high lending growth. That left debt–income and gearing ratios in both the personal and corporate sector at unprecedented levels. Llewellyn and Drake's suggestion is that this represents a stock adjustment correction following an earlier overshooting, and a return to more normal balance sheet positioning by both borrowers and lenders. (Llewellyn had earlier advanced this explanation for Sweden, see Llewellyn, 1992.) Chapter 3, therefore, concentrates on the role of banks in the great growth of credit in the 1980s and in the following 'credit crunch'.

Llewellyn and Drake use a simple but powerful model of bank

behaviour in the period 1975–93. They conclude that supply side-factors, brought about by deregulation stimulating competition, were prominent in the great expansion of credit in the 1980s. The fall in lending that followed is found, not surprisingly, to be explained by lenders sorting out a more sustainable portfolio of risks, and borrowers reducing debt–gearing ratios. But Llewellyn and Drake take this further in an examination of the under-estimating and under-pricing of risk and of the effects of an incipient capital constraint resulting in securitisation and cuts in devidends and so on. They provide econometric support for supply-side impulses and 'dismiss the notion that the decline in bank lending simply reflected a decline in the demand for external funding associated with the course of the business cycle' (p. 156).

The USA–Eichengreen and Grossman

Eichengreen and Grossman in Chapter 2 extend the work of Bernanke (noted above), in that they seek to distinguish between the effect of collapsing asset and commodity prices in causing bank failures and thus increasing the costs of financial intermediation (i.e. thus restricting the supply of lending) and the extent to which collapsing prices operate by reducing the ability of non-financial debtors to borrow, thus reducing demand. Further, they also look for second-round effects, by trying to measure the importance of bank failures in reducing asset prices and thereby depressing consumption, and they compare that effect on consumption with that of reducing consumption by disrupting access to finance.

They are, in effect, trying to distinguish between and assess the importance of supply and demand shifts on credit growth and consumption. These are important and interesting questions, relevant in understanding recent experience and in the still-continuing debate over why the US inter-war recession was so severe. Was it due entirely to monetary shocks, or did disruption of financial intermediation play other than a trivial role?

A crucial aspect of the study is to identify when debt-deflation occurred. Not all bank failures lead to such an episode. The currency–deposit ratio varies – how big a rise in it signals a crisis? Eichengreen and Grossman suggest that one should use a combination measure, looking at numbers of failed banks, their size (as measured by assets), and various other measures. Even such a combination of course requires judgement of how big a shock is a crisis, and the data are not all available before 1916 – a crucial drawback as the authors wish to compare the US experience after the civil war with US experience in the 1929–33 recession. Accordingly, Eichengreen and Grossman use interest rate spreads as a measure of debt-deflation, on the grounds that deflation reduces the value of collateral and thus leads to bigger spreads. By use of vector autoregression (VAR) models, the authors then examine the two periods, and conclude that debt-deflation mattered for recession before 1913, but in the 'Great Depression' contributed nothing in addition to the already widely discussed effects of money, interest rates, exchange rates, and financial panic. Chapter 2 is wide-ranging and fascinating. It does not explain *why* debt deflation mattered before 1913 but not after, and there are doubts over using the spread as a measure of debt-deflation. But the chapter is a pioneering attempt at quantification in this area, raises fascinating questions, and should prompt much further work. In particular, is asymmetric information crucial to the cycle or, as Anna Schwartz suggests (both in her Comment here, pp. 100–5 and elsewhere (1994) is price level unpredictability the crucial influence leading to widespread borrower and lender distress, and the difficulties and sometimes failure of financial institutions?[5]

The USA–Calomiris, Orphanides and Sharpe

Calomiris, Orphanides and Sharpe start their Chapter 4 by noting that '"Debt-deflation" refers to one of the ways in which the cumulative past of the economy matters for its future evolution. In a debt-deflation, existing [non-contingent] debt contracts become a burden on producers, consumers, or intermediaries, and prevent them from achieving levels of activity they would otherwise have achieved' (p. 169).

There are incentives to issue debt, as the authors show from their review of the literature. The US (and other) tax systems provide an incentive by allowing the deduction of interest but not dividends; debt finance limits moral hazard and monitoring costs in the presence of asymmetric information; rapid expansion can sometimes be better than slow, thus leading to accumulation of debt (as well as equity); and firms may simply underestimate the effects of a downturn on their activities.

How important in affecting aggregate activity is the debt accumulated for these reasons? Drawing on previous work by Calomiris and Hubbard (1990), the authors suggest that the effects are asymmetric, depending on whether the firm's sales are growing or shrinking. They then proceed to test whether debt acts as an 'asymmetric conditioning variable' in affecting the response of investment to changes in other variables.

As aggregate debt: asset data may conceal the condition of debt-constrained firms, the authors use panel data – a set of durable goods manufacturers for the years 1959–85. Examining the importance of debt during cyclical expansions and contractions (as identified by the NBER), they find that debt propagates shocks in downturns but not upturns. The authors conclude by suggesting further ways by which the importance of leverage can be measured more accurately.

Sweden–Lars Jonung and Joakim Stymne

It is widely appreciated that around the world in the past 10 years there has been a strong boom in asset prices and a deep and/or long recession following the end of that boom. Sweden and Japan are commonly thought to be extreme examples of either the boom or collapse (or both), and British experience can be taken as an example of the intermediate position.

Chapter 1 by Jonung and Stymne shows why Sweden has often been cited in the recent past as a prime example of boom and bust in its acute form. The 1980s was a decade of solid growth in real output, accompanied by a particularly strong surge in asset prices, notably in the stock market and property. At the end of the 1980s asset prices were falling sharply and the three years of recession, 1991, 1992 and 1993, were the deepest and longest recession in Sweden for 60 years.

It is the interaction between the stock variables, debt and wealth, and flow variables such as income, that interest Jonung and Stymne. They draw attention to a number of explanatory variables, many of them common to other OECD countries with similar experiences. But they emphasise two shifts that took place in Sweden in the 1980s. There was one from a highly regulated economy, and a heavily regulated monetary and financial system, to one that was more market-based. Second, there was a regime change in the conduct of monetary policy; there was a political consensus to turn the Krona into a hard currency. Jonung and Stymne argue that it was the considerably changed competitive environment for financial institutions that led to more aggressive lending: that the boom was created by weak balance sheets and financial fragility. The severity of the ensuing crisis, however, is not really due to the burden of debt built up in the boom. The banking system did have severe problems, and borrowing costs did rise disproportionately for lower quality borrowers. But, the authors conclude, 'It is possible to understand the downturn primarily as a rational response to a rapid and fundamental regimes shift' (p. 52). Debt in their view did play a role, but only a supporting one. Jonung and Stymne's chapter has the further merit of placing recent experience in historical perspective, bringing out the similarities and differences with some inter-war experience.

Japan–Kaku

At the end of the 1980s and beginning of 1990s one of the most striking features of world asset prices was the collapse in the Japanese stock market and its failure to bounce back. The Japanese market came out of the 1987 world stock market collapse in better shape than most, but then from a peak in December 1989 fell more than 50 per cent and has continued at a low level since. Stories of parallel property price experience followed and the true fragility of the banking sector was said to be greater than it appeared.

Kaku provides an abundance of data and a battery of tests on these data in his examination of the Japanese experience, particularly the price experience in goods and assets, concerning the growth of indebtedness in both the household and corporate sector. He also shows the increasing fragility of the financial system.

In contrast to the British experience, Kaku argues that demand factors must be the dominant ones in Japan – essentially since bank lending remained stagnant after big reductions in interest rates. The demand for bank loans was low because the economic outlook remained uncertain. But Kaku accepts that the fragility of the financial system has restrained bank lending to some extent.

CONCLUSIONS

Looking over all the chapters and comments in this volume, the striking common feature is how hard it is to find significant macroeconomic consequences of fluctuations of asset prices. Even the Japanese experience seems to show no more than a hint of such consequences. There may have been effects on the composition of national income, as between consumption and other categories, but effects on the total do not stand out. In general, the behaviour of asset prices both in boom and in slump seemed to be a consequence of prior policy (or policy regime) changes. These changes are in turn sufficient by themselves to explain the behaviour of the economy; asset prices do not need to be invoked as an additional explanatory variable. It may well be, of course, that further work using two (or more) sector models, as in Mervyn King's Chapter 5, changes this conclusion. But on the evidence presented here, the behaviour of asset prices should not be of great concern to policy makers, or to those concerned simply to understand the behaviour of the economy as a whole.

Notes

1.　We are indebted to the ESRC and the Clearing Banks for assistance in organising the conference at which these papers were first presented.
2.　This depresses output, rather than simply changes its composition, as in Mundell (1963) because of Keynes's assumption of some degree of price stickiness.
3.　In her comments on Chapter 2 by Eichengreen and Grossmann (p. 8) Anna Schwartz maintains that Fisher emphasised the importance of debt as a result of his own experience of its effects.
4.　In his Opening Remarks, Gordon Pepper drew attention to this concept (pp. 1–3), and pointed out how it was both ill-defined and often used.
5.　Such price level instability was certainly important in the UK secondary banking crisis of 1979. See Reid (1982).

References

Akerlof, G. and J. Yellen (1985) 'A Near-Rational Model of the Business Cycle with Wage and Price Inertia', *Quarterly Journal of Economics*, 1001, 823–38.
Bernanke, B.S. (1983) 'Non-Monetary Effects of the Financial Crisis in the Propagation of the Great Depression', *American Economic Review*, 73, 257–76.
Calomiris, C.W. and R.G. Hubbard (1990) 'Internal Finance and Investment: Evidence from the Undistributed Profits Tax of 1936–1937', NBER. *Working Paper*, 4288 (March 1993).
Fisher, I. (1932) *Booms and Depressions* (London: George Allen & Unwin).
Fisher, I. (1933) 'The Debt-Deflation Theory of Great Depressions', *Econometrica*, 1 (October), 337–57.
Keynes, J.M. (1936) *The General Theory of Employment, Interest and Money* (London: Macmillan).
Llewellyn, D. (1992) 'Scandinavian Banking: The crises and lessons' *Banking World*, October.
Mundell, R.A. (1963) 'Inflation and Real Interest', *Journal of Political Economy*, 71 (June), 280–3.
Reid, M. (1982) *The Secondary Banking Crisis* (London: Macmillan).
Schwartz, A.J. (1988) 'Financial Stability and the Federal Safety Net', in W.S. Haraf and R.M. Kushmeider (eds), *Restructuring Banking and Financial*

Services in America (Washington, DC: American Enterprise Institute), 34–62.

Schwartz, A.J. (1994) 'Systemic Risk and the Macroeconomy', Conference on Banking, Financial Markets and Systemic Risk, sponsored by the Office of the Controller of the Currency (Washington, DC).

Tobin, J. (1975) 'Keynesian Models of Recession and Depression', *American Economic Review Proceedings*, 65, 195–202.

1 The Great Regime Shift: Asset Markets and Economic Activity in Sweden, 1985–93[1]

Lars Jonung and Joakim Stymne

INTRODUCTION

The Swedish economy has undergone spectacular convulsions since the mid-1980s. Several aspects of the development are common to many industrialised countries: an unusually long period of economic expansion, involving financial liberalisation and characterised by low real rates of interest, rising asset prices, rapid growth in private consumption, declining household saving rates and rising corporate and household indebtedness. Eventually this period of expansion was followed by downturns of varying severity, with increasing real rates of interest accompanied by falling asset prices, balance sheet consolidation, financial fragility, slow or negative income growth, rising unemployment, and expanding public deficits. This cycle is prominent in countries such as the USA, Japan and the UK.[2] In Sweden, the turnaround was particularly dramatic.[3] Therefore, the Swedish case is of special interest when studying the anatomy of the process.

A distinguishing feature of macroeconomic events since the early 1980s has been that the role of asset prices has been more central to cyclical developments than previously in the post-Second World War period, during both the upturn and the downturn. This was unpredicted and, at least initially, poorly understood. Asset market boom–bust cycles are well-known from economic history (Kindleberger, 1978) and did receive early attention (Fisher, 1932, 1933). Such cycles have not been prominent in the post-1945 experience of the industrialised world. As a consequence, the role of assets has in recent decades been subordinated to flow concepts in the analysis of aggregate economic fluctuations. Understandably, macroeconomic events in the past decade have changed this. The downturn of the world's stock markets in October 1987 and rising private indebtedness raised concerns about the fragility of the financial system.[4] The interaction between stock variables such as debt and wealth and flow variables such as investment and consumption has attracted new interest.[5]

This chapter focuses on the recent Swedish experience. Although a downturn was expected after the overheated late 1980s, the severity of the crisis came as a surprise. No commentators had predicted its depth or length. Real GDP exhibited three years (1991–3) of consecutive decline for the first time this century, not excluding war years. By 1993, GDP had fallen to its 1987 level.[6] During this downturn, rising real interest rates exposed the fragility of the financial sector which entered a period of deep crisis, necessitating large-scale government support to ailing banks and financial institutions. Unemployment reached unprecedented levels, and huge public deficits appeared, leading to an increase in the ratio of public debt to GDP by 30 percentage points between 1990 and 1993. Only in 1994 did Sweden start coming out of its deepest recession since the 1930s.

Why were the Swedish events so dramatic? What caused the rapid expansion of asset prices in the second half of the 1980s? What caused the drop in asset prices in the early 1990s, and how was this related to the severe economic contraction? These are key questions for the chapter. A central thesis is that a great – and unexpected – regime shift took place in the early 1990s. A number of more or less permanent policy changes were made, most importantly a rapid transition from a high-inflation to a low-inflation economy. In this chapter, we explore the developments that in effect forced the policy-makers to carry out the regime shift, we discuss its character, and we analyse the immediate consequences. The chapter is organised as follows. We first review briefly some central developments during the expansion period 1985–90 compared with the downturn of 1991–3. The next section discusses the asset inflation period 1985–90, highlighting factors that affected lender and borrower behaviour. The third section analyses factors behind the sharp downturn of 1990–3, with a focus on the financial crisis. In the fourth section the crisis is analysed in a historical perspective. The fifth section draws some conclusions.

KEY DEVELOPMENTS

Table 1.1 highlights the development of some central variables during the boom period of 1985–90 and the bust period of 1991–3. The year

Table 1.1   Macroeconomic indicators for Sweden, 1985–90 and 1991–3

	Boom period (1985–90)	Bust period (1991–93)
Real GDP[1]	2.3	−2.0
Nominal GDP[1]	9.4	1.8
CPI[1]	6.2	5.4
Real private consumption[1]	2.7	−1.6
Exports[1]	3.1	2.3
Stock market, total index[1,2]	17.1	1.9
Total lending[1,2]	20.5	0.0
Commercial property prices (Stockholm office buildings, prime location)[1]	18.2	−26.5
Fixed investment, per cent of GDP[3]	20.6	18.7
Unemployment, per cent of labour force[3]	2.1	5.5
Household saving, per cent of disposable income[3]	−1.9	6.6
Business bankruptcies, no.[3]	6698	19109
Credit losses, per cent of bank lending[3]	0.4	4.3
Public saving, per cent of GDP[3]	1.3	−7.1

Notes:
1. Average annual percentage change.
2. End-of-year changes.
3. Annual averages.

Sources: Statistics Sweden: Swedish Institute for Economic Research; Affärsvärlden; Ljungquist Fastighets Värderingar AB; own calculations.

1985 is chosen as the starting point since it may be classified as a 'normal' year; most of the immediate impact of the large devaluations of 1981 and 1982 had worked its way through the system, and the disequilibrium tendencies appearing in the economy were still minor. Also, the most important deregulation of the domestic credit market took place in 1985. The year 1990 is chosen as the end of the period since this was the last year with positive economic growth before the recession. Furthermore, in 1990 the first signs of an impending financial crisis became apparent with the failure of the finance company Nyckeln ('The Key') in September.

Average GDP growth was 2.3 per cent per annum in 1985–90. During the three following years the economy contracted by 2.0 per cent per year. This may be compared to the average for the OECD, where GDP grew by 3.3 per cent and 1.2 per cent respectively in the two periods. The development of nominal GDP in Sweden is notable: nominal

GDP growth fell from 9.4 per cent per year in the former period to 1.8 per cent in the latter. In fact, nominal GDP growth was negative in both 1992 and 1993. The OECD period averages for nominal GDP growth were 8.0 and 5.4 per cent, respectively. Thus, even in the boom phase, Swedish real growth was not particularly impressive by OECD standards. Furthermore, not only did Swedish real growth slow more than the OECD average, the reduction in nominal growth was even more pronounced, suggesting more rapid disinflation in Sweden.[7]

Private consumption, which had been growing faster than GDP during the second half of the 1980s, contracted dramatically thereafter, and household saving, which had actually been negative, turned sharply positive. Unemployment rose to unprecedented levels. Investment fell, in particular in construction. Many companies experienced financial distress. The average annual number of bankruptcies for the two periods more than doubled. Bank credit losses rose from on average 0.4 per cent of lending to 4.3 per cent.

The stock market index, which had grown at an impressive annual average of 17.1 per cent in 1985–90 grew by an average of 1.9 per cent the following three years. Property prices, especially prices of commercial property, rose rapidly in 1985–90, after which they took a sharp dive. The annual average increase for office buildings in Stockholm was 18.2 per cent between 1985 and 1990, after which they fell by 26.5 per cent per year during the three following years.

THE BOOM PHASE: ASSET INFLATION

The asset market appreciation during the second half of the 1980s was driven by changes affecting both lender and borrower behaviour. On the lender side, two interrelated but nonetheless distinct developments were of importance for the increase in credit supply during the second half of the 1980s. The first was the deregulation of the financial markets and its consequences for the behaviour of financial intermediaries and appearance of financial innovations. The second was the set of factors driving expansionary fiscal and monetary policies. On the borrower side, the behaviour of real interest rates, the relaxation of regulatory constraints on borrowers' access to credits, and the circumstances surrounding the boom in the domestic economy all affected the increased demand for credit.

Lending

In Sweden, the 1980s was a time of important innovations in financial markets as well as a period during which fiscal and monetary policies contributed to rapid credit growth.

Financial Sector Deregulation and Competition

The process of financial deregulation was common to several countries during the late 1970s and through the 1980s. During the inflationary 1970s many financial markets exhibited imbalances. Constraints on interest rates and lending volumes imposed by the regulatory environments became more strongly binding. This created opportunities for new financial instruments and new types of financial intermediaries by raising the potential returns to financial innovations that circumvented the regulations.

In the early post-war period, Swedish policy makers had embarked on a policy of 'low interest rates'. Since this policy led to excess demand for credit, it also required a system of credit rationing (Jonung, 1993). With credit controls and the absence of a market-clearing mechanism, interest rates and credit volumes were controlled separately. Maximum rates on deposits and on lending were set by the Riksbank and 'volume ceilings' determined the size and sectoral composition of credit and capital flows. Financial intermediation took place through banks and a small number of regulated specialised institutions, in particular for funding of housing construction. At the end of the 1970s, the credit market was still unsophisticated, with no secondary bond market and 'a rather dormant stock exchange' (Englund, 1990). Integral to the credit controls was a system of exchange and capital control, which made it possible to some extent to isolate Swedish financial markets from international developments.

But beginning in the second half of the 1970s, a rapidly growing public debt required financing. The volumes were too large to be passed on to the regulated sector at regulated rates. Various instruments were eventually introduced to mobilise resources at market rates. Other important developments at the time were the increased ability of large corporations of using international financial markets and the appearance and rapidly increasing importance of what was called 'grey' financial markets (Jonung, 1993).

Secondary bond markets developed in the early 1980s with the introduction of several new instruments such as treasury bills and a more diversified supply of government bonds. Markets for derivative instruments followed suit. The most significant step toward domestic financial market deregulation came in November 1985 when quantitative restrictions on commercial bank lending were abolished. Simultaneously, a mechanism was introduced by which the central bank determined the liquidity in the economy and the short-term interest rate through a combination of open market operations and the central bank marginal lending rate, which directly determined the inter-bank rate. Sweden deregulated its credit market later than most OECD countries. Of the Scandinavian countries, deregulation came last in Sweden and Finland, and in reaction to events that forced the hand of policy-makers rather than as a result of proactive policy (Åkerholm, 1994).

In the early 1980s, the activities of what are referred to as finance companies grew rapidly. These companies were not subject to the same volume and interest rate restrictions as banks and mortgage institutions, and were thus able to exploit niches that were not directly available to banks. However, by the time of financial market deregulation, banks circumvented quantity restrictions through balance sheet manipulations (af Jochnik, 1987). After the 1985 deregulation, banks and finance companies competed openly.

The shift from a financial system with regulation of prices, quantities and the sectoral composition of lending to a more market based system fundamentally changed the competitive environment for lending institutions. First, it removed a binding constraint on bank lending. Second, it sharpened competition in previously sedate markets. Both developments created incentives for more aggressive lending behaviour by financial intermediaries.

Figure 1.1 illustrates the growth of bank lending, lending by finance companies, and lending by mortgage institutes during 1981–93. At the time of deregulation, it had been expected that the importance of the finance companies would wane (af Jochnik, 1987), but instead all categories of lenders expanded their activities. These figures exaggerate some of the early growth in lending as it became unnecessary for banks to under-state their lending activities, but this was a one-shot adjustment.

The fight for market share took place on a rapidly growing market. Banks, finance companies and mortgage institutes, even discounting some under-reporting of new lending in the pre-1986 period, all expanded their activities significantly after deregulation (see Figure 1.1). The significance of deregulation as an unshackler of credit supply is emphasised by Figure 1.2, which exhibits total lending from all credit institutions as a share of GDP. For many years before deregulation,

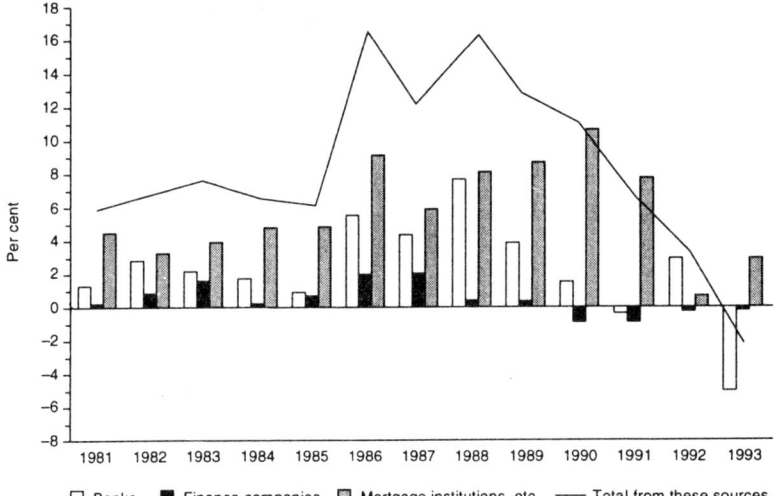

Sources: Svergies Riksbank *Statistical Yearbook*; Statistics Sweden.

Note: 1. Change in end-of-year stocks.

Figure 1.1 Lending to non-bank public: change in loan stock in Kronor,[1] various lenders, as a share of GDP, 1981–1993

Source: Ministry of Finance.

Figure 1.2 Total lending by credit institutions, 1970–93

lending as a share of GDP was almost constant. It then grew from less than 80 per cent of GDP to over 130 per cent in just four years.

Monetary and Fiscal Policy Environment

In 1984–85, the Swedish economy was experiencing capacity constraints and other bottleneck problems. Production costs were increasing more rapidly than for the most important foreign competitors, the current account was weakening, and so was the government budget. The problems were similar to those that had led to a number of devaluations during the 1976–82 period. However, the country was saved by the bell from the choice between devaluation and disinflation as a result of 'OPEC III' in 1986. Oil prices plummeted, and Swedish terms of trade improved by 9.4 per cent. The immediate consequence of this was that the current account improved in spite of deteriorating wage costs. This oil price drop proved to be a mixed blessing. Since employment was already full at 2.7 per cent unemployment and capacity utilisation was high, the reduction in oil prices helped to hide inflationary pressures in the economy without defusing their causes.

After the devaluations of 1981 and 1982, the goal of the government and the Riksbank was to turn the Krona into a hard currency. A credible fixed exchange rate regime was to replace the accommodation strategy (Hörngren and Lindberg, 1994). Thus, monetary policy became more strongly subordinated to the fixed exchange rate commitment. The sectors of the economy exposed to international competition were forced to maintain internationally competitive prices, which was not a constraint on the sheltered sectors (i.e. the production of non-tradables). Thus, because of the ability of the sheltered sector to pass on higher costs into final demand prices, there was a resource pull from the exposed sector to the sheltered sector, especially into construction. And wage pressures in the sheltered sector were not contained.

A consequence of a fixed exchange rate under these circumstances was that a tighter monetary policy would have manifested itself in an increased international interest differential, and thus to capital inflows and an appreciation pressure on the currency. Sterilisation of larger inflows of capital would not have been unproblematic. The strict commitment to a fixed exchange rate reduced the degrees of freedom in monetary policy. This created a conflict between internal and external goals as monetary policy would have needed to be tightened for domestic reasons.

An incentive for private foreign borrowing was provided by the 'foreign borrowing norm' established in the first half of the 1980s. According

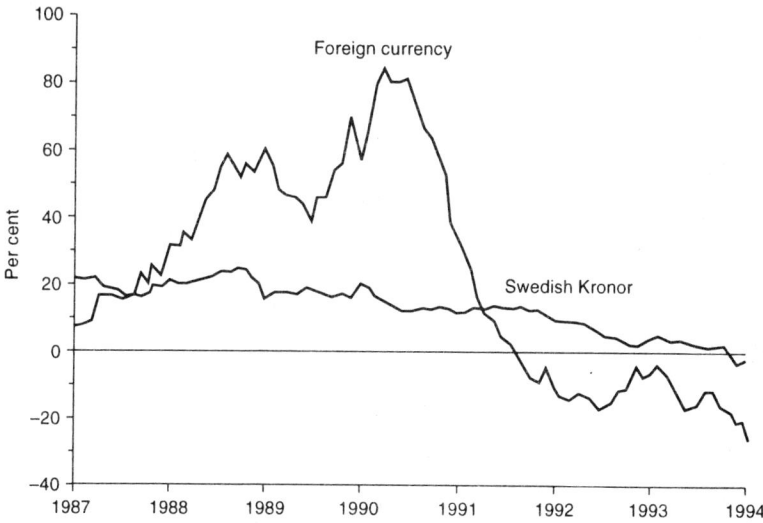

Source: Ministry of Finance.

Figure 1.3   Bank lending to non-bank public by currency 1987–93, 12-month change

to the view of the policy-makers, government borrowing from abroad to finance budget deficits in the 1970s and early 1980s had been excessive. The authorities decided that a commitment not to borrow directly in foreign currencies abroad would make the costs of deficit financing more visible to members of parliament, and thus serve as a disincentive to fiscal laxness. To the extent that foreign financing was needed, it would be up to private agents to borrow in foreign currency. This created what proved to be a strong incentive for domestic agents to borrow abroad and then lend on in Kronor to the Swedish government at higher interest but with a currency risk. In the second half of the 1980s, lending in foreign currency to the non-bank public increased very rapidly (see Figure 1.3).

A hothouse economy was created in the second half of the 1980s since fiscal policy was not tightened enough in response to the explosive credit expansion, given the restrictions on degrees of freedom in monetary policy. The old methods for constraining liquidity growth were unavailable after the credit market deregulation, and the mix of fiscal and monetary policies was inconsistent with reduced demand pressure.

Borrower Behaviour

Real Interest Rates

An important determinant of credit demand is the real interest rate. What matters for decisions by investors is in principle the *ex ante* real rate of interest, i.e. expected nominal interest minus expected inflation, with inflation appropriately defined. However, as the *ex post* real interest rate, the actual nominal interest rate minus realised inflation, is directly observable, it tends to be presented as 'the' real interest rate.

The long-term *ex post* real interest rate is exhibited in Figure 1.4. Real rates measured this way were not particularly low during the 1985–90 period: they tended to fluctuate around 5 per cent.[8] This is a pronounced increase compared to the years immediately after OPEC I, when the real rate was consistently negative.

However, the *ex ante* real rate after 1985 was probably less than the *ex post* rate, allowing for the difference between expected and actual inflation after the credit market deregulation. Unlike several other industrialised countries, Sweden did not go through a disinflationary period

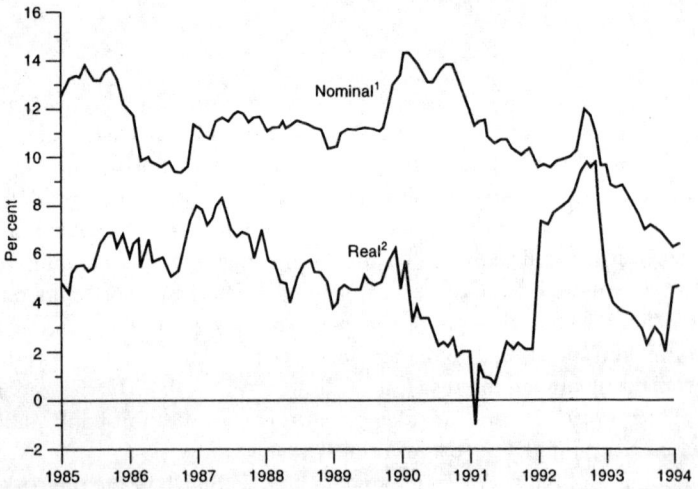

Notes:
1. Nominal interest: return on long-term government bonds.
2. Real interest: nominal interest minus preceeding twelve month change in CPI.

Sources: Ministry of Finance; Statistics Sweden.

Figure 1.4   Nominal and real interest rates 1985–93

in the early 1980s. The relatively rapid rate of inflation was accommodated through a series of devaluations. In 1981 and 1982, the Krona was devalued twice by together more than 25 per cent. The inflation targets announced by the government for 1983 and 1984 of 4 and 3 per cent, respectively, were not met. In fact, between 1974 and 1985, annual consumer price inflation never fell below 7 per cent and was often considerably higher. After 1985, inflation fell somewhat.

Thus, when the credit market was deregulated the political system had not shown a propensity to accept the costs of disinflation. Sweden had proven inflationary credentials. There are therefore reasons to believe that inflationary expectations at the time were persistent and rather high.

Household surveys of inflationary expectations, carried out quarterly since the early 1980s, support this conjecture. In Figure 1.5, the results from these surveys are compared to realised inflation since 1983. Expected inflation exceeded realised inflation by between 1 and 3 percentage points in 1985 to 1988, if the survey data correctly measure anticipated inflation. Therefore, *ex ante* real interest can be estimated

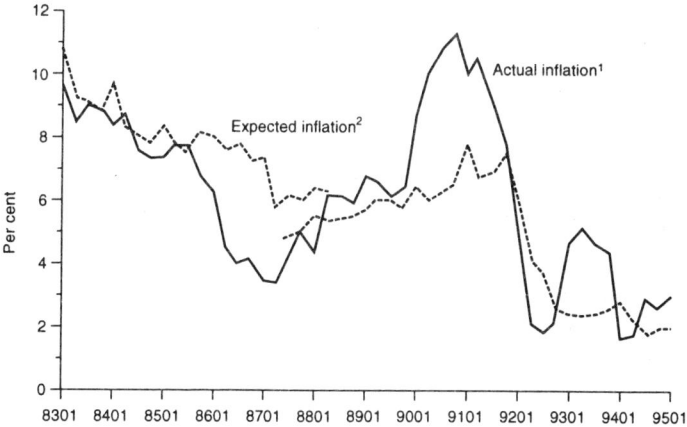

Notes:
1. Actual change in CPI refers to 12-month percentage change. Expected inflation refers to expectation of future prices expressed in household surveys 12 months previously.
2. The break in the series of expected inflation is a consequence of a change in methodology.

Source: Statistics Sweden.

Figure 1.5   Inflation and expectations: expected and actual change in CPI, 1983–95

to have been a few percentage points lower than what is exhibited in Figure 1.4, at least for the years immediately following 1985.[9]

The picture of moderately high real interest rates in the years after 1985 is even further modified when tax deductibility of interest payments is allowed for. The tax treatment of household interest payments has historically been very favourable to borrowers. With high marginal taxes, deductibility of interest payments has had a very strong bite. The marginal tax in the top bracket was 85 per cent in 1982, which as a result of full deductibility meant that interest payments of 100 Kronor reduced disposable income only by 15 Kronor. This 85 per cent deduction was incrementally reduced to 50 per cent by 1985, then again to 40 per cent in 1990, and further to 30 per cent in 1991. Unlike most OECD countries, deductibility is not limited to interest on housing loans. Instead, all types of interest payments by household, regardless of the purpose of the loan, were (and are) deductible.

Figure 1.6 exhibits nominal interest rates before and after tax, and *ex post* real interest after tax for household bank loans, 1985–93. Calculated this way, the real rate of interest for household loans fluctuated around zero until 1991.

To conclude, real interest rates were low during the second half of the 1980s without being exceptionally low in the (recent) historical

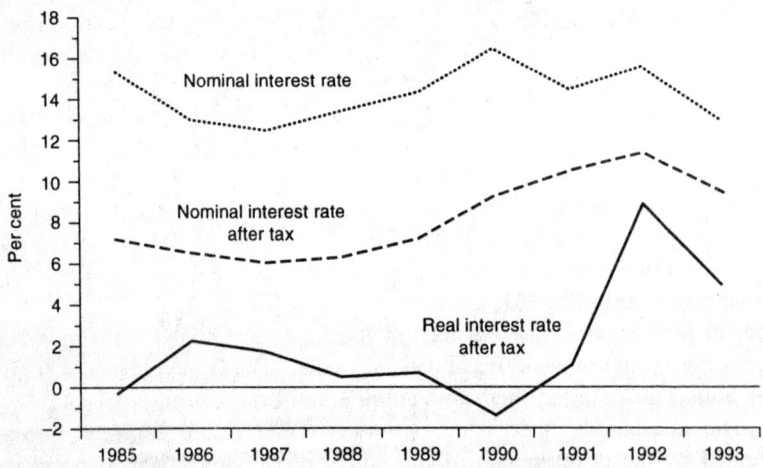

Sources: Ministry of Finance; Statistics Sweden; own calculations.

Figure 1.6   Interest rates for household bank loans, 1985–93

perspective. Additional factors need to be considered when explaining the increase in credit demand after 1985. We will consider households and the business sector separately.

Household Borrowing

First, credit market deregulation led to a significant relaxation of household liquidity constraints. Borrowing against property – or for that matter, borrowing with little collateral – for consumption purposes became easier. Mortgage institutions increased the share of estimated market value of property that could be mortgaged at the most favourable interest rate. Homes could be bought with small or no down payments.

Second, households seem to have maintained expectations of permanent income formed after 1983. After having fallen each year 1981–3, disposable income began increasing more rapidly up to 1986. When growth in disposable income slowed somewhat after 1986, growth in consumption continued at the same rate. At that time, there were weak incentives for precautionary saving. With unemployment of less than 2 per cent, jobs were easy to find, and increasingly generous transfer systems promised to maintain household incomes if household members temporarily chose to exit from the labour market. The commitment by the public sector to finance these systems appeared credible as the public finances improved rapidly and showed a surplus from 1986.

Third, a wealth effect was evident. Real prices of residential property (single-unit dwellings) started increasing after 1985, in particular in urban areas (see Figure 1.7). In the Stockholm area, real prices rose by more than 50 per cent in four years. To the extent that housing price increases were seen as permanent this led to an increase in permanent consumption. In addition, if there were positive feedback loops present such that increases in housing prices led to expectations of further price increases, this effect was strengthened.

A wealth effect was also apparent from households' holdings of financial wealth. In 1985, a period of rapidly rising stock market prices began (see Figure 1.8). Ownership of shares accounted for about 30 per cent of households' gross financial wealth. Thus, the financial wealth of households started increasing significantly.

The households' increasing optimism about future earnings is revealed by the development of the household saving rate (saving as a share of disposable income). Traditionally not very high, saving turned negative in 1987 and dissaving was close to 5 per cent of disposable income in 1988 and 1989 (see Figure 1.9). Private consumption grew

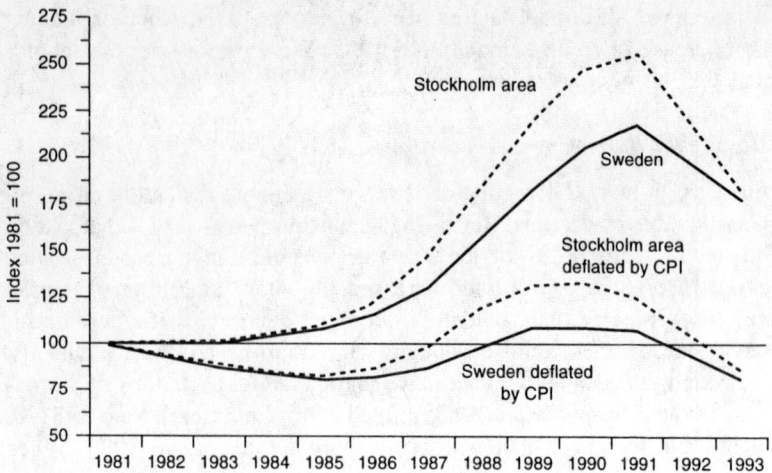

Source: Statistics Sweden.

Figure 1.7   Residential property prices, 1981–93

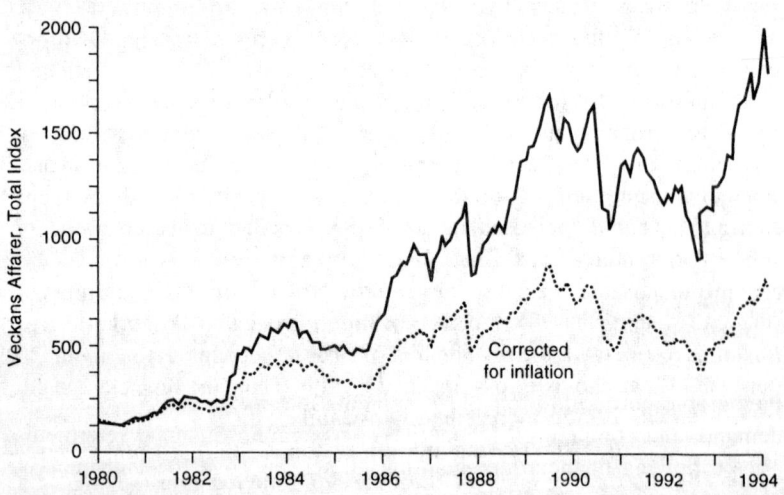

Source: Ministry of Finance.

Figure 1.8   Stock market index, 1980–93

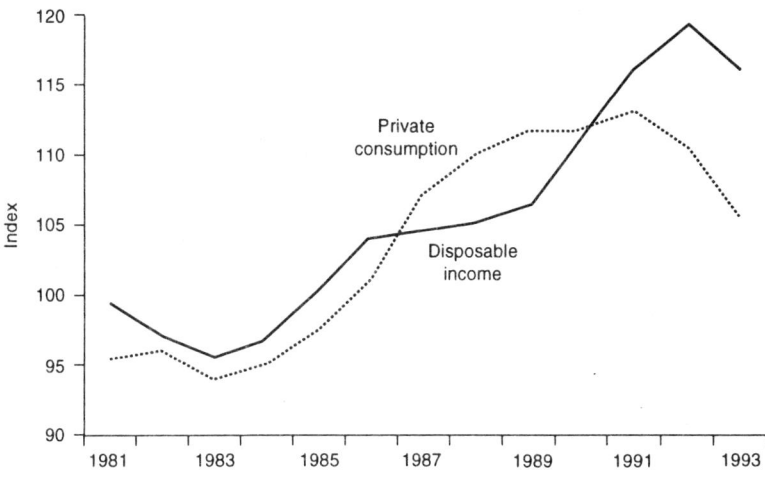

Note:
1. Both series are expressed as a percentage of 1985 disposable income.

Source: Statistics Sweden.

Figure 1.9   Disposable income and consumption, 1981–93[1]

more rapidly than GDP. Investment in consumer durables, often loan-financed, took off: purchases of automobiles were 20 per cent higher in 1989 than in 1985.

The net financial wealth of households was maintained at around 25 per cent of GDP between 1985 and 1989 (Figure 1.10). Increases in the value and volume of financial assets compensated for the increase in indebtedness. Since financial wealth does not include housing own-ership, household net wealth actually increased during the period in spite of very considerable dissaving (in the sense of consumption ex-ceeding disposable income).

Business Sector Borrowing

Favourable corporate profit developments, strong growth of domestic demand, and competition for market share among financial intermedi-aries following financial deregulation all set the stage for asset market expansion. The financial deregulation of 1985 was incomplete, in the sense that exchange controls were kept in place, and were not scrapped until 1989. The capital controls restricted investment in foreign securi-ties and foreign real estate by Swedish investors. This partly accounts

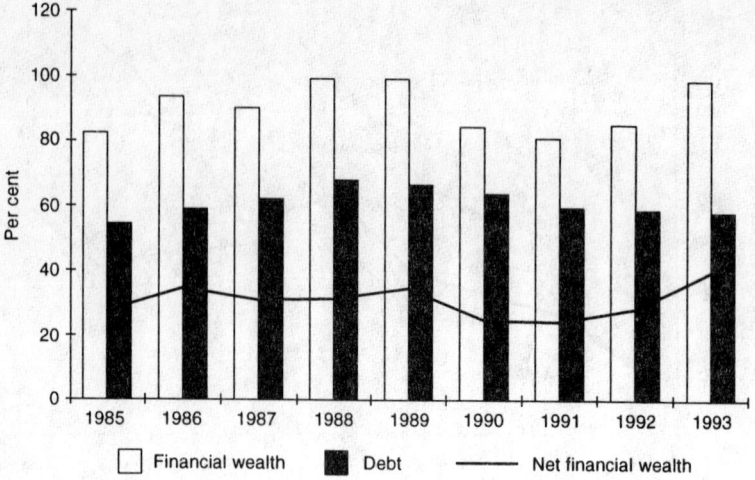

Source: Statistics Sweden.

Figure 1.10   Household sector financial position: financial wealth, debt and net financial wealth as a share of GDP, 1985–93

for the 'hothouse environment' on Swedish capital markets. Swedish investors had become much more liquid, and since important segments of foreign financial markets were restricted to them this put extra pressure on the demand for domestic assets.

A larger share than previously of firms' investments took the shape of acquisitions, often with a significant amount of loan-financing. Also, for tax reasons many listed companies were made private by their main owners because of differences in the tax treatment of ownership in shares between listed and privately held companies. Such repurchases were often highly leveraged.

The stock market took off, as was indicated in Figure 1.8. The resource pull during the second half of the 1980s into the 'sheltered sector', i.e. the production of non-tradables, has already been mentioned. In particular, the construction sector was favoured by the developments in the second half of the 1980s. Businesses in the sheltered sector, such as banking and construction, did much better than the manufacturing industry on the stock market, as shown in Figure 1.11. Between 1985 and 1989, the index for shares in real estate and construction rose by 350 per cent, in banking by 250 per cent, and in the manufacturing industry by 150 per cent.

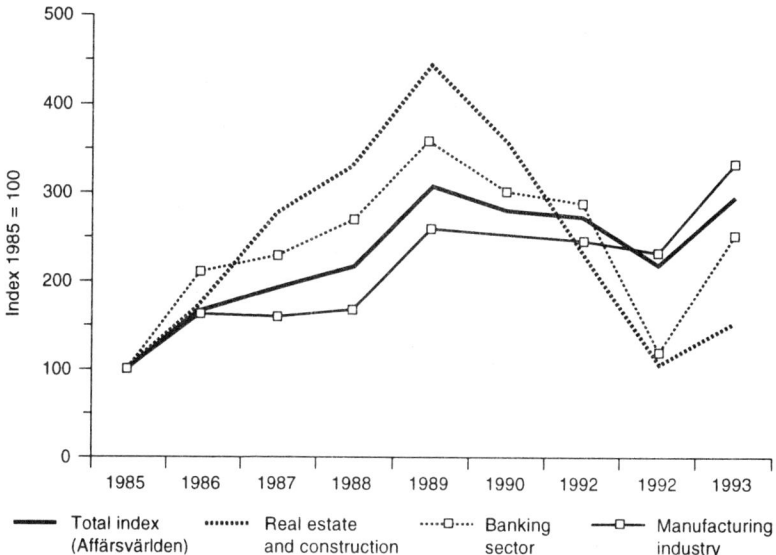

Index 1985 = 100

500 — 400 — 300 — 200 — 100 — 0

1985 1986 1987 1988 1989 1990 1992 1992 1993

— Total index (Affärsvärlden)   ·········· Real estate and construction   ····◻···· Banking sector   —◻— Manufacturing industry

Source: Affärsvärlden.

Figure 1.11   Stock indexes, various sectors: annual averages, 1985–93

Commercial property prices rose even more rapidly than residential property. Figure 1.12 exhibits the price development for commercial property, multi-unit residential property (i.e. apartment blocks) and single-unit residential property (i.e. private homes). Commercial property prices more than doubled between 1985 and 1989. Lending to the property and construction sector accounted for more than half of the lending by banks and credit institutions during the period. Between 1985 and 1989, the price of commercial property in Stockholm rose by about 125 per cent. Rents, however, rose only by approximately 40 per cent during the same period. Just as was the case with households, the behaviour of investors in commercial property seems to have been under the influence of positive feedback loops: borrowing for investment in assets took place against expectations of future increases in asset prices, which further inflated these prices (see Jaffee, 1994 for an account of the developments on the real estate markets).

Corporate debt rose from 120 per cent of GDP in 1985 to 180 per cent in 1990 (see Figure 1.13). Financial wealth grew but at a slower rate, and net financial wealth had thus fallen by some 10 per cent of GDP until 1989 and a further 10 per cent in 1990. Financial saving by

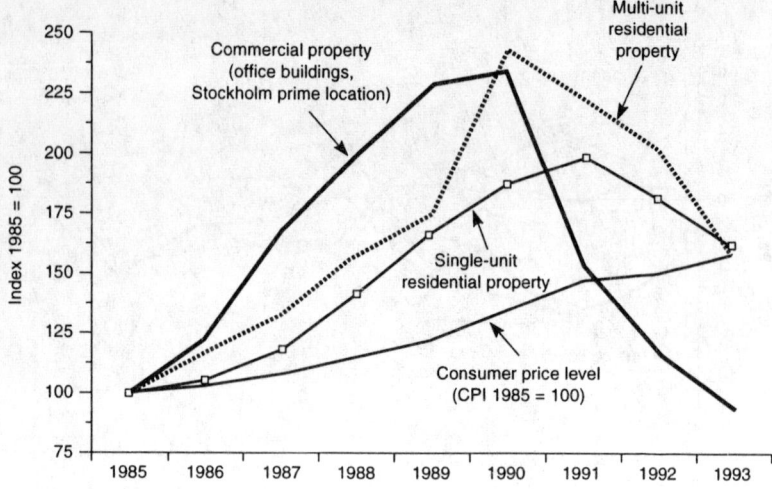

Source: Statistics Sweden; Fastighetsvärderingas jungquist AB

Figure 1.12   Property prices, various categories, 1985–93

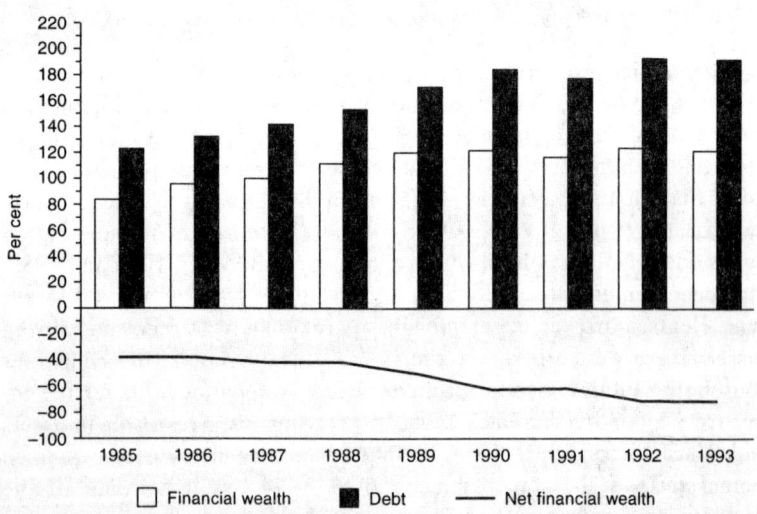

Source: Statistics Sweden.

Figure 1.13   Non-financial corporate sector financial position: financial wealth, debt and net financial wealth as a share of GDP, 1985–93

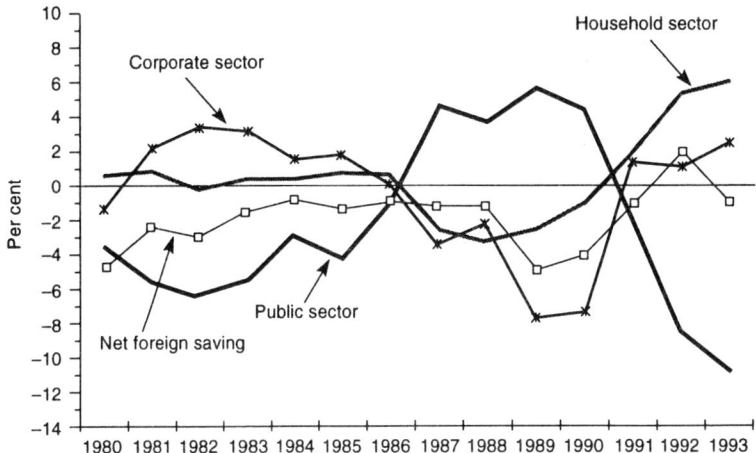

Source: Statistics Sweden.

Figure 1.14   Saving by sector: financial saving as a share of GDP, 1980–93

sector as a share of GDP is summed up in Figure 1.14. Both corporate
and household saving turned sharply negative after 1986, especially
corporate saving. Figure 1.14 reveals that public sector finance was
the mirror image of private saving.[10]

THE BUST PHASE – ASSET DEFLATION

The Turnaround

Macroeconomic imbalances were significant by the end of the 1980s
even if asset market developments are disregarded. As already discussed, there were a number of manifestations of the overheating. The
household saving rate was negative, unemployment was lower than at
any time for more than a decade, and the rate of inflation was higher
than that of important trading partners. Relative unit labour costs had
increased about 10 percentage points in some four years after 1986.
GDP was above trend. In Sweden, annual trend growth of GDP was
1.9 per cent in 1976–90. By 1989, the GDP level exceeded the trend
level by 2.1 per cent. Thus, returning to trend after 1989 required a
cumulative growth deficit compared to the trend rate approximately
equal to one year's GDP growth.

Table 1.2   Decomposition of the change in real GDP of Sweden, 1985–93

Year	Change in GDP[1]	Contribution to the change in GDP accounted for by:				
		Private consumption	Government consumption	Total fixed investment	Inventory investment	Net exports
1985	1.9	1.4	0.7	1.2	0.9	−2.1
1986	2.3	2.5	0.4	0.2	−0.5	−0.3
1987	3.1	2.5	0.3	1.5	−0.3	−0.9
1988	2.3	1.4	0.2	1.2	0.2	−0.8
1989	2.4	0.7	0.6	2.4	0.2	−1.6
1990	1.4	−0.1	0.7	0.2	0.2	0.4
1991	−1.1	0.6	0.9	−1.9	−1.7	1.0
1992	−1.9	−1.0	−0.2	−2.3	1.3	0.3
1993	−2.1	−2.0	−0.2	−3.0	0.3	2.8

Year	Contribution to GDP accounted for by total fixed investment and its components:			
	Total fixed investment	of which residential construction	of which other construction	of which machinery and equipment
1985	1.2	−0.1	−0.0	1.3
1986	0.2	−0.1	0.3	0.0
1987	1.5	0.4	0.1	1.0
1988	1.2	0.4	0.0	0.8
1989	2.4	0.2	0.6	1.6
1990	0.2	0.3	−0.1	−0.1
1991	−1.9	−0.1	−0.5	−1.3
1992	−2.3	−0.3	−0.4	−1.5
1993	−3.0	−1.4	−0.4	−1.3

Note:
1. Percentage change. The columns may not sum to the total because of rounding errors.

Source: Swedish Institute for Economic Research.

The contributions to GDP from changes in its various components are displayed in Table 1.2. Table 1.2 shows that private consumption growth started slowing before investment (in 1989, private consumption eased considerably while investment boomed). However, the proximate cause of the sharp fall in GDP that was initiated in 1991 was plummeting investment, especially investment in machinery and equipment. Private consumption only started falling outright in 1992, and the impact of falling construction investment only became dominant in 1993. Why did what initially seemed like a 'normal' cyclical downturn deteriorate into an outright depression?

A reduction in inflation and an increase in saving rates were required in order to restore macroeconomic equilibrium. Even if there had been no additional effect from adjustment to changing asset prices, such processes would have implied a reduction in economic activity. However, measures to counteract the overheating were not put in place until around the time when economic activity peaked (GDP growth peaked in the first quarter of 1990). Thus, instead of smoothing the cyclical developments, the impact of these measures was to accelerate the downturn.

The process of disinflation can be examined through its most important direct manifestation: a sharp increase in the real rate of interest. A number of policy choices, with the purpose of achieving disinflation, as well as external events, contributed to this increase.

First, the tax system was radically reformed, reducing the deductibility of interest payments and thus directly raising the after tax real interest rates (see Figure 1.6).[11] Second, Swedish policy-makers announced a very strong commitment not to carry out accommodative fiscal and monetary policies in response to the overheated domestic economy and the deteriorating relative cost situation of Swedish export industry. The major political parties as well as most Swedish economists agreed that the devaluation episode of 1981–2 was not to be repeated. In order to strengthen this commitment to reduce inflation, the Krona was unilaterally pegged to the ECU in May 1991, with the explicit intention of precluding future devaluations. Since the remaining capital controls had been finally eliminated in 1989 this commitment was open to be tested by the financial markets. Third, besides these domestic developments, German monetary policies in response to the financing of the unification process raised the floor for Swedish interest rates.

The increase in real rates of interest, in a very short period of time, considerably raised borrowing costs for both households and businesses. As indicated by Figure 1.6 an increase of around 8 percentage points between 1990 and 1992 was typical. Demand for loans both for investment and for consumption was affected negatively. This effect in itself slowed economic activity.

The far-reaching consequences of the regime change were poorly understood by most policy-makers and economists. To take a central example, the huge change in the relative price between current and future consumption could be expected to raise household saving. However, the increase in the saving ratio was substantially and consistently underestimated throughout the recession. Figure 1.15 displays forecast and actual saving as a share of disposable income for the 1988–93 period (with forecasts included up to 1995). According to the forecast in the

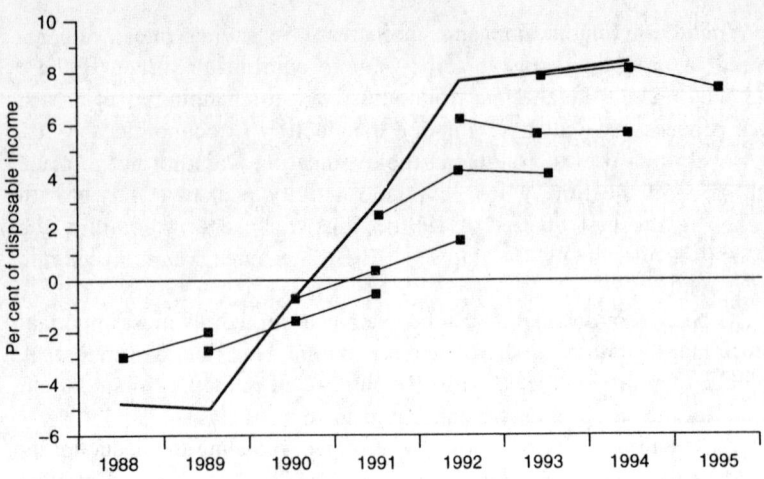

Note:
1. The thick line indicates the actual saving ratio. The short thin lines indicate the saving ratios as forecast in the national budget for the current year and the two following years (in 1988, the one following year).

Source: Statistics Sweden; Ministry of Finance, National Budget, various years.

Figure 1.15   Saving ratio, forecast and realised, 1988–94[1]

National Budget of January 1989 the saving ratio was to increase until 1991 by less than 3 percentage points, from approximately –3 per cent in 1989 to a little below 0 per cent in 1991. In fact, the actual saving ratio in 1989 was –5 per cent and rose to almost 3 per cent in 1991 – an increase by almost 8 percentage points, or 5 percentage points more than the forecast. Similarly, the forecast in 1990 for 1992 under-estimated the outcome by close to 7 percentage points, and the forecast of 1991 for 1993 about 3 percentage points. Thus, a profound change in household behaviour with strong negative effects on economic activity in the short run was not captured in the policy-makers' forecast. To the extent that there should have been a policy reaction to this behavioural change, there was nothing in the policy-makers' understanding of the world that gave any justification for such a reaction.

In addition to the direct effect on aggregate economic activity, the shock to the real interest rate had a far-reaching impact on asset markets. It frustrated the inflationary and real growth expectations that lay behind the asset price inflation. The increasing real cost of capital contributed to the turnaround in asset prices. The stock market had

Table 1.3   Household balance sheets, 1985–93, current prices, billion
Krona

Year	Houses	Apart-ments[1]	Total real assets[2]	Financial assets	Debt	Net financial wealth/net wealth[3]	Debt/ assets[3]	Financial assets/ debt[3]
1985	574	45	619	721	469	28.9	35.0	153.7
1986	607	57	664	888	557	33.3	35.9	159.4
1987	690	74	764	934	631	28.4	37.2	148.0
1988	818	109	927	1104	755	27.4	37.2	146.2
1989	975	138	1113	1196	819	25.3	35.5	146.0
1990	1146	169	1315	1153	861	18.2	34.9	133.9
1991	1257	185	1442	1202	859	19.2	32.5	139.9
1992	1060	156	1216	1245	847	24.7	34.4	147.0
1993	1019	150	1169	1406	827	33.1	32.1	170.0

Notes:
1. The value for apartments 1991–3 is a particularly rough estimate.
2. Real household wealth does not include land.
3. Per cent.

Sources: Ministry of Finance; Statistics Sweden.

peaked in 1989, and the property markets peaked in 1990–1. Thus, asset markets had already begun to contract, or were about to, when the economy peaked.

One important avenue by which falling asset prices fed into a further reduction of economic activity was through balance sheet adjustments. In response to increasing real interest rates and declining asset prices households and businesses adjusted their balance sheets. For households, this meant an increase in household saving rates and a reduction in consumption as well as in leverage. Table 1.3 shows the effects on the household balance sheets. By increasing household saving very substantially households managed to reduce nominal debt after 1990 and thus also to avoid an increasing trend in the debt–asset ratio. A similar process in the corporate sector contributed to the drop in investment. In 1991, corporate sector financial saving as a share of GDP increased by almost 10 percentage points (see Figure 1.14). This exactly reversed the decrease in corporate financial saving that had taken place from 1985 to 1990.

Financial Distress

In spite of, but also partly as a result of, the attempts at balance sheet consolidation, bankruptcies started growing quickly. The number of

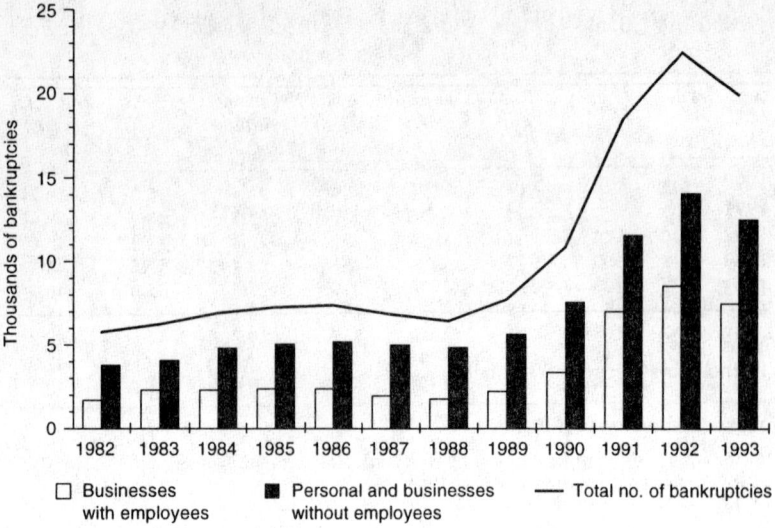

Source: Statistics Sweden.

Figure 1.16   Bankruptcies, 1982–93

bankruptcies increased about 50 per cent per year in each of the years 1990, 1991 and 1992 (see Figure 1.16). This led to a rapid increase in the amount of non-performing loans in the banking system. Credit losses rose from 0.3 per cent of the stock of lending in 1989 to 1.1 per cent in 1990, 3.4 per cent in 1991, and approximately 7 per cent each in 1992 and 1993. The total amount of credit losses in the banking system was approximately 175 billion Kronor in the period 1990–3, which is equal to about 12 per cent of one year's GDP (in either of the years in question). Table 1.4 outlines bank profits before and after credit losses for 1990–3.

Credit losses on corporate sector borrowing accounted for 70 per cent of the total losses during the period, although the corporate sector only accounted for 46 per cent of the banks' loan portfolio at the end of 1990. Losses on loans that were classified as 'property-related' accounted for about two-thirds of the losses on claims on the corporate sector in 1992–3, although less than 30 per cent of claims were property-related (Wallander, 1994). This shows that the downturn on the property market is responsible for more than its share of the problems in the banking sector.

Table 1.4   Banks' profits before and after credit losses, 1990–3, current
prices, billion Kronor

Year	Result before credit losses	Credit losses	Net result
1990	25	12	14
1991	27	36	–9
1992	25	74	–49
1993	35	49	–14
1993[1]	35	63	–30

Note:
1. Including Securum (see below).

Source: Ministry of Finance.

The first sign of an outright threat to the financial system came with the failure of the finance company Nyckeln in 1990. A large share of the company's activities was financed by short-term commercial paper. When its solvency came under question, the market for such instruments quickly dried up. One year later, the solvency of partly government-owned Nordbanken, a major commercial bank, was threatened, and the government for the first time stepped in to support the financial system. Later in 1991, the government guaranteed a large loan for the reconstruction of Första Sparbanken, which in 1992 was complemented with a loan at concessional rates and further loan guarantees. Also in 1992, Nordbanken was split into a 'good bank' and Securum, a 'bad bank' to which the non-performing assets were moved. In September the same year, the capital adequacy requirement of Gota Bank, another major commercial bank, was threatened and the government provided a loan guarantee.

By this time, it was clear that the entire financial system was in danger, and the government issued an explicit guarantee of the commitments of banks and 'certain other credit institutions' with the purpose of guaranteeing the stability of the payments system and the supply of credit. By the end of 1994, at which time the banks appeared to be on solid ground, the total explicit government commitments to bank support amounted to 88 billion Kronor, and total disbursements were a little over 65 billion Kronor.

Although Nordbanken and Gota Bank in effect were declared insolvent, and although other banks were threatened, no credit losses resulted from a bank's inability to fulfil its commitments. This makes it more difficult to claim that the downturn of the Swedish economy is partly explained by a reduced ability of the financial system to carry out its role as an intermediary between lenders and borrowers. However, if asymmetric information problems became more pronounced during the downturn, this may have influenced the depth of the recession. This is discussed in the following section.

Financial Crisis and Interest Differentials

Did financial distress have effects on the real economy? In particular, did debt-deflation of the type described by Irving Fisher (Fisher, 1932, 1933), whereby falling asset prices force the liquidation of collateral for debt which in turn depresses asset prices further, contribute to the downturn? Bernanke (1983) has argued that the bank failures in the USA of the early 1930s precipitated the Great Depression through a resulting large reduction in the volume of bank credit.

Clearly, the response to the falling asset prices contributed to the convulsions of the Swedish economy, as agents adjusted to a changed policy environment. But the fact that a very large adjustment took place rapidly does not in itself necessarily mean that there were secondary effects, related to the process itself, which further depressed the economy. Government support of the banks made it possible to avoid the very serious disintermediation that would have resulted from outright bank failures. The lending activities of banks were as a result not discontinued. Such a discontinuation is likely to have increased the severity of the downturn considerably. Yet, the requirement to strengthen capital adequacy ratios by itself made it necessary for banks to restrict lending while their balance sheets were improved, thus possibly implying a credit crunch.

One possible way of studying this issue is to pursue the question whether problems of asymmetric information arose during the crisis. As emphasised, for example, by Mishkin (1994), the difference in interest paid by low and high quality borrowers is expected to increase during a financial crisis. In a crisis, the problems connected with asymmetric information between borrowers and lenders (moral hazard and adverse selection) become more pronounced. Mishkin (1991) has compared the differential between returns to bonds of varying quality during various financial and 'pseudo-financial' crises in the USA, and finds that increasing interest differentials suggest an impending crisis and worsening problems of adverse selection and moral hazard.

Historically, such comparisons are difficult to carry out for Sweden owing to the lack of depth in the financial system. As in most European countries, the financial system has been bank-based. Corporate borrowing has taken place mainly through banks and not through the bond market. However, a significant exception to this is the debt issued by mortgage institutions. The best example of assets of different quality but with other characteristics in common are government bonds and housing bonds. Since a thick secondary market for housing bonds has developed alongside the secondary market for government bonds, a comparison of these two kinds of debt is meaningful.

In Figure 1.17, the daily spread between the interest on housing bonds and government bonds for the period 28 November 1990 to 24 March 1994 is exhibited.[12] The behaviour of this spread may indicate how financial crises during the period led to more pronounced problems of asymmetric information, and how reductions in uncertainty reduced them.

During the turbulent period of the fall of 1992, the differential between housing bonds and government bonds spiked several times. On 16 September, the Riksbank signalled its strong commitment to defend the exchange rate by increasing the marginal lending rate to 500 per cent. On 21 September, it was reduced to 50 per cent. On 23 September, the differential between government and housing bonds exceeded 200 basis points for the first time, as the exchange rate commitment implied possibly prohibitive interest rates in the future.

As a result of crisis negotiations between the government and the opposition Social Democrats, a 'crisis package' was announced on 24 September 1992 containing a number of economic policy measures, among them a blanket guarantee for the banking system and a (yet vaguely formulated) promise of support for mortgage institutions. In addition, the Riksbank announced on 24 September that it offered loans to the housing institutions on 'special conditions' to aid their short-term financing. 18 billion Kronor were offered at 20 per cent interest for four-week borrowing. The spread fell sharply as a result.

Uncertainty remained on the market as to the extent of the government guarantee of the mortgage institutions. Although credit losses had been small in these institutions compared to the banks, concerns about the future ability of households to service their debts arose. Trade in some mortgage bonds stopped completely. There is a parallel between this and the total disappearance of the market in short-term commercial paper after the failure of Nyckeln. However, a breakdown of the market in mortgage bonds would have had devastating consequences for the entire Swedish financial system.

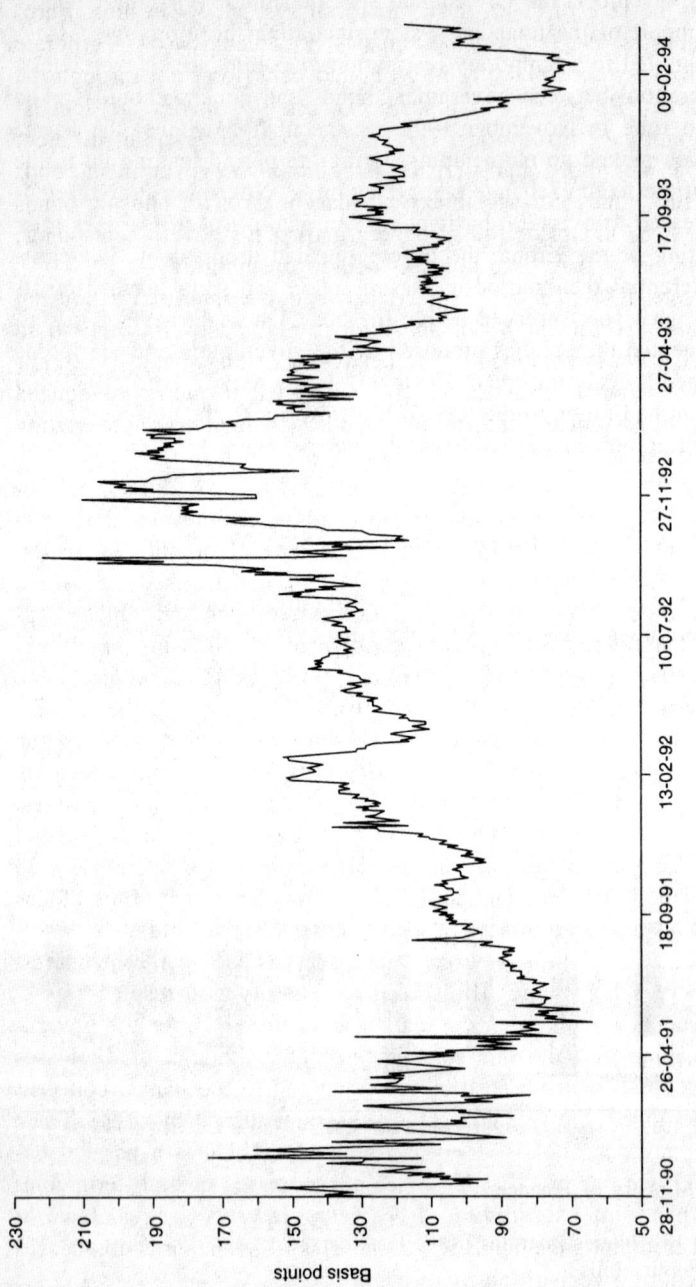

Source: Alfred Berg Transferator AB.

Figure 1.17 Interest differential, mortgage bonds/government bonds

On 5 November, the government specified more fully the contents of its support of the financial system, including the mortgage institutions. This led to a temporary restoration of confidence. Nevertheless, the differential between government bonds and housing bonds spiked a second time in November 1992, as speculation against the Krona once again picked up momentum. During the period leading up to the defeat of the fixed exchange rate policy on 19 November, the differential increased to over 200 basis points yet again. But a few days after the floating of the Krona, the differential had dropped by 50 points. The differential then started increasing again and soon reached levels close to what was observed before the float. On 18 December, parliament accepted the policies proposed by the government and the spread maintained a declining trend. However, it was only in April 1993 that the spread had fallen to the level prevalent prior to the currency crisis.

A similar but coarser comparison can be made by studying bank lending and deposit rates. These are exhibited for 1989 to 1993 in Figure 1.18. The total spread rose from about 5 per cent in 1989 to almost 8 per cent in the fourth quarter of 1992, after which they fell back to about 6 per cent by 1994.

The combination of the breakdown of the fixed exchange rate policy, the government guarantee of the financial system and the provision of

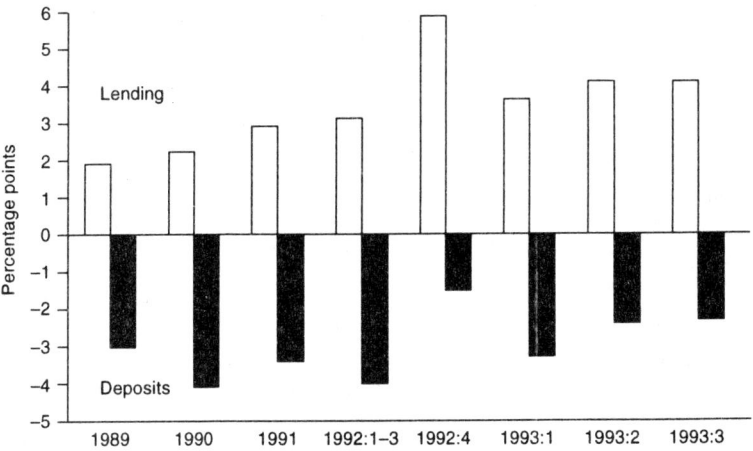

Source: Ministry of Finance.

Figure 1.18   Interest margins in the banking sector: spread against six-month treasury bills

extra liquidity by the Riksbank to the institutions averted an acceleration of the financial crisis as it expressed itself through the spread
between government bonds and housing bonds. No mortgage institution has defaulted on any of its bonds. Still, during the period of increased uncertainty, when the spread between government borrowing
and mortgage institution borrowing rates increased substantially, the
perception of increased risk of the mortgage institutions can be expected to have had especially adverse effects on borrowing costs for
housing, and thus also for the activity on the housing market.

THE CRISIS OF THE 1990s IN A HISTORICAL PERSPECTIVE

Sweden has in the twentieth century during peacetime conditions experienced five major downturns in economic activity, or 'crises': in
1920–2, 1930–2, 1974–7 (OPEC I), 1979–82 (OPEC II) and in 1990–3.
The performance of the Swedish economy during these five crises is
summarised in Table 1.5. This table makes it possible to set the crises
of the 1990s in a historical perspective by comparing it to previous
major recessions.

Such a comparison brings out several conclusions. First, the recession
of the 1990s was deeper and more serious than the two other recessions of the post-Second World War period, judging from most indicators. During the early 1990s private and public sector employment,
real GDP and bank lending fell in absolute terms. This was not the
case during OPEC I and II. The volume of bankruptcies was significantly larger in the early 1990s. Producer price, consumer price and
wage inflation was considerably higher in the 1970s and 1980s than in
the 1990s. In fact, the recessions of the 1970s and 1980s do not stand
out as major crises compared to the events of 1990–3. Unemployment
remained around 2–3 per cent in the period 1970–90. It reached a
level of 8 per cent in 1993. An additional 5–7 per cent of the labour
force was engaged in various labour market programmes.

Second, although the depression of the 1990s is the most severe one
of the post-Second World War period, it does not appear as deep as
those of the 1920s and 1930s. The fall in real and nominal GDP was
larger during the inter-war crises. However, the fall of real GDP of
the 1990s lasted for three years, making it one year longer than the
decline of the 1920s and 1930s.

Third, a major difference between the crisis of the 1990s and the
depressions of the 1920s and 1930s concerns fiscal policy. A balanced

Table 1.5   The contraction phase of five deep economic crises, 1920–93, percentage change from peak to trough.

	Crises of:				
	1920–2	*1930–2*	*1974–7* *OPEC I*	*1979–82* *OPEC II*	*1990–3*
Employment	−5.5	−4.0	4.4	1.0	−11.9
Private sector	−5.4	−4.9	−1.1	−1.6	−15.4
Public sector	−6.8	11.6	15.7	5.1	−6.7
Producer prices	−52.2	−10.9	26.9	39.8	5.3
Consumer prices	−30.5	−5.7	34.9	38.4	17.1
Nominal wage	−31.7	−4.2	42.6	26.5	15.2
Real wage[1]	−1.7	1.5	5.7	−8.6	−1.7
Industrial production	−9.6	−13.3	−7.9	−3.0	−6.8
Real GDP	−16.5	−11.9	2.0	2.7	−5.7
Nominal GDP	−42.2	−16.2	44.5	37.6	5.6
Private consumption	−2.1	−8.6	6.0	−0.7	−5.4
Public consumption	10.1	5.6	11.6	5.6	−0.7
Investment	2.7	−33.2	1.9	−3.2	−29.4
Construction	2.4	−18.1	−6.5	−8.0	−24.0
Export	7.2	−31.8	−4.0	7.2	6.9
Import	−28.2	−23.3	1.3	−2.2	−5.1
Bankruptcies	89.9	45.8	−0.2	33.0	83.8
Stock market index (nominal)	−35.3	−54.3	10.3	160.0	61.2
Stock market index (real)[1]	−6.8	−51.5	−18.2	87.8	37.6
Money supply (nominal)	−9.5	−1.5	36.4	36.3	19.2
Money supply (real)[1]	30.2	4.4	1.1	−1.6	1.8
Bank lending (nominal)	−11.5	−2.4	55.8	47.1	−25.6
Bank lending (real)[1]	27.4	3.4	15.5	6.3	−36.4
Public debt (nominal)	3.6	22.0	58.0	115.3	83.1
Public debt (share of GDP)[2]	9.4	8.2	2.3	21.4	33.3

Notes:
1. Real wage, stock market index, money supply and bank lending are deflated by CPI.
2. Change in public debt share of GDP in percentage points.

Source: Jonung (1994).

budget was the guiding norm for fiscal policy in the inter-war period, even during the 1930s in spite of attempted counter-cyclical fiscal measures.[13] No major changes in the public debt occurred during the inter-war crises.

This picture changed dramatically in the post-Bretton Woods period with the acceptance of a Keynesian view of counter-cyclical fiscal policy. Starting with OPEC I, the fiscal authorities have responded to recessions by expanding government expenditures sharply and relying on loan financing. Consequently, the volume of public debt measured as a ratio of nominal GDP has risen markedly during the recessions in the past 20 years. Currently, the Swedish debt: GDP ratio is among the highest of the OECD countries. The fall in both investment and in private consumption during the crisis of the 1990s was large compared to that of OPEC I and II. The fall in private consumption would have been larger without the significant rise in transfers through the public sector.

As argued above, the depression of the 1990s owes much to the rapid and unexpected rise in real interest rates. The policy of turning the Krona into a hard currency contributed to this. After high wartime inflation, the depression of the early 1920s was due to the policy of the Riksbank of returning to the pre-1914 dollar rate. This precipitated a deflationary process with sharply rising real rates, widespread bankruptcies and financial distress. Thus, there are considerable similarities between the crises of the 1920s and of the 1990s.

SUMMARY AND CONCLUSIONS

In this chapter we have explored macroeconomic developments in Sweden 1985–93 and analysed them with a special focus on asset markets. We see the regime shift of the early 1990s as an understandable reaction to, maybe even unavoidable consequence of, the preceding events. Still, the unexpectedness of the regime shift explains part of the sharpness of the consequent downturn.

To recapitulate, in the late 1980s and early 1990s the Swedish economy went through a dramatic process. First, during a boom phase in the second half of the 1980s, real rates of interest were low or negative, asset prices rose rapidly, household saving rates turned negative, the gross indebtedness of the private sector rose, unemployment reached exceptionally low levels, and – given the pegged exchange rate – the tradable sector was squeezed while the non-tradable sector, in particular the construction and the financial sector, expanded.

The economy peaked in the first quarter of 1990 and soon deteriorated into a severe bust phase. Real interest rates rose sharply, inducing households and businesses to adjust their balance sheets by increasing financial saving. Property prices plummeted, and the stock market fell. Investment demand fell significantly and unemployment increased. There was an explosive rise in public debt as a result of automatic stabilisers as well as government support to the ailing financial sector. By 1992 the Swedish economy was in the deepest crisis of the post-Second World War period. The severity of the recession was close to that of the early 1920s and 1930s.

The boom and bust cycle of 1985–93 represents a unique chain of events, different from the experience of previous business cycles as collectively remembered. The depth of the downturn was not expected. An indication of this is the government's forecasts for the economy, in which the magnitude of the contraction was consistently and significantly under-estimated.

What accounted for this extreme process? Three conclusions emerge here. First, financial market developments were central to the anatomy of the boom phase. Second, an unexpected regime change precipitated the depression. Third, although asset prices fell dramatically during the downturn it is not necessary to use debt-deflation arguments to explain the depth of the recession.

To begin with the first of these conclusions, the constraints on both borrowers and lenders were radically relaxed during the 1980s, which had important consequences for their behaviour during the boom phase. On the lender side, the deregulation of the domestic credit market that took place most prominently in 1985 led to competition between financial intermediaries and the appearance of new instruments. On the borrower side, deregulation relaxed the previously constrained access to credit for both households and firms. As a result of low or negative after-tax real rates of interest, credit demand remained high. In addition, weak incentives for precautionary saving, the wealth effect of rising asset prices, and strong profit opportunities in the non-tradables sector all contributed to rapid credit expansion. As long as asset prices increased at a rapid rate, new borrowing could be taken on seemingly without weakening balance sheets.

The process was sustainable only as long as expectations were maintained of low real interest rates, almost non-existent unemployment, and strong demand growth. Until the end of the 1980s there were few reasons to revise these expectations. However, a series of events quickly frustrated the prevailing expectations. In addition to a 'normal' cyclical downturn, policies were put in place that raised real interest rates significantly and paved the way for permanently higher real interest. This was an unexpected regime shift and it precipitated the deep recession that followed, which is our second main conclusion.

The Swedish political establishment expressed, across party lines, the intention to turn the Krona into a hard currency. This required a change of monetary regime not only from a regime of strongly regulated financial markets, low real interest rates, and monetary accommodation to one based on internationalized financial markets and market-determined real interest rates. In addition, the hard currency commitment required a rate of inflation that was no higher than that of Sweden's major trading partners. Given the high inflation rates at the end of the 1980s, the only way to realise the goal was through rapid disinflation.

The combination of the disinflationary commitment, a tax reform that made borrowing and consumption more expensive, changes in the system for subsidies of construction, and internationally rising interest rates added up to a huge increase in the real interest rate. This was a regime shift in the sense that several of the policy changes that led to the increase were structural and permanent rather than cyclical in nature.

The regime shift raised return requirements on assets, and thus required a down-valuation of asset prices generally. It also revealed that a significant amount of over-investment had taken place, which reduced investment demand. And it forced households and businesses to increase saving in order to consolidate their bloated balance sheets. All of this led to sharp reductions in economic activity.

Are debt-deflation arguments of the type associated with Irving Fisher necessary to explain the depth of the downturn? Our answer to this question is 'no', which is our third main conclusion. It is possible to understand the downturn primarily as a rational response to a rapid and fundamental regime shift that involved a huge change in the relative price between current and future consumption and in the return requirements on assets. The rapid fall in asset prices did cause a crisis in which the entire banking system was threatened. And asymmetric information problems regarding borrowers of varying quality probably did become more pronounced during the crisis, which to the extent that it raised borrowing costs for lower quality borrowers and constrained their access to credit is likely to have affected economic activity. However, since the banking system was saved by a combination of financial support and guarantees from the government and the relaxation of monetary policy that resulted from the floating of the Krona, this was not allowed to deteriorate into a meltdown of the financial sector. Thus, a reduction in credit supply as a result of falling asset prices was not *the* central feature explaining the depth of the recession of the early 1990s.

Notes

1. An earlier version of this chapter was presented at the City University Debt-Deflation Conference, London, 14–15 April 1994. We are grateful for comments on various versions of this chapter by Andrew Bain, Erik Berglöf, Michael D. Bordo, Lennart Erixon, Patrick Foley, Per Frennberg, Lars Hörngren, Karl-Göran Lemne, Allan Meltzer, Mancur Olson, Mats Persson, Jan Wallander and David Weil.

2. See, for example, Schinasi and Hargraves (1993) for an overview.

3. For a comparison of developments in Sweden to Finland, a country with an even deeper downturn than Sweden, see Jonung, Söderström and Stymne (1995).

4. For collections of papers, see Hubbard (1991) and Feldstein (1991). For a recent discussion of financial crises in a historical perspective, see White (1991).

5. Borio, Kennedy and Prowse (1994) examine the role of credit for asset market fluctuations since the early 1980s and its consequences for monetary policy.

6. All real national accounts data for Sweden in this paper are based on 1985 prices.

7. In a historical perspective, the downturn was also particularly sharp, and unprecedented in Sweden in the post-Second World War period.

8. The OECD calculates and publishes, in *OECD Historical Statistics*, real long-term and short-term interest rates for various OECD countries, where the change in GDP deflator is used as the measure of inflation. The results from these calculations of *ex post* real interest for Sweden are of the same magnitude as those shown in Figure 1.4. According to the OECD's calculations, Sweden's real interest rates tended to be below the average of OECD real interest rates in the second half of the 1980s, however without being dramatically lower than in the typical OECD country.

9. It should also be recalled that although credit demand was high during the 1970s as a result of low real rates of interest, regulated quantity constraints reduced access to credit, and non-price mechanisms determined the allocation of loans.

10. Public finances improved in the late 1980s and then deteriorated rapidly through the workings of automatic stabilisers. It is difficult to argue that there was a Ricardian equivalence mechanism present with causality running from public saving to private saving. In practice, it was the other way around, at least for the fluctuations we study here.

As private saving rose, economic activity slowed, and unemployment increased. This led to reductions in tax revenues and increases in expenditures, in particular for unemployment benefits, which caused rising budget deficits.

11.   In addition, consumption taxes were increased in order to finance income tax reductions, further stimulating saving. Also, a large reduction of subsidies to the construction sector, to take place over a number of years, was initiated.

12.   The securities are chosen in order to be as comparable as possible, i.e., with the goal of making them differ only in quality. The government bond is the benchmark bond referred to as ro 1020, which matures on 23 January 1997. There is no identical housing bond. Three different housing bonds have been used: For the period 28 November 1990–23 December 1992, Caisse 96: for the period 28 December 1992–2 February 1994, Caisse 97; for the period 3 February 1994–25 March 1994, Caisse 98. For the days of change between two different housing bonds, the spread between the two bonds has not exceeded 5 basis points.

13.   The 'crisis' policy of the Social Democratic government that came into power in 1932 was explicitly based on budget deficits to be financed through government borrowing. The fiscal stimulus had a minor impact on the public debt for two reasons. The magnitude of the measures was small, and they lasted for a short period, 1933–5. See Jonung (1994).

References

Åkerholm, J. (1994) 'Financial Deregulation and Economic Imbalances in the Scandinavian Countries', Korea Institute of Finance, *Working Paper Policy Issue Series*, 94–7.

Bernanke, B.S. (1983) 'Non-Monetary Effects of the Financial Crisis in the Propagation of the Great Depression', *American Economic Review*, 73; 257–76.

Borio, C.E.V., N. Kennedy and S.D. Prowse (1994) 'Exploring Aggregate Asset Price Fluctuations Across Countries', Bank for International Settlements, *Economic Papers*, 40.

Englund, P. (1990) 'Financial Deregulation in Sweden', *European Economic Review*, 34, 385–93.

Feldstein, M. (ed.) (1991) *The Risk of Economic Crisis* (Chicago: The University of Chicago Press).

Fisher, I. (1932) *Booms and Depressions* (London: George Allen & Unwin).

Fisher, I. (1933) 'The Debt-Deflation Theory of Great Depressions', *Econometrica* (October), 337–57.

Hörngren, L. and H. Lindberg (1994) 'The Struggle to Turn the Swedish Krona into a Hard Currency', in J. Åkerholm and A. Giovannini (eds), *Exchange Rate Policies in the Nordic Countries* (London: CEPR) 133–72.

Hubbard, R.G. (ed.) (1991) *Financial Markets and Financial Crises* (Chicago: The University of Chicago Press).

Jaffee, D.M. (1994) 'The Swedish Real Estate Crisis', *Occasional Paper*, 59 (Stockholm: SNS).

af Jochnik, K. (1987) 'The Credit Market in 1986 – First Year with Unrestricted Lending', *Sveriges Riksbank Quarterly Review*, 1.

Jonung, L. (1993) 'The Rise and Fall of Credit Controls: The Case of Sweden, 1939–89', in M. Bordo and F. Capie (eds) *Monetary Regimes in Transition* (New York: Cambridge University Press) 346–70.

Jonung, L. (1994) '1990-talets ekonomiska kris i historisk belysning' (The crisis of the 1990s in a historical perspective), *Occasional Paper*, 57 (Stockholm: SNS).

Jonung, L., H.T. Söderström and Stymne, J. (1995) 'Depression in the North. Boom and Bust in Sweden and Finland, 1985–93', paper prepared for the 40th anniversary symposium of the Yrjö Jahnsson Foundation.

Kindleberger, C.P. (1978) *Manias, Panics and Crashes* (New York: Basic Books).

Mishkin, F.S. (1991) 'Asymmetric Information and Financial Crises: A Historical Perspective', in R.G. Hubbard (ed.), *Financial Markets and Financial Crises* (Chicago: The University of Chicago Press) 69–108.

Mishkin, F.S. (1994) 'Preventing Financial Crises: An International Perspective', NBER, *Working Paper* 4636.

Schinasi, G.J. and M. Hargraves (1993) '"Boom and Bust" in Asset Markets in the 1980s: Causes and Consequences', in International Monetary Fund, *Staff Studies for the World Economic Outlook* (Washington, DC: International Monetary Fund) 1–27.

Schwartz, A.J. (1986), 'Real and Pseudo-financial Crises', in F. Capie and G.E. Wood (eds), *Financial Crises and the World Banking System* (London: Macmillan) 11–31.

Wallander J. (1994) 'Bankkrisen – Omfattning. Orsaker, Lärdomar' (The Banking Crisis – Its Extent, Its Causes and Its Lessons) in H. Lindgren *et al.*, *Bankkrisen* (Stockholm: Bankkriskommittén).

White, E.N. (ed.) (1991) *Crashes and Panics. The Lessons from History* (Homewood, Ill.: Dow Jones-Irwin).

Comment

Andrew Bain

We need to begin by attempting to distinguish *debt-deflation* from the characteristics of the ordinary business cycle. Both are, of course, associated with changes in financial flows and asset values, which have significant implications for the behaviour of economic activity and prices.

In the course of a typical business cycle there is an acceleration of credit in the upswing followed by a deceleration later, with consequential changes in the pace of monetary expansion. The trigger for credit expansion may be found in 'real' factors, such as investment opportunities or tax incentives, or it may come from monetary factors such as low interest rates: in either case there is a discrepancy between the natural and market rates of interest.

Once the process is underway both monetary and real factors are normally present. Monetary factors cause interest rates to lag behind the perceived rate of return on capital, which normally rises in the upswing; and again, when the expected return on investment falls during the downswing, interest rates – particularly *real* rates – are generally slow to follow.

As a result, asset values rise in the upswing and fall in the downswing.[1] Thus a fall in the value of assets which have been purchased by the issue of debt, or which provide the security relied upon by lenders, is a normal feature of the business cycle and is not confined to conditions of debt-deflation.

Apart from these changes in asset prices there is also a tendency for current output prices to rise relatively quickly in the upswing of the cycle and to rise relatively slowly (or fall) in the downswing. The real value of debts fluctuates accordingly. To the extent that changes in the rate of inflation are unanticipated or are not fully incorporated in interest rates, asymmetric responses to changes in the real values of financial instruments contribute to the cyclical behaviour.

All this is well understood. If debt-deflation simply described the consequences for economic activity of the contraction in credit in the downswing, of the concomitant fall in asset values, and of the rise in the real value of debts, there would not be much that is novel to say. We could also rely on the usual explanations to explain why both output and the general price level were likely to be affected.

As Minsky (1982) has pointed out, however, the special interest in debt-deflation lies in the analysis of pathological situations, where the economy lapses temporarily into incoherence. As a consequence of both over-indebtedness and the decline in asset values, economic behaviour lies for some time outside the normal range of experience.

An economy undergoing debt-deflation may be expected to experience some or all of the following characteristics:

- The normal cyclical fall in physical and financial asset values may be exaggerated by distress selling.
- Markets for assets may dry up – uncertainty about future asset values combined with extrapolative expectations can lead to a dearth of buyers.
- There is a possibility that some financial institutions will fail, with the risk of a more general financial crisis.
- The losses experienced by banks, or other lenders, and investors may significantly reduce their *appetites* for risk. Thus the supply of risk and loan capital may be curtailed by a shortage of capacity in the financial sector, which cannot readily be augmented in the prevailing financial conditions. On the demand side, balance sheet weakness may curtail entrepreneurs' appetites for new risky projects.
- The same goes for lenders' *perceptions* of risk – banks have an exaggerated perception of risk in a recession, but act like lemmings in a boom! Abnormal losses are liable to lead to an excessive tightening of credit standards.
- A falling general price level may exacerbate the effects of the fall in the relative price of long-term financial assets.

With these thoughts in mind, I turn now to Chapter 1. Jonung and Stymne have set out very clearly the characteristics of the debt-deflation from 1990 to 1993 in Sweden.

The first point to make is that what occurred went well beyond the normal range of business cycle experience: it is certainly worthy of the description 'debt-deflation'. Moreover, in contrast with the cycles associated with OPEC I and OPEC II, the most recent recession had its roots in a monetary disturbance – deregulation, its associated credit boom, and an inability or failure of the monetary authorities to counter it by raising interest rates sufficiently. While shocks in the real economy can trigger business cycles, in the absence of at least an accommodative monetary policy it is doubtful whether anything of the severity of debt-deflation will ensue.

The sharp fall in property values was evidently exaggerated by distress selling – there was much more than a normal fall in commercial and residential (particularly rented) property prices (Figures 1.7 and 1.12). The fall in stock market prices overall (peak to trough 1989–92) also seems to have been as great as in the Great Depression of 1930–2 (Figure 1.8). It would be interesting to know whether there is any evidence that here too distress selling (or equivalent phenomena such as the forced liquidation of hedge positions) contributed to the fall.

To what extent did markets simply dry up? Was there a sharp reduction in turnover in the property markets so that sales could not be made quickly at any tolerable price? The fact that the company CD market dried up will have led to reintermediation through the banks – presumably it reflected greater risk aversion on the part of holders of this paper as well as perceptions that the risk of default had risen.

The losses experienced by the banks and other financial institutions clearly threatened to cause a financial crisis, or more accurately a series of financial crises. The Riksbank had its work cut out in ensuring that a general financial collapse was avoided. But, thanks to its efforts and to support from the government, a financial collapse was prevented.

However, even if individual financial institutions can be preserved, and domino effects from one institution to another prevented, there is a limit to what a central bank can (and perhaps should) do to make private financial institutions lend more. The central bank can encourage commercial banks not to call in loans or force clients into making distress sales of assets, on the basis that others will do likewise and the quality of all their assets will benefit. But the central bank can hardly press institutions into making new loans which they judge to be excessively risky, or to make even low-risk loans when their exposure to risk is already uncomfortably high.

Jonung and Stymne show that the banks and other lenders suffered severe losses, that bank lending fell sharply and that mortgage institute lending followed later (Figure 1.1). Is it possible to identify the respective contributions of supply and demand factors to this reduction in lending, and within the latter to distinguish real from financial causes?

Was there evidence of banks tightening up to a greater extent than in other recessions, so that credit was simply unavailable to certain categories of borrower? Were banks under pressure to contract their loan books in order to meet prudential capital ratios? Did they regard as very risky (when asset prices were relatively low) lending which during the boom (with over-valued assets) they would have regarded as reasonably safe? How did the mortgage institutions behave after the

crisis? (The figures for the interest differential on housing bonds –
Figure 1.17 – show that for a couple of years the perception of risk on
mortgage bonds appears to have been well above the normal level.)

Alternatively, was the decline in borrowing mainly a result of demand factors? Had the boom created a greater over-supply of fixed
capital than in previous business cycles, so that the opportunities for
investment were few and far between – a *real* cause of the deep recession? Or did the weakening of balance sheets and uncertainty about
income flows lead to demand for credit drying up – a *financial* cause
more closely linked to debt-deflation?

On this occasion, in contrast with the inter-war period, while the
relative prices of long-term assets fell sharply, Sweden did not apparently suffer from the additional problems caused by a fall in the
general price level. Equally, there was much less assistance – Figure
1.5 – from general inflation than in the OPEC I and OPEC II recessions, and real interest rates rose significantly. There are therefore likely
to have been some adverse distributional effects on demand as borrowers
responded more strongly than asset holders to their altered circumstances.

Nevertheless, while Fisher (1933) placed considerable emphasis on
the role of a fall in the *general* price level in his account of the debt-
deflation process, it is surely the size of the reduction in the *relative*
price of long-term assets which is more important. It is this which
forces borrowers into insolvency, which undermines the assets of the
banking sector, and which erodes the net worth of future investors. It
is the prevalence, scale and risk of insolvency, and their consequences
for economic behaviour, which distinguish debt-deflations from the recessions of ordinary business cycles.

Jonung and Stymne's analysis of the economy of Sweden in the
early 1990s has demonstrated the depth and length of the recession in
the absence of a fall in the general price level – the economy was
clearly suffering from debt-deflation in this period. It follows that a
fall in the general price level cannot be regarded as a necessary condition for debt-deflation.

Note

1. This rise (fall) in asset values is inherent in the process of monetary and
   credit acceleration (deceleration), and, although it implies a change in
   the *relative* price of long-term versus short-term assets, in my view it is
   properly regarded as a monetary phenomenon.

References

Fisher, I. (1933) 'The Debt-Deflation Theory of Great Depressions', *Econometrica*, 1 October, 337–57

Minsky, H.P. (1982) 'Debt Deflation Processes in Today's Institutional Environment', *Banca Nazionale del Lavoro Quarterly Review*, 143, 377–93.

Comment

Patrick Foley

Sweden's recent economic development is in many respects similar to that of the UK. Deregulation in the second half of the 1980s led to a surge in private sector borrowing from banks, with the outstanding stock of banks' private sector lending rising by 140 per cent. As in the UK, much of this lending appears to have been used to support asset purchases (property and stock market).

The scale of the change is larger in Sweden than in the UK. On average, asset prices rose by much more in Sweden than in the UK during the 1980s – in real terms by around 100 per cent in the UK but over 200 per cent in Sweden. By 1990, the ratio of private credit to GDP had risen to over 140 per cent in Sweden, compared with less than 100 per cent in the UK at the same time.[1]

Like the UK, the boom in lending was brought to a halt by a sharp tightening of monetary policy, with tax changes contributing to that tightening. Interest rates had to be kept high, despite a weakening economy, as a result of the government's decision to link the Krona with the ECU. The weakening economy has caused the government's budget deficit to widen sharply, which contributed to growing speculation against the Krona, again much like the UK situation. The slowdown, together with high interest rates, has caused a sharp decline in asset prices, a surge in bad debt and deepening problems for Swedish banks. In the UK we have also seen declining asset prices and a big surge in bad debt, though neither on the same scale as Sweden,[2] nor with such dire consequences for the banks.

The chapter provides much discussion of the surge in borrowing and asset prices that resulted from deregulation and inappropriate monetary policies. But it would be interesting to see more discussion in the chapter of several issues:

1. Mervyn King points out in Chapter 5 that debt-deflation in the household sector probably owes much to distributional shocks – if savers and borrowers have different propensities to consume out of marginal income, a shock such as that caused by a change in real interest rates or a decline in asset prices will affect aggregate demand

even if it leaves aggregate household wealth unchanged. Is there any survey evidence on the behaviour of individuals in different financial circumstances during the recession?

2. The sequence of developments during the downturn is important. For instance, there is some evidence for the UK that the downturn was precipitated by a decline in business investment, and falling employment which accompanied it. In the first year of the UK downturn, the investment decline by itself would have accounted for 97 per cent of the drop in GDP. Businesses also managed to cut stocks by over 1 per cent of GDP, despite the downturn in aggregate demand being more severe than any had forecast. Consumer spending was by comparison slower to turn down, its eventual fall presumably in part reflecting the worsening employment situation. The same appears to be true for Sweden. Private consumption appears to have held up reasonable well until 1992. In 1992, for instance, it grew by just under 1 per cent. By contrast, industrial investment fell by 16 per cent in 1991, stocks fell by the equivalent of 1 1/2 per cent of GDP in the same year, and unemployment rose from 2.8 to 4.9 per cent. This is an important issue because it sheds light on the propagation mechanism, the route by which the initial shock reverberates through the economy. It appears to me that the propagation mechanism, at least in the early stages, works more through the business sector than the household sector.

3. Related to this, it would be interesting to have more discussion of the impact of adverse selection in credit markets. As the chapter briefly discusses, spreads between government bonds and housing bonds widened from around 100 basis points to close to 200 basis points on occasion during 1992. Bank loans spreads have also widened. According to OECD figures, loan spreads rose from an average of 5.3 per cent across all sectors in 1989 to 7.5 per cent in 1992, an increase of over 200 basis points. During that time, lending rates rose by an average of 3.1 per cent for businesses compared with 1.5 per cent for households, suggesting, as one would expect, that adverse selection was more of a problem in commercial lending than in personal lending. But this is only part of the impact of increasing adverse selection during the recession. There may be an increasing number of borrowers who are unable to raise loans at any price. Whilst the growth of bank lending in the UK slowed sharply during the recession in aggregate it has remained positive. In Sweden there has been a very substantial decline in lending. Based on figures from the Swedish Central Bank, my calculations

suggest a change in the lending stock (ignoring the effect of debt write-offs) of +2 per cent for businesses and -1 per cent for households, but -25 per cent for unincorporated businesses, which again is evidence of growing adverse selection, since one would expect the effect to be more severe in the small business sector.

In my view there appear to be at least three routes by which credit-related factors can affect real spending. First, there is the 'banking crisis' route, which can cause a credit crunch. In this case, bad debt weakens bank balance sheets, and this leads them to reduce lending. But this not really debt-deflation. Second, if asset prices fall, the value of loan collateral will also be reduced. Lending risk is increased, and this again leads to a reduction in bank lending. In the third case, a decline in asset values leads individuals and firms to attempt to reduce debt, thereby reducing the demand for loans. It is only these second and third cases which are true 'debt-deflation'. It would be interesting to know how important the authors feel each of these factors was in the Swedish case. In his presentation, Joakim Stymne argued that 'the downturn was a direct consequence of debt consolidation in response to reductions in wealth', i.e. route 3. But surely the banking crisis must have had some effect also.

I wonder how much the length and depth of the recession was simply a consequence of following a particularly long boom – what the OECD call 'the longest and strongest output boom since 1960'? Of course, the boom itself was in part the result of financial regulation, but may also have owed much to inappropriate monetary policy.

The chapter describes Sweden in the late 1980s as a 'hothouse' economy. Perhaps one lesson is that policy-makers in hothouse economies shouldn't throw stones! By that I mean that financial deregulation makes economies more unstable – as Mervyn King suggests in his chapter there may be multiple equilibria in such a world, not all of them stable. In such a world, policy-makers have to use the instruments at their command – which in a deregulated world probably means just interest rates – with more caution.

By the same token, private individuals will probably now have revised their ideas about the potential instability of the economy. This will presumably make them more cautious borrowers – and lenders – than was the case in the 1980s, thereby helping to reduce macroeconomic instability once more. It is perhaps inevitable that any period of financial deregulation in any economy will be followed by a period of volatility, because the actions of policy-makers and private individuals are conditioned by their past experience of the way the economy works rather than the new potentially more unstable world which we now believe they live in. But such volatility may not last if policy-makers, and others, including banks, learn from their mistakes.

Notes

1. BIS, 63rd Annual Report, June 1993.
2. For instance, six largest Swedish banks made loan loss provisions equal to 3.2 per cent of total assets in 1992, compared with 1.5 per cent for the four largest UK banks.

2 Debt-Deflation and Financial Instability: Two Historical Explorations

Barry Eichengreen and Richard S. Grossman[1]

INTRODUCTION

Recent research, both historical and contemporary, has broadened existing analyses of the connections between financial markets and macroeconomic conditions to encompass a broader menu of debt, credit and intermediation linkages between real and nominal variables. It is useful to distinguish two categories of contributions to this literature. In the first, which we label 'bank failure' explanations of cyclical fluctuations, one finds research linking bank failures, bank runs and other disturbances to the operation of financial intermediaries to fluctuations in output and employment. Bernanke's 1983 article on non-monetary effects of the financial crisis in the propagation of the Great Depression, emphasising the role of bank failures in disrupting financial intermediation and worsening the US depression, is an influential member of this school.[2] In the second category, which we label 'debt-deflation' theories, one finds studies seeking to establish the relevance for the business cycle of downward movements in asset and commodity prices, movements which, by affecting the net worth of non-financial borrowers, alter spending by households and firms. Calomiris and Hubbard's 1989 article on the real effects of price-level movements in the *postbellum* USA is a leading example of this genre.[3]

While it is useful to distinguish the effects of banking problems from those of movements in asset and commodity prices, clearly the two phenomena are related. In the pre-First World War USA, each of the episodes of financial crisis identified by Sprague (1910) was characterised by an upsurge of bank failures, a collapse of asset prices and a decline in the general price level. The temporal coincidence of these events suggests that banking panics and debt-deflation may have been causally connected, although the direction of causality is unclear. Similarly, during the Depression of the 1930s the banking panics identified

65

by Bernanke and James (1991) follow on the heels of the collapse of equity prices and a dramatic decline in the world price level. Again, historical accounts suggest that debt-deflation and banking crises may have been related, although whether they were two independent responses to a common underlying shock or there were causal connections between them remains an open question.[4]

The possibility of such connections has not escaped previous investigators. Minsky's (1977) emphasis on financial fragility is compatible with the argument that debt-deflation, by eroding the collateral against which banks lend, heightens financial institutions' vulnerability to destabilising shocks. Gorton (1988) shows that the downturn in prices and output associated with recessions tended to provoke financial crises in the 19th century. Bernanke, while focusing on bank failures, supplements his analysis of these factors with a discussion of debt deflation. Calomiris and Hubbard, in focusing on the real effects of price-level changes, cite the tendency for deflation to cause borrowers to default and banks to fail. Bernanke and James, while concentrating on banking panics, argue that the correlation between deflation and output declines in the 1930s, which survives even after controlling for other channels through which deflation operates, suggests the presence of a debt-deflation effect.

Although previous work has acknowledged the temporal coincidence of bank failures and collapses in asset and commodity prices, it has not analysed them in ways that facilitate attempts to differentiate their effects or to draw out their connections. One would like to be able to distinguish the extent to which collapses in asset and commodity prices adversely affect output by provoking bank failures and thereby reducing the efficiency of financial intermediation, versus the extent to which they erode the credit-worthiness of non-financial debtors, undermining the ability to borrow of agents on the other end of the transaction. One would wish to compare the importance of bank failures in depressing asset and commodity prices, and thereby inducing reductions in desired levels of consumption and investment, with disruptions in access to finance which prevent agents from achieving the levels of consumption and investment they desire.

In this chapter we explore two episodes on which much previous historical work has focused: the *post-bellum* USA and the global depression of the 1930s. We seek to distinguish the effects of bank failures and debt deflation and to probe the connections between them. The next section lays out some theoretical considerations and discusses problems of measurement. The third section then analyses economic fluctuations in the *post-bellum* USA. The fourth examines cross-country evidence from the Great Depression.

We adopt an agnostic perspective on the importance of debt-deflation. We do not wish to be interpreted as attempting to show that debt-deflation was necessarily important in the episodes analysed here. We think this sceptical approach is warranted for several reasons. One is the difficulty of conceptualising debt-deflation and of distinguishing it from alternative macroeconomic mechanisms. Formalising debt-deflation as a decline in asset and commodity prices that induces reductions in desired levels of consumption and investment on the part of households and firms is surely not sufficiently refined for definitive analysis. Caution is warranted on empirical grounds as well. Any empirical difficulties that hamper attempts to measure concepts such as, say, the money supply or the incidence of bank failures are dwarfed when one considers debt deflation. How does one measure the relevant debts in light of data limitations? While this is a problem for all attempts empirically to analyse debt-deflation, it poses special difficulties for historical work. Given the limitations of historical data, we therefore focus on the prices associated with the quantities that theory suggests should be relevant for debt-deflation. But this renders our results contingent on a further set of assumptions, which we describe on pp. 67–71. Inevitably, ambiguity arises concerning the interpretation of our evidence. Surprisingly, however, there does not appear to exist a previous empirical study that seeks to distinguish the effects of debt-deflation from those of bank failures and policy variables. We therefore think that out approach, despite the inevitable ambiguities, is useful in pushing the debate forward.

THEORY AND MEASUREMENT

Any attempt to distinguish the effects of 'banking crises' and 'debt-deflation' is handicapped by the difficulty of conceptualising and measuring the two concepts. In the case of the former, it is far from straightforward to identify banking 'panics' or 'crises' independent of their effects. Schwartz (1986) distinguishes 'real' from 'pseudo-' financial crises, maintaining that not all instances of deposit liquidation, bank runs and bank failures necessarily constitute a crisis in the sense of exercising an adverse impact on the real economy. While upsurges in bank failures tend to be one of the criteria investigators since Sprague have invoked when indentifying distress among financial intermediaries, it is clear that not all bank failures connote a panic or crisis of a sort that is likely to significantly affect economic activity. Limiting one's attention to episodes in which bank failures are accompanied by declines in output, on the other hand, would bias one toward finding an association between banking panics and cyclical fluctuations. Grossman (1993), in analysing US experience from 1874 through 1913, experiments with a number of proxies for banking problems, including the number of bank failures and the assets of failed or suspended banks. While this approach is free of the selection bias alluded to earlier in this paragraph, it runs the risk of conflating isolated bank failures with full-fledged panics. Schwartz (1986) and Bordo (1990) focus on the currency – deposit ratio as a measure of the severity of crises. This does not eliminate the need to invoke ancillary information, however, since a judgement still must be made about the critical threshold through which a change in that ratio must pass before qualifying as a 'crisis'.

Investigations of debt-deflation are similarly handicapped by difficulties of defining and measuring the concept. Fisher (1933) when coining the term failed to provide a clear definition, instead pointing to nine aspects of indebtedness and deflation with possible implications for the business cycle. While some subsequent investigators have associated the concept with a falling aggregate price level which raises the real value of nominally denominated debts, others have emphasised asset price deflation – a drop not in the general price level but in the market value of financial assets – which raises the value of net debt (gross debt net of assets).

In a single Chapter it is not possible to provide definitive solutions to these problems. Rather, we adopt as working conventions the following definitions and measures. By a 'banking crisis', we mean an increase in the incidence of distress among financial institutions which disrupts their ability to carry out their intermediation function. We measure the incidence of this distress in a number of alternative ways: as a function of the number of national bank failures and the assets of failed banks, and as binary indicator variables based on both qualitative and quantitative information. By 'debt-deflation', we mean a fall in the prices of either assets or goods and services that raises the real value of net debt, thereby worsening the net wealth position of non-financial borrowers and discouraging them from consuming or investing. Define the real value of net debt as $[(D-A)/P$, where D is gross debt, A is assets, and P is the price of goods and services. Then the real value of net debt, which we will also refer to as the 'real debt burden', can be raised by increasing indebtedness (a rise in D),] by asset-price deflation (a fall in A), or by commodity-price deflation (a fall in P). (An alternative measure of the debt burden that might appeal more to some readers is the net debt – income ratio $(D-A)/PY$, where Y is real income or output. In this case the debt burden can also be raised by a fall in Y.[5])

Measuring the debt burden poses difficulties for historical research. Time-series estimates of real net debt can be constructed for times and places like the 20th century USA on the basis of individual and corporate tax returns, but for periods preceding the adoption of personal and corporate income taxes, no comparable information is available.[6] While earlier information is available for public debt issues and the debts of publicly listed and traded companies, there is only scattered information on the debts of privately held companies (which dominate earlier periods) and households (limited mainly to spotty information on mortgage debts). On the asset side it might be possible to assemble time series on the value of publicly traded securities and on the assets of joint-stock companies publishing balance sheets, but doing so for private companies and estimating the asset position of households would be more difficult.[7]

Historical data on the market prices of assets and debts is more readily available than information on their quantities. The approach we take in this chapter is therefore to use information on prices and yields as indirect indicators of debt-deflation. Following Calomiris and Hubbard (1989) and Mishkin (1991), we focus on the information content of interest rate spreads. In an environment of asymmetric information, adverse selection can arise.[8] Consider a situation in which lenders have incomplete information about the risk characteristics of the projects that borrowers wish to undertake. As the interest rate rises, borrowers with relatively risky projects will become the likeliest to want to take out loans. This gives rise to the possibility of a backward-bending supply curve of loans and rationing in credit markets (Stiglitz and Weiss, 1981).

Lenders can reduce adverse selection by requiring borrowers to provide collateral.[9] If a borrower defaults, the lender takes title to the collateral and is compensated at least partially for the loss. If the collateral is of sufficiently good quality, the danger of loss and hence the existence of asymmetric information are no longer relevant; all borrowers should be able to obtain funds at the rate on risk-free loans.[10] As emphasised by Greenwald and Stiglitz (1988) and Bernanke and Gertler (1990), a collapse in asset prices, due say to a stock market crash, by eroding the value of collateral magnifies the implications of asymmetric information and adverse selection. The more the value of collateral falls, the less the compensation available to lenders in the event of default, and the larger the spread over the risk-free rate that will have to be paid by prospective borrowers when information is

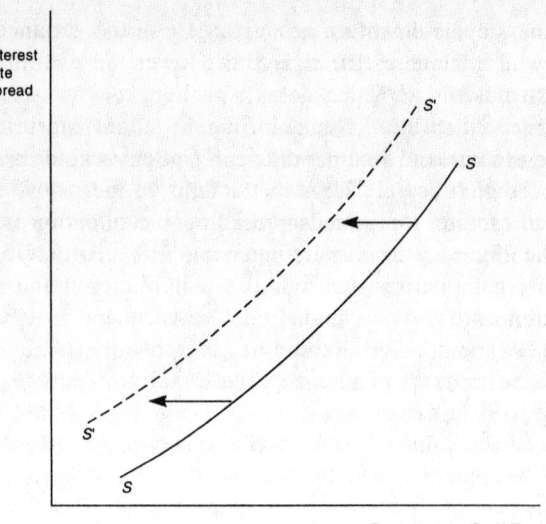

Figure 2.1   Debt-spread space

incomplete. Similarly, a fall in the general price level increases the real value of debt (reduces the real value of collateral) for potential borrowers, requiring them to pay larger interest rate spreads.

Figure 2.1 displays this schedule in debt-spread space. As the value of collateral declines ($[D-A]/P$ rises), larger spreads are demanded of potential borrowers.[11] This suggests that, other things being equal, the spread can be taken as a measure of the debt burden and hence of debt-deflation pressures.[12]

Importantly, other variables can shift the SS locus in debt-spread space. A banking crisis, for example, can be expected to shift the entire locus leftward from SS to $S'S'$. As Diamond (1984) and others emphasise, banks can engage in delegated monitoring and establish long-term relationships with borrowers in order to attenuate adverse selection and asymmetric information problems. A shock to the banking system which disrupts the ability of financial intermediaries to assemble information and screen borrowers will consequently increase the spread corresponding to any level of collateral. Thus, the impact of a change in spreads on output can be interpreted as a debt-deflation effect only if one controls for bank failures and other variables capable of shifting the SS locus in debt-spread space.

Some readers may remain uncomfortable with our use of interest rate spreads to proxy for debt-deflation. They may worry, for example, that a business cycle downturn or an increase in the variance of output or prices, which increases the size of the lower tail of the wealth and income distributions at which default on liabilities occurs, may also increase observed spreads. Our point is that output and prices so low as to erode income and wealth sufficiently to provoke default by non-financial borrowers is precisely what should be meant by 'debt-deflation.' Spread captures this effect so long as one controls for other factors affecting the efficiency of financial intermediation. The addition of such controls is what distinguishes our use and interpretation of interest rate spreads from other work, such as Calomiris and Hubbard (1989), Mishkin (1991), and Bordo, Rappaport and Schwartz (1992) where they are interpreted in terms of a range of financial problems including but not limited to debt-deflation.

Others may object that spreads, insofar as they reflect the term structure of interest rates, are picking up expectations of future price-level trends and liquidity preference effects. To minimise the contamination of spreads by these effects, we compute them from higher- and lower-grade railroad bonds of comparable maturities for the *post-bellum* USA; for the inter-war period we compare central bank discount rates and commercial paper rates rather than mixing bond and commercial paper rates. And insofar as spreads rise in business cycle downturns because default risk on low quality bonds rises disproportionately, this reflects the rise in $(D-A)/PY$ (the erosion in the real value of collateral) that is at the centre of debt-deflation analyses.

In the following sections we employ this model of the relationship between interest rate spreads and debt-deflation in an effort to marshall evidence on the operation of the latter.

EVIDENCE FROM THE *POST-BELLUM* USA

The *post-bellum* USA is a natural laboratory for analysing the connections between debt-deflation, banking panics and business cycles. Cyclical instability was pronounced – although how much more pronounced than in the post-Second World War period remains a matter of dispute.[13] Wholesale prices fell steadily, by more than 1 per cent per annum, for fully two decades prior to the mid-1890s, which itself could have elevated the real burden of existing debts.[14] On a number of occasions the price level declined abruptly, telescoping the effects of general price deflation into shorter periods. The *post-bellum* years saw waves of bank failures, most notable in 1873, 1893 and 1907. On each occasion asset prices plummeted, eroding the value of borrowers' collateral. Influential accounts (see Sprague, 1910; Kindleberger, 1978) emphasise the importance of asset and debt-market collapses and banking panics in the business cycles of the period.

Two attempts to elucidate the connections between these variables are Calomiris and Hubbard (1989) and Grossman (1993). Calomiris and Hubbard use monthly data for the period 1893–1909 and a structural vector autoregression model to analyse the contribution of credit market disruptions to business cycle fluctuations. Their analysis focuses on the correlation between measures of credit market distress like the spread between interest rates on high- and low-risk assets and economic activity (their preferred measure being pig iron production).[15] They document significant correlations between credit market disturbances and output fluctuations.

For our purposes, their approach and results are subject to two limitations. The first, noted above, is that their formulation does not lend itself to the distinction between debt-deflation and banking crises. As shown in Figure 2.1, an increase in the interest rate spread could result from either debt-deflation or a banking crisis which shifted the relationship between real net indebtedness and observed interest rates. A second problem is that the authors find that an increase in the interest rate spread is contemporaneously associated with increases in output and prices, seemingly inconsistent with interpretation of the spread as a measure of debt deflation.

Grossman (1993) focuses not on debt-deflation but on banking crises. Using quarterly data for a longer period than Calomiris and Hubbard, he estimates a structural macroeconomic model designed to extend the *IS-LM* framework to incorporate monetary and nonmonetary effects of bank failures. In Grossman's model, bank failures can reduce output by prompting a shift into currency from deposits, depressing the money multiplier, reducing the money supply and shifting the *LM* curve to the left. Alternatively, bank failures can depress output through nonmonetary (confidence or spending) channels that shift the *IS* curve to the left. Grossman presents evidence consistent with the operation of both channels. For present purposes, the limitation of this approach is again that it does not enable us to distinguish the effects of banking panics from those of debt-deflation, since asset- and price-level collapses, whose effects are not treated explicitly, tended to coincide with upsurges in bank failures.

This correlation is plotted in Figure 2.2 for the period 1876–1913. Its two panels juxtapose two measures of bank failures (assets of bank

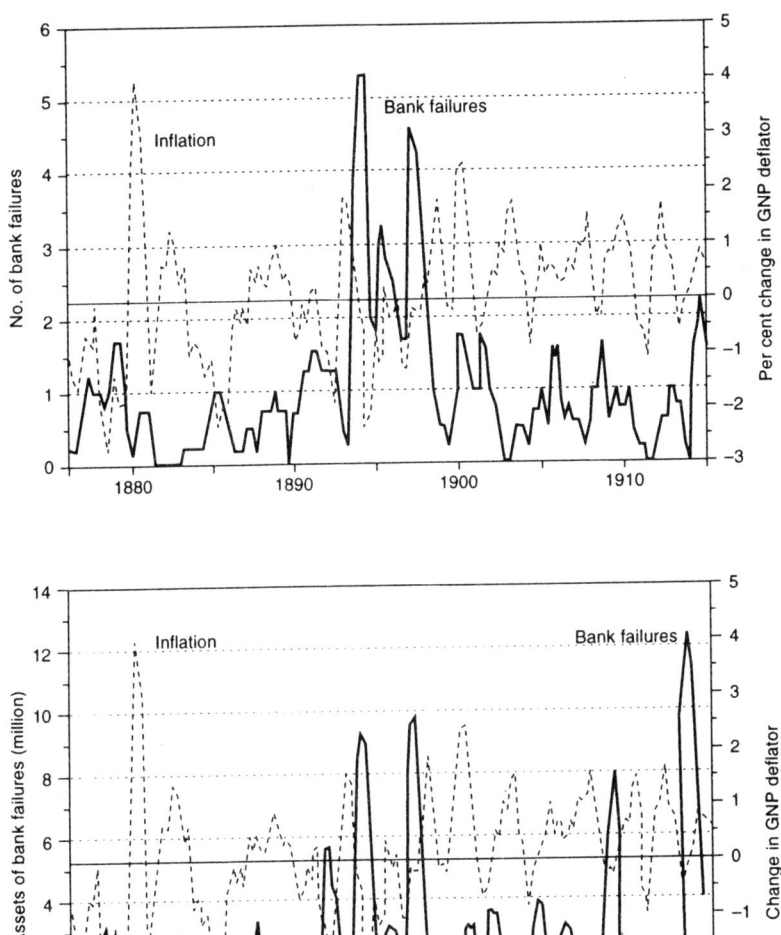

Figure 2.2   Bank failures and inflation/deflation, four-quarter moving average

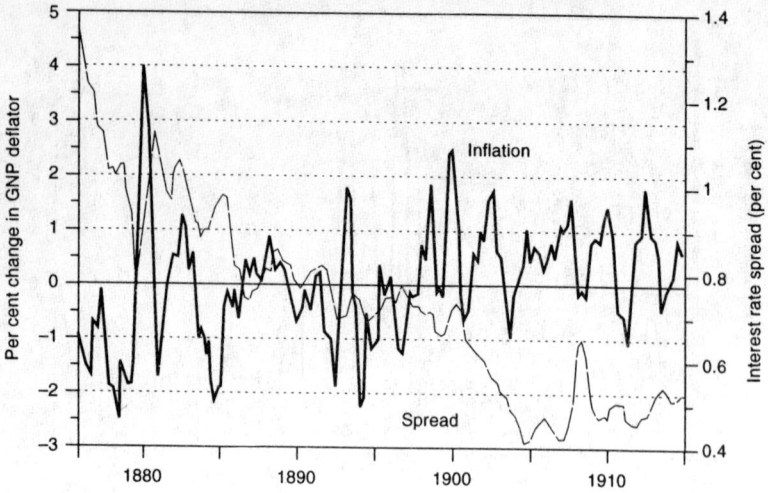

Figure 2.3   Inflation/deflation and spread, four-quarter moving average

failures and number of bank failure) against the percentage rate of
change of the GNP deflator. All variables are expressed as four-quarter
moving averages. A negative correlation between the number of bank
failures and the rate of inflation is apparent, consistent with the notion
that deflation is conducive to financial instability (and vice versa). The
correlation coefficient of -0.12, however, is not significantly different
from zero. Figure 2.3 shows the analogous relationship between the
interest rate spread and the rate of inflation. This correlation is a mar-
ginally stronger -0.20, although it is still not significantly different from
zero; the sign is not inconsistent with our interpretation of the spread
in terms of debt-deflation. Figure 2.4 plots the spread and the number
of bank failures. Although the two variables appear to move together
during certain episodes, over the entire period they are uncorrelated.[16]

   We also ran bivariate Granger causality tests between these pairs of
variables.[17] The only statistically significant relationships were those
between inflation and the spread. Prior declines in the price level significantly predicted subsequent increases in the spread (at the 99 per
cent confidence level), again consistent with out interpretation of the
spread in terms of debt-deflation. In addition, increases in the spread
predicted deflation, as if the process fed on itself in a vicious circle.
There was no bivariate relationship, in contrast, between the interest
rate spread and the number or assets of failed banks. We found no

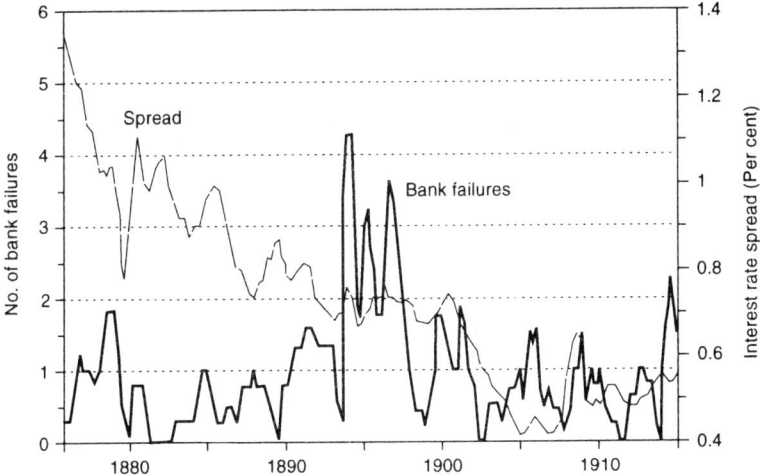

Figure 2.4   Bank failures and spread, four-quarter moving average

support, in other words, for the idea that debt-deflation heightened the fragility of the banking system or that bank failures were conducive to debt-deflation.

One way of more precisely distinguishing the various effects is to augment Calomiris and Hubbard's vector autoregressions to incorporate the effects of bank failures. Holding constant shocks to the bank failure equation, we can interpret the effects of shocks to the interest rate-spread equation in terms of debt-deflation, in the spirit of Figure 2.1 above.[18] Holding shocks to the spread constant, we can interpret shocks to the bank failure equation in terms of financial market disruptions narrowly defined.

The data used in this analysis are described in the Data Appendix. We consider the same variables as Calomiris and Hubbard, augmenting their specification to include bank failures. Our implementation differs slightly. Rather than monthly data spanning the 1890s and 1900s, we use quarterly observations for the period 1881:1–1914:1. This enables us to utilise a more comprehensive measure of output, Balke and Gordon's (1989) quarterly estimates of real GNP. Rather than the structural VAR approach, we use the Choleski decomposition, considering different orderings to test the sensitivity of our results.

The F-statistics for the joint significance of four lagged values of the explanatory variables in the various equations are reported in Table 2.1.[19]

Table 2.1 VAR estimates:[1] F-statistics (sign of sum of coefficients), dependent variables

Independent variables	Loan flow	Commercial paper	Spread	Prices	Output	Bank failures	Business failures
Loan flow	0.460 (+)	0.099 (−)	0.304 (−)	0.970 (+)	0.526 (−)	0.199 (−)	0.031 (+)
Commercial paper rate	0.757 (−)	11.7 (+)	0.351 (+)	0.872 (−)	2.50 (−)	2.52 (−)	3.24 (+)
Interest rate spread	0.168 (+)	1.61 (−)	28.7 (+)	0.379 (−)	1.82 (−)	0.368 (−)	0.157 (−)
Change in prices	1.94 (−)	1.35 (+)	1.77 (+)	0.885 (−)	0.984 (−)	1.38 (−)	2.75 (+)
Change in output	0.790 (+)	2.04 (+)	0.711 (+)	0.545 (+)	4.83 (−)	2.28 (−)	0.197 (−)
Bank failures (no.)	0.684 (−)	3.62 (−)	0.843 (−)	1.57 (−)	2.83 (−)	2.38 (+)	0.37 (+)
Business failures (nominal assets)	0.779 (+)	1.26 (−)	1.82 (−)	0.797 (−)	1.87 (+)	0.059 (+)	6.52 (−)

Note: VAR uses quarterly data over the period 1881:1–1914:1. All regressions include quarterly dummies and a time trend.

Sources: See text.

An increase in the number of bank failures and in the spread both have negative impacts on subsequent output movements. The coefficient on bank failures differs significantly from zero at standard confidence levels, while that on the spread approaches but does not quite achieve significance. These results are not inconsistent with financial instability and debt-deflation theories. In addition, output responds negatively to lagged values of the interest rate and the price level, although only the coefficients on the first of these variables are jointly significant at standard confidence levels.[20]

The variables considered here have less explanatory power in the other equations. Bank failures, in addition to showing considerable persistence, rise when output falls, when prices decline, when business failures increase, and when there is a prior disruption to the flow of loans. But only the commercial paper rate and output, in addition to lagged failures, have a statistically significant effect on failures in a single-equation setting.[21] The spread is most strongly affected by lagged prices and business failures. Commercial paper rates depend significantly on lagged output and bank failures. While their positive response to output is intuitive, their negative response to bank failures is not; we return to this point below.[22] Business failures respond positively, as expected, to interest rates; surprisingly, they increase when prices rise. The real flow of loans responds negatively to increases in the price level, perhaps reflecting the tendency of price increases to raise the deflator rather than to reduce the nominal flow of loans.

Impulse-response functions based on moving average representation of these regressions provide a more comprehensive picture of the interaction of these variables. We summarise the results in two ways: in the form of plots of the responses to disturbances of variables of interest, and in the form of variance decompositions which measure the share of the forecast-error variance attributable to each innovation. Consider the responses to innovations to bank failures and the spread.[23] The spread, when shocked, takes a considerable period to decline back toward initial levels (Figure 2.5); in comparison, bank failures decline rapidly following a shock to their number (Figure 2.6).[24] Output falls on impact in response to both shocks (Figure 2.7), for the reasons described above. In response to an increase in the spread, output takes four quarters to recover; in the case of bank failures that recovery is immediate. Prices also fall in response to both shocks. Their reaction to a bank failure shock is short and sharp, that to a spread shock shallower but more persistent, mirroring the response of output. Interest rates fall in response to both shocks, bottoming out after two quarters (Figure 2.8).

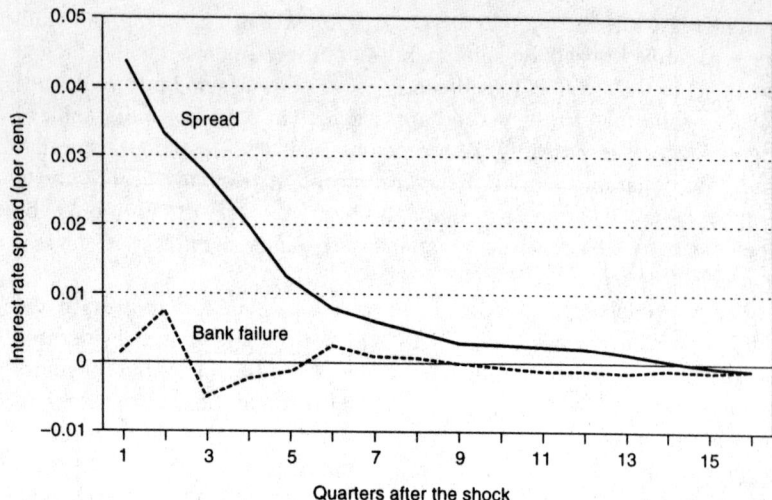

Figure 2.5   Impulse-response of spread to spread and bank failure shocks

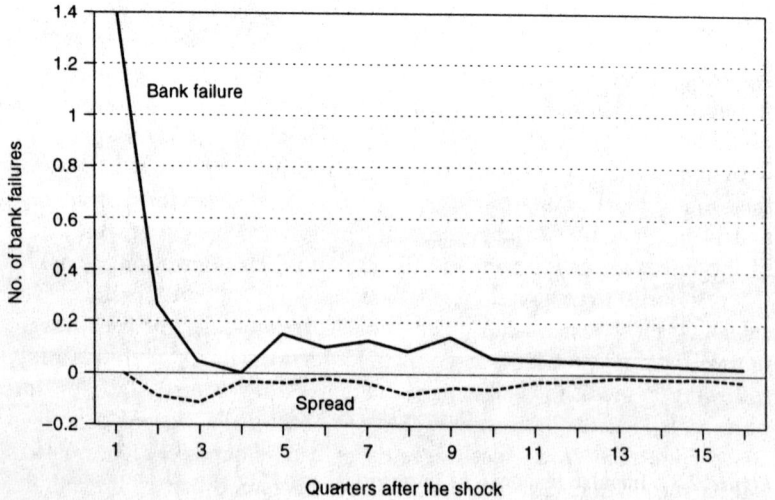

Figure 2.6   Impulse-response of bank failures to spread and bank failure shocks

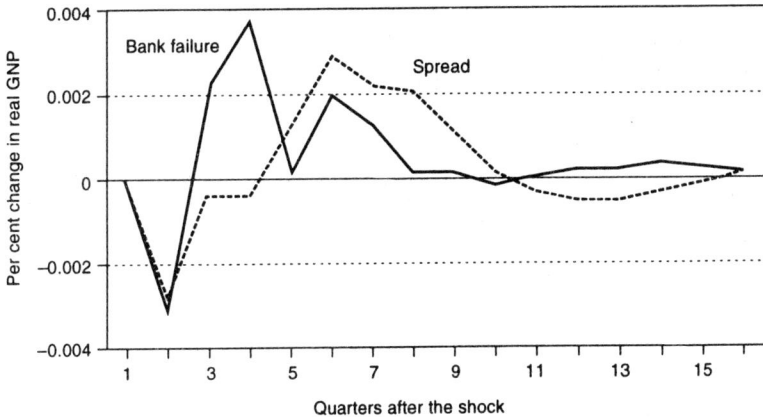

Figure 2.7   Impulse-response of output to spread and bank failure shocks

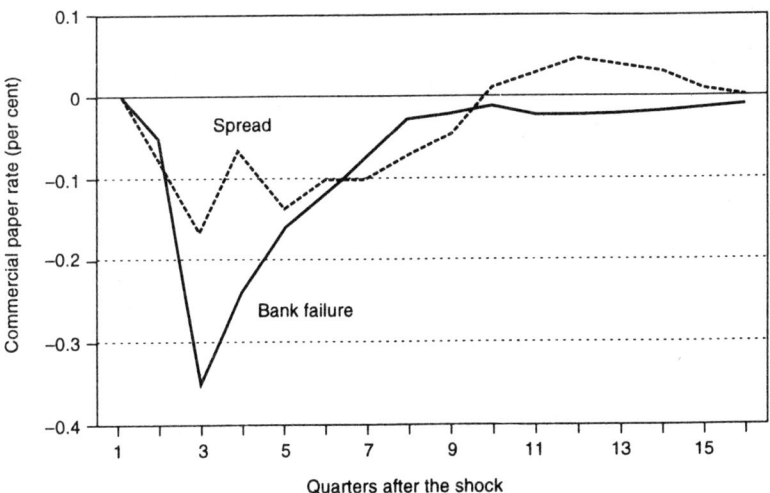

Figure 2.8   Impulse-response of commercial paper to spread and bank failure shocks

This reflects both the direct negative effect of bank failures and the spread that was noted above and the indirect effect operating through output (which declined in response to the shocks, further depressing interest rates).

Especially interesting from the present point of view is the response of the spread and bank failures to one another. An increase in bank failures causes, on impact, a small uptick in the spread, but the response is minimal (Figure 2.5). Table 2.1 showed that the direct effect of bank failures on the spread was negligible; the impulse-response function shows that the absence of a link remains after incorporating indirect effects operating through prices, output and interest rates.[25] An interpretation is that spillovers from financial instability to debt-deflation were insignificant in this period. Similarly, we find a very small response of the number of bank failures to a positive shock to the spread (Figure 2.6). The interpretation is the same: the direct effect of the spread on bank failures in Table 2.1 is small, negative and statistically insignificant; in the impulse-response functions this effect is not significantly modified by indirect effects operating through output, prices or interest rates. Again, it would seem that spillovers from debt-deflation to financial instability were not noticeable during this period.

Another perspective on the impulse-responses can be obtained from the associated variance decompositions. Table 2.2 summarises these after 12 quarters. The row for output shows that more than 60 per cent of forecast error variance for output at this horizon is attributable to output innovations themselves, not surprisingly given the persistence in this variable (which shows up in the output equation in Table 2.1 in the form of a large F-statistic on lagged output).[26] But the next most important determinant of output variance is innovations to the spread, which account for 15 percent of the total. The contribution of bank failures, in contrast, is only a third as large, comparable to that of interest rates and price-level changes and larger than that of business failures and the flow of loans.

The variance decompositions also support our findings concerning the interaction of bank failures and the spread. Bank failure shocks account for less than 2 per cent in the forecast error variance of the spread after 12 quarters.[27] Shocks to the spread account for less than 5 per cent of the analogous variance of bank failures.[28]

To test the robustness of the results, we deflated the assets of business failures by the price level (those assets are in nominal terms in the regressions discussed above); this had minimal effect. Following Bordo, Rappoport and Schwartz (1992), we added the money supply

Table 2.2 Variance decomposition, per cent, after 12 quarters

Equation	Loan flow	Spread	Interest rate	Output	Prices	Bank failures	Business failures
Loan flow	84.33	1.24	0.52	2.82	6.10	1.47	3.49
Spread	0.15	89.54	1.73	1.21	4.51	1.42	1.44
Interest rate	1.20	21.97	37.06	14.30	6.76	17.95	1.65
Output	1.16	15.70	5.46	61.95	5.76	5.76	4.21
Prices	3.20	2.94	4.17	2.36	78.76	4.97	3.60
Bank failures	0.98	4.39	12.73	5.83	3.45	72.13	0.50
Business failures	1.99	13.40	9.84	2.64	7.20	6.01	58.92

Sources: See text.

to our vector of regressors.[29] The response of the other variables to bank failure and spread shocks remained essentially unchanged.[30] In addition, the money supply fell in response to both spread and bank failure shocks.[31] Different orderings did not alter impact effects and only modestly affected the contours of the subsequent response. One change that made a difference was to substitute the assets of bank failures for the number of bank failures. Lagged values of this variable, somewhat implausibly, have a positive impact on output in regressions like those of Table 2.1; in the associated impulse-response functions output rises on impact in reaction to a bank failure shock. The spread and the commercial paper rate behave as before.

What are the implications of these findings? Controlling for bank failures and several additional variables that might plausibly shift the *SS* curve in Figure 2.1, we find a negative impact on output of interest rate spreads, which we interpret as the effect of debt-deflation.[32] This fall in output is short-lived: it reaches its maximum after one quarter, and output has fully recovered after four quarters, although it continues to cycle. The impact effect on output of a one standard deviation shock to the spread is almost exactly the same as that of a one standard deviation shock to the number of bank failures, but the recovery of output from a bank failure shock is faster. A plausible interpretation of these results is that both financial instability and debt-deflation mattered for output movements in the USA prior to 1913, but that neither helps greatly in explaining the persistence of business cycle fluctuations.

Finally, we find no evidence of connections between bank failures and debt-deflation. There is scant indication of causality running in either direction. Insofar as historical accounts suggest a temporal coincidence of financial instability and debt-deflation, this is most likely to have reflected the response of bank failures and asset – debt positions to common underlying shocks.

EVIDENCE FROM THE GREAT DEPRESSION

Another episode in which the effects of debt-deflation may be evident is the global slump of the 1930s. This was, after all, the experience that led Fisher to develop his debt-deflation theory of Great Depressions. The period was characterised by the collapse of asset prices, most prominently in the USA following the Great Crash on Wall Street but in other countries as well. It featured a dramatic decline in the general price level in a range of countries linked together by the international gold standard. If the effects of debt-deflation are hard to discern in this period, it is difficult to imagine another in which they might more plausibly operate.

A problem for empirical analysis is that debt-deflation is only one of several transmission mechanisms running from monetary deflation to output. Bernanke and James (1991) enumerate several possible channels. One is the tendency of declining producer prices to put upward pressure on real wages and reduce profitability, a pattern which was evident in all the industrial countries. If money wages adjust incompletely to the fall in the price level, firms should be induced to move down their upward-sloping supply curves to lower levels of production. This is a mechanism stressed by Eichengreen and Sachs (1985), Newell and Symons (1988) and Sumner (1994), among others. Problems with this explanation include the possibility that the rise in real wages was simply a corollary rather than an independent cause of the Depression and the fact that the sluggishness of money wages was apparently so persistent.

A second channel is real interest rates. If the post-1929 deflation was largely unanticipated, deflation would have raised real interest rates, discouraging consumption and investment. Research on the USA (see Cecchetti, 1992; Hamilton, 1992) suggests that the deflation was at least partly unanticipated. Moreover, even a fully anticipated deflation of the magnitude of that of the early 1930s could have raised real interest rates because of the zero floor on the nominal interest rate. For how long and for how many countries this constraint was binding is unclear, however, because some nominal interest rates in gold standard countries rose rather than falling after 1932.

A third conceivable channel is the direct effect on expenditure of declining money supplies. Schwartz (1981) and others argue, most prominently for the USA but by implication for other countries, that the contraction of the money supply contributed to the severity of the Depression by depressing spending. Authors adopting this perspective emphasise the impact of monetary contraction on demand operating through channels other than the interest rate.

A fourth channel, emphasised by Bernanke (1983) and Bernanke and James (1991), is banking crises. These authors stress the tendency for deflation to undermine the stability of financial institutions. The consequent banking crises disrupted the ability of financial institutions to undertake their intermediation function, cutting the access to external finance of even credit-worthy borrowers and depressing demand.

In comparison with banking crises, 'much less has been written' on debt-deflation.[33] Debts are difficult to measure, notwithstanding the work of Mishkin (1978) on the household sector in the USA and Goldsmith's efforts (described above).[34] Bernanke and James suggest that the residual effects of price level movements – once real wages, real interest rates and real exchange rates have been controlled for – may be attributable to debt-deflation. The problem with this approach, as the authors are aware, is that the residual effect of prices is a catch-all for omitted price-level effects and measurement errors.

The obvious way of dealing with the existence of multiplicity of explanations is multivariate analysis. Thus, Bernanke and James estimate multiple regressions using pooled time-series and cross-section data for 24 countries over the period of 1930–6. They estimate their equations by ordinary least squares on the grounds that the deflation driving the movement of the independent variables was imposed by exogenous monetary forces associated with the operation of the international gold standard.

We extend their approach, building on their data and specification, but adding a measure of the interest rate spread in an attempt to directly estimate debt-deflation effects. Insofar as their measure of banking panics adequately controls for events in financial markets that shift the relationship between spreads and the real debt burden, we can interpret the coefficient on the spread as a measure of the importance of debt-deflation.

We measure spreads as the difference between rates on commercial paper and central bank discount rates. Commercial paper rates are available only for a subset of countries, necessarily reducing the size of the sample.[35] We experimented with the difference between the rate of interest on government bonds and a non-governmental bond rate; this did not produce consistent results, which we attribute to the especially small sample for which long-term rates were available (70 observations) and the fact that the 1930s was characterised by problems of sovereign default, rendering the yield on government bonds a highly imperfect measure of the risk-free rate.[36]

Figures 2.9–2.11 juxtapose this measure of the spread against the change in industrial production relative to 1929. there is no robust bivariate relationship between the two variables.[37]

Table 2.3 reports the basic regression estimates. The dependent variable is the change in the log of industrial production; the independent variables are proxies for the various channels of transmission discussed above. We come close to replicating Bernanke and James's results. The change in output is positively related to the change in the whole-sale price level, positively related to the rate of exchange rate depreciation, and negatively related to the change in the central bank discount rate, although the statistical significance of some of these effects varies across specifications. The sign of the coefficient on money wages seems particularly sensitive to the inclusion of the dummy for financial panics. The panic variable – Bernanke and James's dummy variable for number of months in the year in which a country experienced a financial panic, based on the incidence on bank failures and bank runs – is negative, statistically significant at standard confidence levels, and

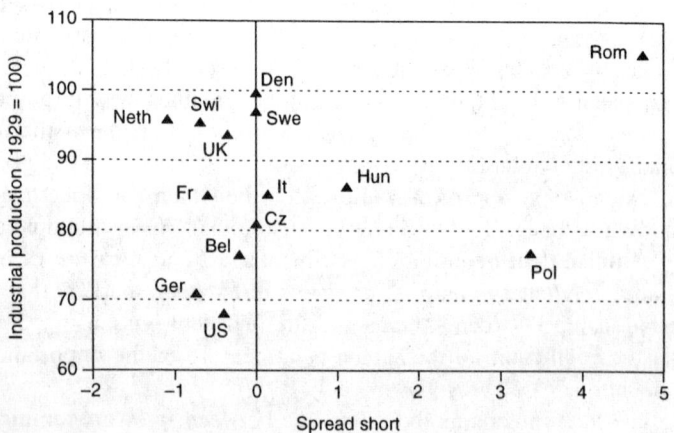

Figure 2.9   1931: commercial paper – central bank discount rate spread and industrial production

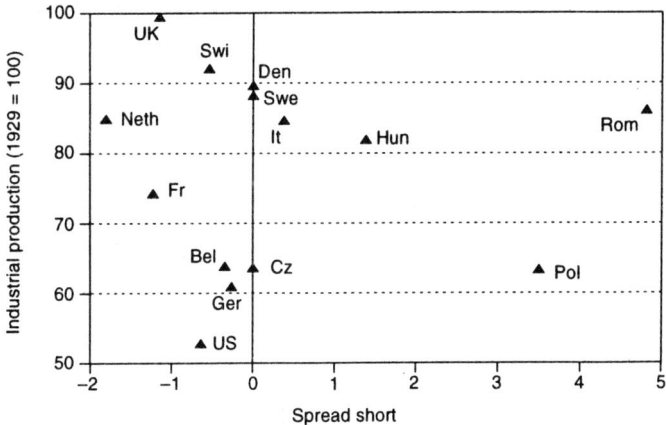

Figure 2.10   1932: commercial paper – central bank discount rate spread and industrial production

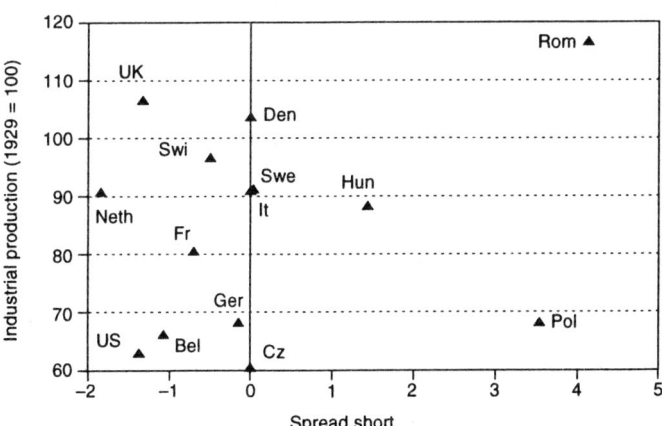

Figure 2.11   1933: commercial paper – central bank discount rate spread and industrial production

Table 2.3 Inter-war regression results[1] (standard errors) dependent variable is log-difference of industrial production

Constant	dln(WP')	Panic	dln(EX)	dln(W)	DISC	dln(M)	N	R^2
1 -0.001 (0.038)	0.805 (0.094)	—	—	—	—	—	167	0.270
2 0.058 (0.036)	0.639 (0.090)	-0.015 (0.002)	—	—	—	—	167	0.402
3 -0.004 (0.031)	0.300 (0.102)	—	0.305 (0.039)	—	—	—	167	0.487
4 0.0279 (0.032)	0.305 (0.099)	-0.008 (0.002)	0.247 (0.042)	—	—	—	167	0.516
5 -0.005 (0.031)	0.272 (0.110)	—	0.336 (0.044)	0.043 (0.170)	—	—	147	0.529
6 0.029 (0.033)	0.310 (0.109)	-0.008 (0.003)	0.238 (0.047)	-0.160 (0.182)	—	—	147	0.552
7 0.106 (0.046)	0.188 (0.111)	—	0.270 (0.046)	0.0908 (0.171)	-0.200 (0.646)	—	140	0.562
8 0.164 (0.046)	0.237 (0.108)	-0.009 (0.003)	0.208 (0.048)	-0.171 (0.184)	-0.200 (0.061)	—	140	0.565
9 -0.033 (0.036)	—	—	0.348[2] (0.528)	0.369 (0.184)	—	0.264 (0.101)	146	0.395
10 0.006 (0.038)	—	-0.010 (0.003)	0.281[2] (0.056)	0.114 (0.200)	—	0.276 (0.098)	146	0.428

Note:
1. The regression results replicate those of Bernanke and James (1991).
2. Real exports.

Source: See text.

has an economically important effect. The change in the log of the money supply has significant effect on output even after controlling for financial panics, interest rates and the price level.

We then added the spread to these equations. We ran the final two equations from Table 2.3 on three samples of countries: the full sample, the full sample minus Romania (since the scatter plots indicated Romania to be a consistent outlier), and the full sample minus France and Italy (Table 2.4).[38] Evidence of a debt-deflation effect, as captured by the coefficient on the spread, is inconsistent. While this coefficient is negative more often than not, it varies in sign and often differs insignificantly from zero at standard confidence levels. Only when money supply is included among the independent variables, as in Table 2.4, is the coefficient on the spread consistently negative, as predicted by debt-deflation theories, and does it approach statistical significance at standard confidence levels.[39] If these results are to be believed, they suggest that both monetary and financial (debt-deflation and panic-related disintermediation) shocks, and not just one or the other, were important for the propagation of the Great Depression. Were one forced to choose, however, the coefficients on money and panics are considerably more robust than those on the spread.

Is it plausible that our spread variable is capturing the (seemingly weak) effects of debt-deflation? This will be the case only if the regressions control adequately for disruptions to the financial system that shift our *SS* curve (the relationship between the spread and real net debt). The danger is that Bernanke and James's dummy variable for financial panics does so imperfectly. Although this variable is based on precisely the factor which we argue is the most likely candidate to shift the *SS* curve, namely serious banking problems, it is derived from a subjective judgement of years and nations in which banking problems were 'serious'. Clearly, there is scope for error here.[40]

Bernanke and James point out that in a model which controls adequately for debt-deflation, the coefficient on the change in the log price level should be equal and opposite in sign to the sum of the coefficients on the change in the log exchange rate, the change in the log money wage, and the change in the central bank discount rate.[41] This is not the case of Bernanke and James's results, even when they include their financial panic measure. It is true, however, when we also control for the interest rate spread, supporting our belief that we have succeeded in capturing effects of debt-deflation.

A proponent of the null hypothesis would say that we have found some evidence, especially after controlling for the effects of monetary

Table 2.4 Inter-war regression results including spread[1]

	Constant	Panic	$dln(EX)$	$dln(W)$	$dln(M)$	Spread	N	R^2
Full sample								
1	-0.077 (0.044)	— —	0.300 (0.064)	0.431 (0.218)	0.368 (0.143)	-0.040 (0.027)	97	0.377
2	-0.031 (0.044)	-0.014 (0.004)	0.213 (0.066)	-0.087 (0.257)	0.420 (0.135)	-0.050 (0.025)	97	0.449
Omitting Romania								
3	-0.086 (0.049)	— —	0.317 (0.065)	0.490 (0.223)	0.383 (0.153)	-0.049 (0.033)	90	0.519
4	-0.050 (0.048)	-0.012 (0.004)	0.234 (0.068)	0.038 (0.260)	0.428 (0.146)	-0.063 (0.032)	90	0.573
Omitting France and Italy								
5	-0.086 (0.046)	— —	0.301 (0.068)	0.368 (0.242)	0.315 (0.158)	-0.053 (0.028)	83	0.501
6	-0.039 (0.049)	-0.013 (0.006)	0.245 (0.071)	-0.120 (0.325)	0.350 (0.155)	-0.057 (0.028)	83	0.534

Note:
1. All equations include real exports.

Sources: See text.

shocks, that debt-deflation mattered in the Great Depression. The evidence supporting that view is far from conclusive, however. In comparison, the evidence that alternative channels, including monetary effects, interest rate effects, exchange rate policy and financial panics, played an important role in the propagation of the Depression is considerably more robust.

SUMMARY AND IMPLICATIONS

Our ambition in this chapter has been to advance the discussion of the role of debt-deflation in two historical periods: the *post-bellum* USA and the global depression of the 1930s. Given the difficulty of assembling historical data on the net debts of households and firms, we have focused on the asset prices that should be associated with the relevant quantities and sought to control for other factors also likely to affect those prices. The results reinforce the sceptical perspective with which we approached the question. While we find in the data for the *post-bellum* USA some evidence of a negative impact of our measure of debt-deflation on real GDP, that impact is short-lived; it can hardly account for the persistence of pre-war business cycles. Strikingly, we find little evidence of connections between debt-deflation and the incidence of bank failures. Our analysis of cross-section data for a range of countries in the Great Depression similarly provides some evidence consistent with the debt-deflation thesis, but this finding is sensitive to changes in specification; in particular, it hinges on controlling for monetary shocks. And even then the evidence of a distinct debt-deflation effect is far from robust.

Does this mean that debt-deflation should be purged from the agenda of macroeconomic historians, who are better advised to concentrate on other transmission mechanisms? Inevitably, it is possible for true believers in debt-deflation as well as sceptics to draw support from our results. Resolving this debate will ultimately require the development of better historical data.

Data Appendix

For our analysis of the *post-bellum* USA, we attempted to replicate and extend the data set of Calomiris and Hubbard (1989). The authors provided us with their data on the monthly change in loans outstanding for banks in New York City, Philadelphia and Boston. These were assembled on a monthly basis from weekly reports in the *Commercial and Financial Chronicle*. We use the figure for the last month of each quarter. We deflate the change in loans by the current period's price index. The commercial paper rate, also using end-of-quarter months, is taken from Macaulay (1938). Data on interest rates spreads was provided by Frederick Mishkin. The Mishkin measure is the spread between high and lower grade railway bonds, calculated from data in Macaulay (1938); for details, see Mishkin (1991). Again, end-of-quarter months were used. Quarterly data on the change in the GNP deflator and real GNP are from Balke and Gordon (1986). The change in the assets of business failures are from US Department of Commerce (1949, Appendix 30). The number and assets of national bank failures (including those eventually restored to solvency) were compiled from the list of receiverships reported in the Comptroller of the Currency's *Annual Report*. Assets of banks placed in receivership and subsequently restored to solvency were frequently not reported in the list of receiverships; assets of these institutions were taken from previous *Annual Report* statements of the condition of banks. The money supply is M2, taken from Friedman and Schwartz (1963).

Our inter-war data set, following Bernanke and James (1991), was compiled mainly from publications of the League of Nations and the International Labour Organisation. We use the log difference of industrial production and of the wholesale price index, as in Bernanke and James (1991, Tables 2.2 and 2.4).

The log difference of money wages was measured using nominal hourly wages from the International Labour Organisation wherever possible. The central bank discount rate, the commercial paper rate, and the log difference of notes and currency in circulation are from the League of Nations' *Statistical Yearbook* (various issues).

Notes

1. This Chapter was prepared for the City University's Debt-Deflation Conference (14–15 April 1994). Much of the work was undertaken during Eichengreen's visit to the International Monetary Fund and Grossman's sabbatical at the Hebrew University. We thank both institutions for their hospitality, Charles Calomiris and Rick Mishkin for help with data, David Selover and Nathan Sussman for technical assistance, and Nick Crafts, Charles Calomiris and Anna Schwartz for comments. For financial support, Grossman thanks the German Marshall Fund of the United

States, Eichengreen the Center for German and European Studies of the University of California.

2.   For our purposes, theories that link bank failures to business cycles via a contraction of the money supply, *à la* Friedman and Schwartz (1963), fall into a separate category ('monetary explanations') from that emphasising debt, credit and intermediation linkages. We return to this distinction below.

3.   The literature on cyclical fluctuations is replete with other theories, for example those that emphasise monetary and technological shocks. Our purpose here is not to provide a complete catalogue, however, but simply to distinguish between two theories focusing on credit, debt and intermediation.

4.   While we do not comment in this chapter on recent experience, we cannot resist pointing to the coincidence in recent years of banking crises and asset price collapses in countries like Sweden, Finland, Israel, Japan and the UK.

5.   In the present context, this measure may be problematic, since as a matter of arithmetic, debt-deflation (defined as a rise in the net debt: income ratio) can result from a fall in the level of activity, heightening simultaneity problems for debt-deflation theories of the business cycle.

6.   Thus, US Department of Commerce (1976) provides time-series estimates of the net debt of the public, corporate and household sectors for the periods 1916–70. For details on sources, see Kuvin (1936).

7.   Goldsmith (1985) made an heroic attempt to assemble national balance sheets for more than a dozen countries for the relevant period, but his estimates exist only for benchmark years and are disaggregated only to a limited extent.

8.   Asymmetric information can also give rise to moral hazard and produce the credit market conditions we describe below. In the interest of simplicity, we concentrate in the text on the adverse selection mechanism. Inevitably, a decision to focus on asymmetric information as the source of debt-deflation is controversial. Schwartz's Comment argues that unexpected shifts in monetary policy are a more important cause of debt-deflation. Borrowers and lenders predicate their investment decisions on a particular set of price forecasts, in this view; if the monetary authorities pursue unexpectedly contractionary policies, prices fall relative to expectations, and debtors and creditors become distressed. In our view, a fall in prices relative to expectations should render borrowers worse off but lenders better off. As King (1993) notes, a further element such as asymmetric information must be added to prevent the impact on the spending decisions on debtors and creditors from cancelling one another out. Thus, while not questioning the importance of the monetary policies emphasised by Schwartz, we prefer to think of them as monetary disturbances rather than debt-deflation shocks of the sort we are concerned with here.

9.   Borrowers with the best reputations may be able to borrow free of collateral. Large, well established corporations for which the asymmetric information problem is attenuated may be able to float unsecured corporate securities, for example. The borrowers on which we focus here

are best thought of as those who find entry to the market for unsecured corporate securities blocked because of informational asymmetries.

10.   This abstracts from litigation and other fixed costs of default.

11.   The reader will note that here we discuss net debt and (negative net) collateral interchangeably. This is sensible if one defines D and A comprehensively, so that A includes all of the relevant collateral.

12.   As noted above, it is possible for the 'supply of debt' schedule to bend back. If the backward-bending portion intersects with a downward-sloping demand schedule, there is the possibility of two equilibria. Only the low interest rate equilibria of this pair is stable.

13.   On this controversy see Romer (1989) and Balke and Gordon (1989).

14.   This is strictly true, of course, only if the deflation of the period was unanticipated and hence not incorporated into interest rates. On the debate over whether pre-war inflation could be forecast, see Barsky and De Long (1991).

15.   To guard against the possibility that interest rate spreads on various grades of commercial paper are imperfect indicators of the cost of credit, they also include quantity flows (the change in the real flow of loans) and the monthly percentage change in the liabilities of failed businesses. We follow this precedent in our analysis below (see Table 2.1, p.000).

16.   The correlation coefficient between the spread and number of bank failures is 0.03.

17.   These used four lagged values of both variables.

18.   Readers concerned that variables like output, prices and interest rates might also shift the SS curve should be reassured by the fact that we hold these variables constant as well when interpreting the effects of the spread in terms of debt-deflation.

19.   In addition, we included a constant, a time trend and quarterly dummies in the regressions. To allay confusion, not that these are *not* the results of bivariate Granger causality tests like those discussed above; rather, the F-statistics test the joint significance of all lags on a particular variable in the multivariate regressions that make up our VARs.

20.   An anomaly is the positive response of output to lagged business failures.

21.   A surprise here is that increases in the commercial paper rate tended to be followed by a decline in bank failures. This is in contrast to Gordon (1988) who finds, using an entirely different methodology, that interest rates are not useful for predicting financial panics during this period.

22.   Grossman (1993) explores the possibility that the response of interest rates to bank failures may be non-linear.

23.   Confidence intervals grow quite large after the initial quarters; this makes it prudent to focus mainly on the impact effects of a shock.

24.   This last result is also evident in Grossman (1993). The general tendency is emphasised by Schwartz (1986).

25.   These results are also consistent with the bivariate Granger causality tests reported above.

26.   This same finding is reported by Bordo, Rappoport and Schwartz (1992), using monthly data.

27.   Aside from own lagged values, the price level explains the largest share of the variance, consistent with our debt-deflation interpretation.

28. Here interest rates are the most important explanatory variable aside from own lags.
29. Bordo *et al.* (1992) criticise Calomiris and Hubbard for omitting monetary variables from their vector autoregression. Our basic specification, designed to follow Calomiris and Hubbard as closely as possible, also omitted this variable. Clearly, a large historical literature, of which Friedman and Schwartz (1963) is the definitive statement, suggests that bank failures may matter by reducing the money supply, and that monetary shocks may be important for both bank failure rates and spreads. See also Cagan (1965).
30. After 12 quarters, monetary shocks account for 10 per cent of the forecast error variance of output, while the spread accounts for 11 per cent and bank failures account for 4 per cent. The shares accounted for by the spread and bank failures are little different than in Table 2.2. Thus, the inference we drew from Table 2.2, that debt-deflation effects exercised a noticeable effect on output, appears to survive the addition of money. Note that when we add money, our approach continues to differ from that of Bordo, Rappoport and Schwartz by our inclusion of bank failures and the distinction this permits between debt deflation and financial instability effects. The main difference between our results and theirs appears to lie in the even smaller effect of the loan flow in our specification, much of the effect of which appears to be captured by variations in the number of bank failures.
31. We refer to the impact effect. In both cases, the behaviour of the money supply mirrors the responses of output and (especially) prices: a brief fall and a quick recovery in the case of bank failure shocks, a more extended decline in the case of spread shocks. Prices account for 28 per cent of the forecast error variance of money after 12 months, more than any other variable than money itself. It is tempting to follow Calomiris and Hubbard in interpreting these money stock variations as reflecting endogenous responses to changes in the determinants of money demand, presumably operating from the operation of the gold standard.
32. The reader should bear in mind the caveats raised on p. 67–8.
33. Bernanke and James (1991, p. 56).
34. For example, bankruptcy procedures change at different times in different countries, often as a function of the severity of the slump and the extent of bankruptcy problems.
35. From 167 to 98 observations. The countries for which we have data are Belgium, Bulgaria, Czechoslovakia, Denmark, France, Germany, Hungary, Italy, Japan, the Netherlands, Poland, Romania, Sweden, Switzerland, the UK and the USA. This change in sample size had little impact on the coefficients on other variables, since we obtained essentially the same results when we estimated equations excluding the spread on the larger sample.
36. Of the countries for which we have long-term rates, the default problem is likely to be particularly severe for Germany and Poland. In addition, Bernanke and James note fears of sovereign debt problems in France in the 1930s. On the experience of other countries, see Eichengreen and Portes (1987).

37.   For 1931, a regression of the change in the log of industrial production
       (since 1929) on the spread produces a positive coefficient with a
       t-statistic of 1.97; for 1932 and 1933, however, the analogous coeffi-
       cients are zero (with *t*-statistics of 0.27 and 0.66). A constant is in-
       cluded in each regression.
38.   Since, as Bernanke and James observe, there is some uncertainty about
       whether they are properly classified as crisis countries.
39.   The *t*-statistics on the spread in Table 2.3 range from 1.43 to 2.03.
40.   Grossman (1994) constructs a different measure of the incidence of
       banking panics for this period, which we intend to use in future work.
41.   This is because theory suggests that it is the real exchange rate, real
       wage and real interest rate that matter, whereas the nominal values
       appear in the basic specification.

References

Balke, N. and R.J. Gordon (1986) 'Historical Data', in R.J. Gordon (ed.), *The
    American Business Cycle: Continuity and Change* (Chicago: The Univer-
    sity of Chicago Press).
Balke, N. and R.J. Gordon (1989) 'The Estimation of Prewar Gross National
    Product: Methodology and New Evidence', *Journal of Political Economy*,
    97, 38–82.
Barsky, R. and J.B. De Long (1991) 'Forecasting Pre-World War I Inflation:
    The Fisher Effect and the Gold Standard', *Quarterly Journal of Economics*,
    106, 815–36.
Bernanke, B. (1983) 'Non-Monetary Effects of the Financial Crisis in the Propa-
    gation of the Great Depression', *American Economic Review*, 73, 257–76.
Bernanke, B. and M. Gertler (1990) 'Financial Fragility and Economic Per-
    formance', *Quarterly Journal of Economics*, 105, 87–114.
Bernanke, B. and H. James (1991) 'The Gold Standard, Deflation and Financial
    Crisis in the Great Depression: An Historical Comparison', in R.G. Hubbard
    (ed.), *Financial Markets and Financial Crises* (Chicago: The University of
    Chicago Press), 33–68.
Bordo, M.D. (1990) 'The Lender of Last Resort: Alternative Views and His-
    torical Experience', *Federal Reserve Bank of Richmond Economic Review*,
    76 (January–February), 18–29.
Bordo, M.D., P. Rappoport and A.J. Schwartz (1992) 'Money versus Credit
    Rationing: Evidence from the National Banking Era, 1880–1914', in C. Goldin
    and H. Rockoff (eds), *Strategical Factors in Nineteenth Century American
    History: A Volume to Honor Robert W. Fogel* (Chicago: The University of
    Chicago Press), 189–224.
Cagan, P. (1965) *Determinants and Effects of Changes in the Stock of Money*
    (New York: National Bureau of Economic Research).
Calomiris, C. and R.G. Hubbard (1989) 'Price Flexibility, Credit Availability,
    and Economic Fluctuations: Evidence from the United States, 1894–1909',
    Quarterly Journal of Economics, 104 (August), 429–52.
Cecchetti, S. (1992) 'Prices During the Great Depression: Was the Deflation of

1930–1932 Really Unanticipated?', *American Economic Review*, 82, 141–56.

Diamond, D. (1984) 'Financial Intermediation and Delegated Monitoring', *Review of Economic Studies*, 51, 393–414.

Eichengreen, B. and R. Portes (1987) 'The Anatomy of Financial Crises', in R. Portes and A. Swoboda (eds), *Threats to International Financial Stability* (Cambridge: Cambridge University Press), 10–58.

Eichengreen, B. and J. Sachs (1985) 'Exchange Rates and Economic Recovery in the 1930s', *Journal of Economic History*, 45, 925–46.

Fisher, I. (1933) 'The Debt-Deflation Theory of Great Depressions', *Econometrica*, 1 (October), 337–57.

Friedman, M. and A.J. Schwartz (1963) *A Monetary History of the United States, 1867–1960* (Princeton: University Press).

Goldsmith, R. (1985) *Comparative National Balance Sheets: A Study of Twenty Countries* (Chicago: The University of Chicago Press).

Gorton, G. (1988) 'Banking Panics and Business Cycles', *Oxford Economic Papers*, New Series, 40, 751–81.

Greenwald, B. and J. Stiglitz (1988) 'Information, Finance Constraints, and Business Fluctuations', in M. Kahn and S.C. Tsiang (eds), *Expectations and Macroeconomics* (Oxford: Oxford University Press).

Grossman, R.S. (1993) 'The Macroeconomic Consequences of Bank Failures Under the National Banking System', *Explorations in Economic History*, 30, 294–320.

Grossman, R.S. (1994) 'The Shoe That Didn't Drop: Explaining Banking Stability During the Great Depression', *Journal of Economic History*, 54, 654–82.

Hamilton, J. (1992) 'Was the Deflation During the Great Depression Anticipated? Evidence from the Commodity Futures Market', *American Economic Review*, 82, 157–78.

International Labour Organisation (various years) *Yearbook of Labour Statistics* (Geneva: ILO).

Kindleberger, C.P. (1978) *Manias, Panics and Crashes* (New York: Basic Books).

King, M. (1993) 'Debt Deflation: Theory and Evidence', Presidential Lecture delivered to the European Economic Association (Helsinki) (August).

Kuvin, L. (1936) 'Prices, Long-Term Debt and Interest in the United States', *National Industrial Conference Board Study*, 230.

League of Nations (various years) *Statistical Yearbook* (Geneva: League of Nations).

Macaulay, F. (1938) *The Movements of Interest Rates, Bond Yields and Stock Prices in the United States Since 1856* (New York: National Bureau of Economic Research).

Minsky, H.P. (1977) 'A Theory of Systemic Fragility', in E.I. Altman and A.W. Sametz (eds), *Financial Crises: Institutions and Markets in a Fragile Environment* (New York: Wiley), 138–52.

Mishkin, F.S. (1978) 'The Household Balance Sheet and the Great Depression', *Journal of Economic History*, 38, 918–37.

Mishkin, F.S. (1991) 'Asymmetric Information and Financial Crises: A Historical Perspective', in R.G. Hubbard (ed.), *Financial Markets and Financial Crises* (Chicago: The University of Chicago Press), 69–108.

Newell, A. and J. Symons (1988) 'The Macroeconomics of the Interwar Years:

International Comparisons', in B. Eichengreen and T.J. Hatton (eds), *Interwar Unemployment in International Perspective* (Dordrecht: Kluwer Nijhoff, 61–96.

Romer, C. (1989) 'The Prewar Business Cycle Reconsidered: New Estimates of Gross National Product, 1869–1908', *Journal of Political Economy*, 97, 1–37.

Schwartz, A.J. (1981) 'Understanding 1929–1931', in Robert Gordon (ed.), *The Great Depression Revisited* (Boston: Kluwer Academic), 5–48.

Schwartz, A.J. (1986) 'Real and Pseudo-Financial Crises', in F. Capie and G.E. Wood (eds), *Financial Crises and the World Banking System* (London: Macmillan), 11–31.

Sprague, O.M.W. (1910) *History of Crises Under the National Banking System* (Washington, DC: National Monetary Commission, US Government Printing Office).

Stiglitz, J. and A. Weiss (1981) 'Credit Rationing in Markets with Imperfect Information', *American Economic Review*, 71, 393–410.

Sumner, S. (1994) 'Bold and Persistent Experimentation: Macroeconomic Policy During 1933', unpublished manuscript (Bentley College).

United States Department of Commerce (1949) *Historical Statistics of the United States 1789–1945* (Washington, DC: US Government Printing Office).

United States Department of Commerce (1976) *Historical Statistics of the United States from Colonial Times to the Present* (Washington, DC: US Government Printing Office).

Comment

Nick Crafts

Eichengreen and Grossman's Chapter 2 is a stimulating piece of empirical research which sheds new light on the role of debt-deflation as a propagation mechanism in business cycle fluctuations. Debt-deflation is conceptualised in terms of a rise in the real value of debt. To circumvent data problems the empirical work uses interest rate spread variables as a proxy while seeking also to control for other variables impacting on the efficiency of financial intermediation. The basic conclusion is that in both the late nineteenth-century USA and in the industrialised countries during the Great Depression of the 1930s changes in the interest rate spread had small and statistically quite weak effects on changes in output. The authors are cautiously sceptical of the claim that debt-deflation *per se* (as opposed to banking collapses) was a major factor historically in exacerbating demand shocks.

Despite the care with which the empirical work has been carried out, the reliance on the interest rate spread proxy variable means that some aspects of debt-deflation may not be adequately captured and that the results must be taken as quite provisional. If debt-deflation is taken to centre on balance sheet–wealth effects on consumption as in King (1993) and other discussions of the recent recession or as in the pioneering analysis of 1930s' America in Mishkin (1978), then I am rather doubtful that the interest rate spread between commercial paper and the discount rate will be closely related to the relevant changes in household debt positions.

Table D2.1 underlines this worry as far as the American depression is concerned where Mishkin (1978, p. 930) estimated balance sheet effects on housing and consumer durables expenditure equal to about a quarter of the total fall in aggregate demand in 1930–2. Similarly, while interest rate spreads as seen, for example, in the 3-month inter-bank rate minus the Treasury Bill rate (Bank of England, 1993) moved in much the same way during the UK recessions of the early 1980s and the early 1990s, household debt positions were very different before and after the 1980s' credit boom and in 1979–81 real personal consumption rose by 0.2 per cent while in 1990–2 it fell by 2.2 per cent (CSO, 1994).

Table D2.1   Debt-deflation and consumer spending in the USA, 1929–32,
$1958 billion

Year	Interest rate spread (percentage points)	Real household Liabilities	Real household Financial assets	Estimated spending effect
1928	0.34			
1929	0.68	65.3	637.8	
1930	0.54	78.1	613.0	−5.2
1931	0.55	79.5	578.6	−5.0
1932	0.03	81.0	533.7	−5.8

Sources: Interest rate spread is the variable used by Eichengreen and Grossman (chapter 2, p. 000) in their 1930s regressions while all other data is from Mishkin (1978, Tables 1 and 4).

Table D2.2   The UK personal savings ratio in two recessions, 1929–33 and 1989–93, per cent

Year	Ratio	Year	Ratio
1929	4.6	1989	6.6
1930	3.7	1990	8.6
1931	3.2	1991	10.1
1932	3.8	1992	12.6
1933	4.8	1993	11.3

Sources: Feinstein (1972); CSO (1994).

Nevertheless, the Eichengreen–Grossman conclusions may be basically right for the past episodes at which they look. For earlier times it may be that the American experience in the 1930s is an outlier because balance sheet effects on consumption were generally weak in the days when relatively few households had mortgages or substantial financial assets and the proportion of expenditure on durables was much lower. Certainly in Britain where real personal consumption rose by 2.0 per cent between 1929 and 1932 (Feinstein, 1972), the conventional wisdom is that Pigou (real balance) effects dominated Fisher (debt-deflation) effects (Hendry, 1983). The behaviour of the personal savings ratio shown in Table D2.2 is suggestive of this outcome and makes a strong contrast with recent experience.

The key requirement is clearly to obtain more information on household balance sheets in the past. In the meantime, it may be worth remembering that the scope for debt-deflation effects on consumption has doubtless changed substantially over time and probably varies considerably across countries.

References

Bank of England (1993) *Bank of England Statistical Abstract Part 1* (London: Bank of England).

Central Statistical Office (1994) *Economic Trends Annual Supplement* (London: HMSO).

Feinstein, C.H. (1972) *National Income, Expenditure and Output of the United Kingdom, 1855–1965* (Cambridge: Cambridge University Press).

Hendry, D.F. (1983) 'Econometric Modelling: the Consumption Function in Retrospect', *Scottish Journal of Political Economy*, 30, 193–220.

King, M. (1993) 'Debt Deflation: Theory and Evidence', Presidential Lecture delivered to the European Economic Association Meeting (Helsinki) (August).

Mishkin, F. (1978) 'The Household Balance Sheet and the Great Depression', *Journal of Economic History*, 38, 918–37.

Comment

Anna J. Schwartz

The task Eichengreen and Grossman have set for themselves in Chapter 2 is to distinguish the extent to which collapses in asset and commodity prices adversely affect output by provoking bank failures and thereby reducing the efficiency of financial intermediation, versus the extent to which they erode the credit-worthiness of non-financial debtors, undermining the ability to borrow of agents on the other end of the potential transaction.

In addition, the authors seek to compare the importance of bank failures in depressing asset and commodity prices and thereby inducing reductions in desired levels of consumption and investment, versus disruptions in access to finance which prevent agents from achieving the levels of consumption and investment they desire.

Before laying out the groundwork for their study, the authors note problems in defining the issues of concern. Not all bank failures generate a panic. Relying on a rise in the currency–deposit ratio to identify a crisis requires a judgement on how big the rise must be to qualify. Debt-deflation has been interpreted, on the one hand, as a fall in the price level that raises the real value of nominal debt, and on the other, as asset price deflation that raises the amount of gross debt net of assets.

The authors' definition of a banking crisis is financial institution distress, measured by number of bank failures, assets of failed and suspended banks, and quantitative and qualitative information variables. They define debt-deflation as a rise in indebtedness, a fall in asset prices, or a fall in commodity prices that increases the real debt burden. Measures of debt, however, are not readily available before 1916. The authors therefore substitute interest-rate spreads as indicators of debt deflation.

The rationale for using spreads is that a collapse in asset prices erodes the value of collateral supplied by borrowers. The greater the collapse, the less are lenders compensated in the event of default, and the larger the spread over the risk-free rate that borrowers will have to pay, given that lenders have incomplete information about the riskiness of the projects that borrowers intend to undertake. Hence the spread can be regarded as a measure of the debt burden and of debt-deflation pressures.

The spread, however, may also increase, according to the authors, in the event of a shock to financial intermediation that impedes the ability of banks to screen borrowers. For this reason the authors find it necessary to control for bank failures before interpreting a change in spreads as a debt-deflation effect.

The study then focuses on the effects of bank failures and debt deflation during the USA *post-bellum* period and the Great Depression of 1930–33. The authors are restrained in their claims for the results of their study. Their findings for the *post-bellum* period are that, according to Granger bivariate casualty test, prior declines in the price level significantly predicted subsequent increases in the spread and increases in the spread predicted deflation, which they conclude are consistent with the debt-deflation interpretation of the spread. However, they find no support for the notion that debt-deflation heightened the fragility of the banking system or that bank failures led to debt deflation.

The authors summarise the results of VAR quarterly regressions with four lags of seven explanatory variables as confirming that both financial instability and debt-deflation mattered for output movements before 1913, but neither contributes to the explanation of business cycle persistence. Further, bank failures and debt-deflation may be responding to common underlying shocks but otherwise do not seem related.

With respect to the 1930–3 depression, the authors conclude that the evidence is more robust that monetary, interest rate, exchange rate, and financial panic effects were important in propagating the Depression than the evidence on debt deflation.

GENERAL COMMENTS

Let me add my own reservations about (1) the meaning of debt-deflation, (2) the use of interest rate spreads to measure it, (3) the compatibility of debt-deflation with robust economic growth during the post *bellum* commodity price decline until the mid-1890s, and (4) its role in the decline in the investment–output ratio during the Great Depression.

Debt-Deflation

Debt-deflation in the recent literature on the subject relates the phenomenon to asymmetric information. Lenders are not as well informed as

borrowers about the viability of the projects borrowers want to undertake. Hence lenders require collateral. A collapse in asset prices that
erodes the value of collateral, however, on this view, magnifies the
problem of asymmetric information and adverse selection.

Asymmetric information in my view is not the central problem in
studying debt-deflation. I believe lenders and borrowers both evaluate
the prospects of projects by extrapolating the prevailing price level of
inflation rate. A subsequent decision by monetary authorities to pursue
contractionary policies will undermine the price-level assumptions of
both lenders and borrowers. That is why borrowers default and lenders
become distressed.

Interest Rate Spreads

The spread before it got to be interpreted as providing information on
adverse selection problems in debt markets was regarded in its term
structure guise as a forward-looking variable. The spread in the latter
interpretation reflected both liquidity and expectational forces. Liquidity preference accounts for a pecuniary yield differential of long-term
over short-term securities.

But liquidity preference also has implications for rates of interest in
general. Low quality bonds ought to yield more, apart from the cycle,
than high quality bonds, because they are relatively less liquid. Their
price variance is greater because default risk is greater. So we observe
that high quality bonds yield less than low quality bonds generally,
and that the yield differential between high and low quality bonds increases from trough to peak and decreases from peak to trough.

How do yield differentials between low and high quality bonds vary
over the cycle as a result of changes in the level of interest rates?
During contractions the level of interest rates falls and the market tends
to regard issuers of low quality securities as more default-vulnerable.
During expansions the level of interest rates increases and the market
tends to lower its estimate of default risk. Liquidity and cyclical forces
thus have opposite effects on yield differentials.

Both pre-Second World War and post-Second World War, the spread
has increased with the level of interest rates. Does this regularity be-
speak debt-deflation? I doubt it.

Post-bellum Experience

Interpreting the interest rate spread as a measure of debt-deflation is problematic, the authors note, in commenting on an earlier study by Calomiris and Hubbard (1989). The latter found that an increase in the interest rate spread, using monthly data for 1893–1909, was contemporaneously associated with increases in output and prices, hardly the appropriate finding if the spread is a measure of debt-deflation.

During the greenback period before 1879 and throughout the 1880s, declining prices did not prevent a rapid rise in real income. The forces making for economic growth over the course of several business cycle seems to have been independent of the trend in prices. The banking panics of 1873 and 1893 were temporary disruptions, undoubtedly related to preceding price deflation, but the period as a whole is not marked by the consequences of price deflation that the contemporary literature envisages. The price decline during the greenback period was probably anticipated as a measure that resumption of adherence to gold enforced to bring US prices into line with prices in the gold standard world. The price decline until the 1890s was understood to be a feature of the gold standard that a commodity standard in time would reverse.

Why is the landscape not littered with failed projects that interest rate spreads suggest should have occurred?

An awkward fact for the spread as a measure of debt-deflation is that realised returns are higher on low quality corporate bond issues than on high quality issues. Heavy capital losses result when bonds are purchased at offering and sold at default but, for investors who purchase at default and hold until extinguishment of the issue, the returns are equally large. The same is true of bankrupt projects that exact heavy capital losses from the initial owners. Those who buy these projects after default and bring them to completion earn large returns. So-called restructuring, if rapid, makes for a mild cyclical downturn.

The Great Depression

The Great Depression was anything but a mild cyclical downturn. Why was the impact of the fall in prices then so different from the impact of the *post-bellum* fall in prices? In the Great Depression the ratio of investment to output declined; *post-bellum*, it grew. Crucial for this outcome was that price behaviour in the Great Depression, unlike the earlier case, was determined by Federal Reserve discretion.

What was different about the Great Depression was that a series of negative shocks, monetary in origin, reduced real output and the demand for labour and shifted the demand for securities to short-term instruments and high grade long-term securities. The increase in the spread reflected the monetary climate. During interludes in the course of the contraction real output and prices rose, but unanticipated monetary shocks, associated with banking panics and restrictive policies, aborted the tentative moves to recovery.

MINOR COMMENTS

The authors footnote the recent episodes of banking crises and asset price collapses in Sweden. Finland, Israel, Japan, and the UK. This is clearly a subject for a study that the authors ought to write.

The authors state that lenders can reduce adverse selection by requiring borrowers to provide collateral. W. Braddock Hickman (1958) notes that the market regarded unsecured corporate securities more favourably than secured issues (issues secured by mortgage, collateral, or leasehold). Only the best credit risks could float unsecured debentures; corporations whose future earnings were doubtful had to provide a lien on assets for investor protection in possible default situations.

The authors say that 'the experience that led Fisher to develop his debt-deflation theory of Great Depressions' was the global slump of the 1930s. It would be more accurate to say that he derived his analysis from his own experience. In 1923, Fisher sold to a concern that eventually became Remington Rand a small manufacturing business that he had established. The value of his stock soared as the New York bull market took off. Fisher bought heavily on margin the stock of small and medium-sized enterprises producing innovative products. The market crash of 1929 left him bankrupt. He borrowed well over a million dollars from a wealthy sister-in-law, and the burden of the debt, which he was never in a position to repay, became heavier as the price level and his nominal income fell. The sister-in-law forgave the debt in her will.

The authors comment on incomplete adjustment of money wages as a channel running from monetary deflation to output. They note a problem with this possible channel: the rise in real wages may not have been an independent cause of the Depression and the fact that the sluggishness of money wages was apparently so persistent. We do know what produced 'sluggishness of money wages': it was the Hoover administration's successful attempt to forestal money wage reductions in 1930. Downward money wage adjustments became substantial in 1931 and beyond.

References

Calomiris, C. and R.G. Hubbard (1989) 'Price Flexibility, Credit Availability and Economic Fluctuations: Evidence from the United States, 1894–1909', *Quarterly Journal of Economics*, 104 (August), 429–52.
Hickman, W.B. (1958) *Corporate Bond Quality and Investor Experience* (Princeton: Princeton University Press for the National Bureau of Economic Research).

3 Credit Crunch: A British Perspective

Leigh Drake and David T. Llewellyn[1]

INTRODUCTION AND ISSUES

There are pressures on banks to contract their balance sheets and withdraw from markets.

The difficulties being faced by banks have led them to exercise greater caution in extending new credit.

The financial weakness of banks' customers is reflected in the quality of their assets and could affect banks' ability or willingness to continue supporting customers through difficult times. (Bank of England, 'Banking Act Report for 1989/90', *Quarterly Bulletin*, 1990)

The period since 1989 has witnessed a dramatic decline in bank lending in the UK despite a sharp fall in interest rates. This follows several years of exceptionally high volumes of bank lending with corporate and personal borrowers' debt–income and gearing ratios rising to unprecedented levels. This itself suggests a possible line of enquiry: that the recent sharp deceleration is a reaction to previous 'excessive' borrowing (unsustainable gearing ratios) and lending (recent loan-loss experience of banks). Perhaps what has recently been happening is a stock-adjustment correction following an earlier stock-adjustment and over-shooting of long-run sustainable positions, and a return to more normal balance sheet positions by both borrowers and lenders.

The general theme in analyses of UK experience focuses on the demand side of the credit market and, in particular, that the recent deceleration reflects either a cyclical or stock-adjustment effect on the demand for credit. Unlike in the USA, where the literature on credit crunch is voluminous, there has been remarkably little analysis in the UK of supply-side effects, i.e. the independent role of bank behaviour. And yet in 1992, Congdon argued: 'The British financial system is more fragile today than it has been for many decades.' Later sections demonstrate that British banks' capital positions have been seriously eroded by loan losses. It is also the case that rating agencies have downgraded their ratings of banks, the relative cost of equity and debt capital has risen, the equity market seems hesitant to supply banks with more capital, massive provisions have been made by banks, overall losses have been reported in some years, two clearing banks have cut their dividends, asset sales have been made, senior bankers have stated that banks' risk analysis and management has been weak, and banks have been withdrawing from some markets. All of these are symptoms of actual or potential distress.

Our starting point is that this can hardly have failed to have an impact on bank behaviour, and that supply-side factors are part of the explanations for the recent sharp deceleration in bank lending in the UK. A later section of the chapter (p. 143 reports on statistical tests to determine whether supply-side factors have been operating and the conclusion is that, while demand factors have been evident, changed behaviour patterns of banks have also contributed. In this sense, and contrary to a general consensus, the concept of a 'credit crunch' is relevant in the UK. The opening quotations are all taken from the *Bank of England Quarterly Bulletin* and relate to the world position of banking rather than specifically to UK experience. Nevertheless, our view is that the UK cannot be excluded. An important perspective is that banking problems are certainly not unique to the UK and pale into significance compared with, for instance, the experience of Scandinavia though there are powerful parallels (Llewellyn, 1992b).

The focus of this chapter is on the position of banks and we attempt to demonstrate that supply-side factors have operated. It must, however, be noted at the outset that analysis in this area is severely hampered by the absence of data that in the USA is derived from the Senior Loan Officer's *Opinion Survey* published by the Federal Reserve. Comparing the analysis of bank behaviour in the USA with what is possible in the UK indicates that substantial benefit would be derived if such exercises were regularly undertaken here.

Structure of the Chapter

The structure of the chapter is as follows. The remainder of this section considers the nature and significance of credit-crunch issues. In the next section we present a simple framework of the economics of the banking firm (including credit rationing) and, given its potential importance, the role of capital in the banking firm and the strategic options faced by banks with a capital constraint. One theme of the chapter is that the recent deceleration in bank lending is in part a reflection of stock adjustments and over-shooting during the 1980s and, therefore, the third section offers an analysis of credit trends in that decade. *En passant*, it needs to be said that, as with Friedman's (1989) comment on US experience, there is no clear understanding of the reasons for the apparent change in attitude towards debt and leverage that was · evident in the 1980s. The fourth section reviews the loan-loss and capital position of four major British banks. The fifth section considers, in the framework of the banking firm, why bank lending might decline and offers statistical analysis indicating that a credit crunch is a relevant concept for the UK and at least part of the explanation for the recent sharp decline in bank lending. The sixth section offers an overall assessment, and draws some conclusions.

Nature and Significance of 'Credit Crunch'

Much of this chapter concentrates on the business behaviour of banks in the growth of credit in the 1980s, and the subsequent sharp fall in bank lending. Our main purpose is to identify the possibility of a credit crunch in the early 1990s in the UK. Clearly, it is necessary to distinguish demand and supply effects as the sharp decline in bank lending may be either beause borrowers chose to borrow less (movement along or shift in the demand curve for loans due either to recession or their balance sheet positions) or that, for their own portfolio reasons, banks chose to lend less (shift in the supply curve of loans).

In practice, it is difficult to isolate the separate effects in the absence of clearly specified and robust models of the supply and demand for bank credit. This is because given economic conditions (e.g. recession) are likely to simultaneously affect both supply and demand behaviour, and because of feedback effects. For instance, the demand curve for loans may shift to the left because the supply curve of banks has shifted: given transactions costs, borrowers may be deterred from putting propositions to banks because they detect that their banks are less likely to be accommodating. Similarly, an exogenous shift in the supply curve of loans may itself induce a decline in the level of economic activity and hence an endogenous reduction in the demand for credit.

In the US literature different definitions of credit crunch have been applied. Bernanke and Lown (1991), for instance, define it as: 'a significant leftward shift in the supply curve of bank loans, holding constant the safe real interest rate and the quality of potential borrowers'. The US Council of Economic Advisers (1992) observes that: 'Credit crunch occurs when the supply of credit is restricted below the range usually identified with prevailing market interest rates and the profitability of investment projects'. In a similar way, Llewellyn (1992c) defines the concept as: 'an *inability* or *unwillingness* of banks to supply credit (i.e. to meet the demand for credit that in other circumstances they would be prepared to satisfy)' (emphasis added). The common theme is that the concept relates to *exogenous* shifts in the supply curve of banks credit.

It can be useful to distinguish between 'hard' and 'soft' credit crunch. The former relates to an *inability* to supply credit because of clear balance sheet constraints: lack or erosion of bank capital in relation to (perhaps new) regulatory or balance sheet requirements, regulatory limitations, etc. The latter refers to an *unwillingness* to supply loans (e.g. due to increased risk aversion as opposed to increased perceptions of risk). Although related to credit rationing, the concepts of credit rationing and credit crunch are not synonymous as non-price credit rationing may be a normal feature of bank behaviour (Stiglitz and Weiss effects, etc.). However, Owens and Shraft (1991) define credit crunch as periods of sharply rising non-price rationing.

Credit crunch becomes economically significant in three conditions: (1) bank loans and other forms of credit (e.g. capital market finance) are not perfectly substitutable; (2) when, for some borrowers (e.g. small firms), they are not substitutable at all and borrowers are totally dependent on bank finance, and (3) when the global banking market is not perfectly integrated (and hence is segmented into national systems) implying that constraints applying to a subset of banks are not circumvented by other bank lenders. In this last respect, several analysts note the same phenomenon within the USA which, because of regulatory constraints, is not a truly national banking market. The evidence indicates that credit crunch has been more evident in some states than others. Thus an exogenous reduction in the banks' willingness to lend either severely constrains bank-dependent borrowers entirely or, where substitutions can be made, forces borrowers to employ more costly forms of credit (Bernanke and Lown, 1991). In terms of the standard *IS–LM* paradigm, the effect is to shift the *IS* curve to the left.

The significance of a credit crunch is particularly evident if, contrary to efficient markets views, banks are regarded as 'special'. New theories of banking (emphasising, *inter alia*, their roles as solving information and asymmetric information problems, their role as evaluators of credit propositions, their delegated-monitoring roles, and the signal effect they give to other potential lenders) emphasise the special role of banks due to incomplete and less than perfect markets (Llewellyn,

1992a). For a discussion of the special 'credit view' of banks, see Bernanke and Lown (1991) and Bernanke (1993).

The emergence of a credit crunch could be significant because two related vicious circles can be created. Firstly, if banks reduce their lending to companies it accentuates companies' difficulties and this is likely to emphasise any cyclical downswing in the economy. This in turn impairs the value of bank assets and tightens the constraint on bank lending yet further. Secondly, a decline in credit growth is likely to reduce the value of real assets purchased on borrowed funds and hence again may lower the value of bank assets, either directly or indirectly via the financial position of the borrower.

THE BANKING FIRM

Credit trends necessarily reflect the interaction of the aggregate demand for credit by borrowers, their portfolio preferences between alternative forms and sources of credit, and the ability and willingness of lenders to supply credit. An analysis of the divergent credit trends in the 1980s and 1990s therefore needs to incorporate the portfolio behaviour of lending institutions. This section draws heavily on the framework given in Llewellyn and Holmes (1992).

A simple model of a competitive credit market comprising fairly homogeneous institutions is given in Figure 3.1. Assets are funded by deposits and capital. Holding all other interest rates constant, deposit-taking intermediaries face an exogenous upward-sloping supply curve of deposits (S_D). For a given supply curve of deposits, the institutions' endogenous supply of loans (S_L) is also a rising function of the loan rate. The interest margin (AB) (the supply price of financial intermediation) is determined by non-deposit costs (management and technology costs, etc.), the cost of capital (which increases as either the required capital–assets ratio or the price of capital rises), risk premia charged on loans, tax payments, and the institutions' distributed and undistributed profits. The margin will also be influenced by competitive pressures within the banking sector, and from actual or potential external competitors: non-bank financial institutions, non-financial banking institutions, and the capital market. Competitive pressures impact on costs and profits but may also, in the short run and. in order to maintain market share, induce banks not to fully reflect risk premia in loan rates. The demand curve for loans is given by D_0. In equilibrium the volume of deposits and loans is OT with a deposit rate of i_0 and a loan rate of

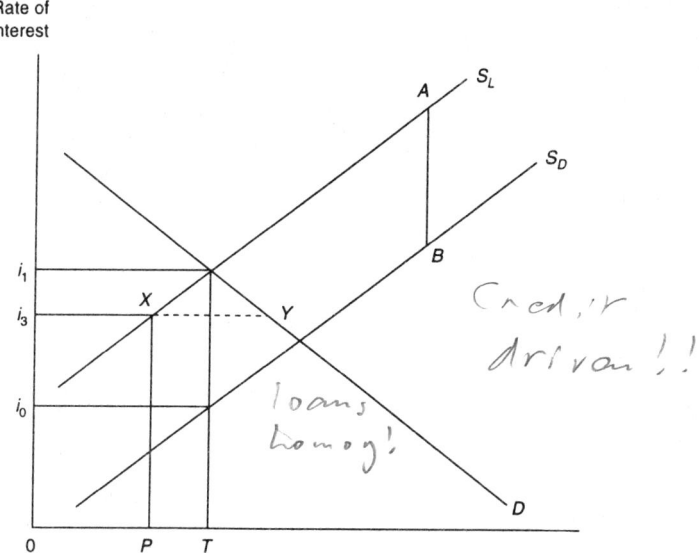

Figure 3.1 The banking firm (∑ firm !)

i_1. The positions of S_L and S_D are determined by the level of alternative interest rates, as determined in part by monetary policy. If the general level of interest rates rises the two schedules shift upwards as banks need to offer higher deposit rates to remain competitive.

Credit Rationing

When considering the concept of credit crunch, the issue of *credit rationing* needs to be incorporated. Banks ration loans as, in practice, the volume of loans is always less than that which borrowers would choose. Banks do not in practice clear the market via interest rates and they sustain an element of excess demand with some borrowers being prepared to pay higher rates of interest than the banks charge. Three forms of credit rationing are identified:

- *risk-threshold rationing* (i.e. where banks set an absolute limit on the risk they are prepared to accept);
- *disequilibrium rationing*, where, in a situation of market collusion, institutions maintain evident and measurable excess demand for credit (e.g. *XY* at i_3 in Figure 3.1); and

- *equilibrium* or *market-clearing rationing*, where other terms of lending (such as collateral, loan/value or loan/income ratios) are set which have the effect of shifting the effective demand curve for loans.

In this last case, adjustments are made to non-interest rate terms which are sufficient to equate the demand and supply of loans when the loan rate is otherwise set below its market-clearing level. *Disequilibrium* rationing occurs when such terms are not sufficient to clear the market. The distinction between *equilibrium* and *disequilibrium* rationing is identified in Oztas and Zahn (1975), Kent (1980), and Nellis and Thom (1983). There are many reasons (not mutualy exclusive) why credit rationing may exist, and these can be reduced to banks being either risk averse or having imperfect information.

These concepts of credit rationing are relevant to an understanding of credit trends in the 1980s because banks' lending criteria may be stable for long periods but change discretely from time to time. The force of competition may induce such changes and may compete away the various forms of credit rationing. The thesis of a later section is that the erosion of these concepts of credit rationing was a major factor in the growth of credit during the 1980s.

Bank Capital

Many studies of credit crunch in the USA identify a deficiency of bank capital as a major contributory factor (Baer and McElravey, 1993; Clair and Yeats, 1991; Jones, 1993). Syron (1991) in particular emphasises a 'capital crunch'. However, the magnitude of the capital crunch is disputed. Thus, Bernanke and Lown (1991) (while recognising that the magnitude of the effect is not insignificant), argue that the 1988–90 fall in capital in New England banks explains only 2–3 percentage points of that region's precipitous decline in lending.

As a capital constraint may be a major factor in restraining the supply of credit (a credit-crunch condition), and the internal generation of bank capital was weak in the late 1980s and early 1990s, a consideration is given to the role of capital within the banking firm. Bank assets are funded by capital (equity and debt) and deposits, and the cost of capital is one of the ingredients determining the supply price of financial intermediation (*AB* in Figure 3.1). And yet capital does not feature predominantly in traditional textbook analyses of bank credit expansion which focus on credit creation on the basis of the supply of bank reserves (the bank component of high-powered money). The position has been put well by Friedman (1993):

When a banking system involves minimum capital *requirements*, along with the more familiar minimum reserve requirements, it is at least possible that the effective limitation on the expansion of deposits and credit may be capital, not reserves. In this case, it is necessary to write the familiar balance-sheet relationships subject to *two* inequality constraints. Only by accident would both always be binding, or not, exactly in concert. And only by presumption would the reserve constraint always be binding and the capital constraint not. Further, if what binds is the capital constraint, then issues of distribution become important in ways that have no ready analog under the more familiar reserves story. There is no equivalent of a federal funds market to enable banks with excess capital to make transfers to banks with insufficient capital, so that the systemwide total is all that matters. (emphasis added)

Capital is a key dimension in banking for several reasons. First, because it is the ultimate determinant of banks' lending capacity: assets cannot be expanded beyond the limit of the multiple of the minimum required capital–assets ratio. The availability and cost of capital therefore determine the maximum level of assets. Second, because capital has to be serviced, it represents a significant cost to banks and hence the amount of capital a bank needs to hold (and its price) has an impact on the pricing of banking business. Third, the structure of capital (especially the balance between debt and equity) may have an impact on various aspects of the banking business because the cost of different components varies as they are not perfectly substitutable. Fourth, capital is a principal aspect of regulation which defines minimum capital adequacy standards, the form in which capital can be issued, the characteristics of allowable capital instruments, and the balance between different forms of capital. Fifth, the cost of capital together with the amount of capital banks maintain has a decisive impact on their competitive position, especially compared with the capital market. There is, therefore, no aspect of the business of banking that is not directly or indirectly influenced by the cost and availability of capital.

The central, strategic role of capital is illustrated by a very simple identity:

$$\frac{P}{A} \equiv \frac{P}{E} \times \frac{E}{A}$$

P is profits, A is the average level of assets, and E is the equity capital base. P/A (rate of return on assets, ROA) is a crucial dimension in banking in that it reflects the pricing of assets and liabilities. In general, the wider is the interest spread (the difference between the average rate of interest on assets and liabilities) the greater will be the ROA. Two simple conclusions follow from this. First, if banks are required to hold more equity capital (a rise in E/A) this must imply either: (1) the requirement to raise the rate of return on assets (with implications for pricing); or (2) a lower rate of return on equity to the detriment of shareholders and hence the likely future supply of equity capital. In this way, regulation and capital have an impact on the fundamental business decisions of the bank. As competitive conditions might not allow a change in pricing to raise the ROA, capital regulations may undermine the competitive position of banks. A second property of the identity is that if the cost of equity capital rises (i.e. the required P/E rises) either the ROA must be raised (implying a higher interest margin) or the bank must lower its capital ratio, which might be hazardous both on risk and regulatory grounds.

As both internal and external sources of equity capital depend ultimately upon profitability, the imposition of equity capital requirements has powerful implications for the required profitability of banking, the ability of banks to compete, and the type of business they are likely to conduct. The Bank for International Settlements (BIS) in its 1989 *Annual Report* recognises this: 'since a higher capital ratio reduces the extent to which a bank can rely on debt finance, the argument that the convergence agreement will lead to an increase in bank costs is well founded.'

A capital constraint for a bank can emerge for three main reasons: (1) internal profitability is too low to generate sufficient profits to both make dividend payments and retain an amount sufficient to back an expansion of the balance sheet; (2) the capital market becomes unwilling to supply new capital at a cost that enables the banks to compete in credit markets, or (3) because provisions or asset wide-offs have to be made. Capital was not a constraint for UK banks for most of the 1980s as the sharp rise in lending generated buoyant profits; regulation was eased to allow new forms of capital to be issued, and profits were over-stated by the failure to make sufficient provisions. However, as noted below, capital became a potential constraint in the early 1990s.

Overall, faced with a capital constraint, banks must either raise more capital or economise on its use. It follows that a credit crunch, as defined at the outset, can have its origin in a capital constraint faced by banks. A substantial US literature views capital crunch as a subset of credit crunch.

BANK LENDING IN THE 1980s

Before considering the recent experience of a sharp cutback in bank lending (Figure 3.2), the context of the 1980s is reviewed as the deceleration has been in part both a supply and demand reaction to an unsustainable growth of indebtedness of both the personal and corporate sectors during the 1980s. A stock-adjustment interpretation of trends during the 1980s is relevant to the analysis of the factors behind the decline in bank lending after 1989.

The 1980s experienced one of the fastest growth rates of bank and building society lending of any decade this century. Personal sector debt rose by around £350 billion (a five-fold increase) and lending to the personal sector expanded at an average annual rate of 19 per cent. Figure 3.3 shows that (most especially in the second half of the decade) the corporate sector's borrowing requirement rose sharply and to unprecedented levels and subsequently declined substantially. At the same time, borrowing from the banking sector (Figure 3.2) also rose sharply (again especially in the second half of the decade) and until 1991 was a high proportion of total borrowing during the 1980s (Figure 3.4).

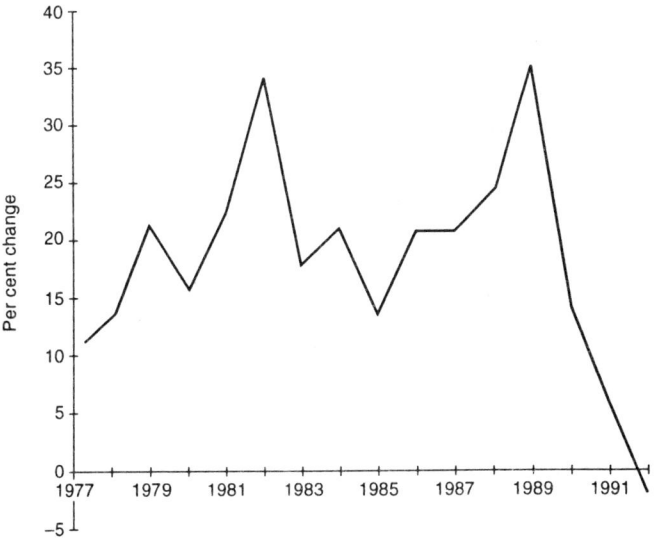

Figure 3.2   Growth in UK bank lending, 1977–91

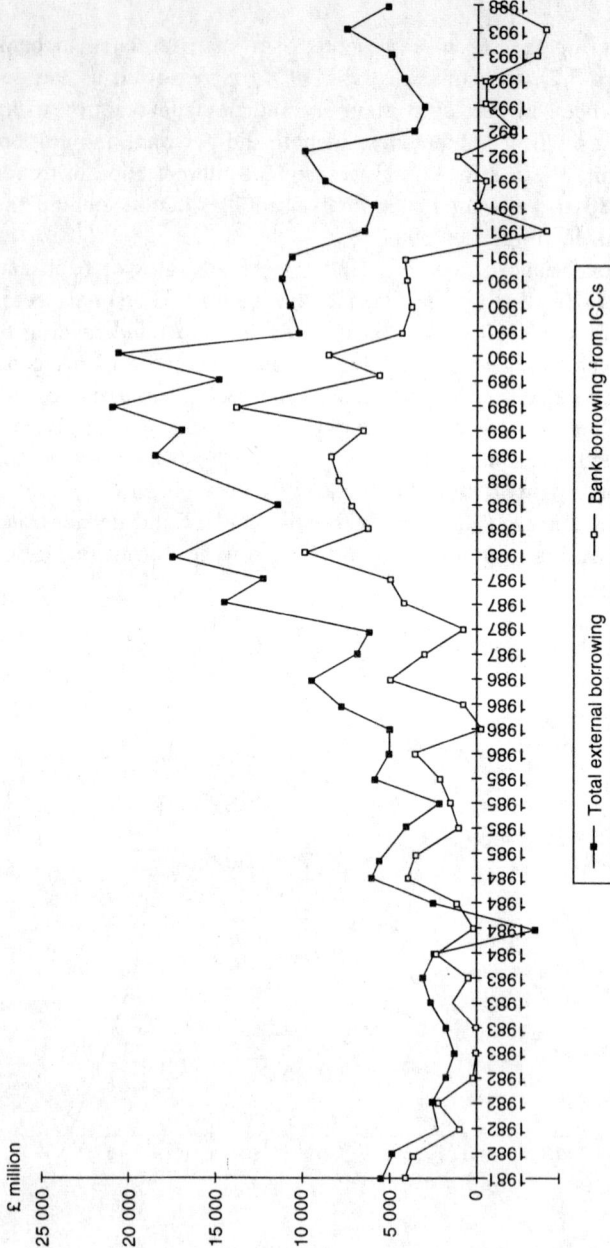

Figure 3.3 Evolution of total external borrowing and bank borrowing from ICCs, 1981–93

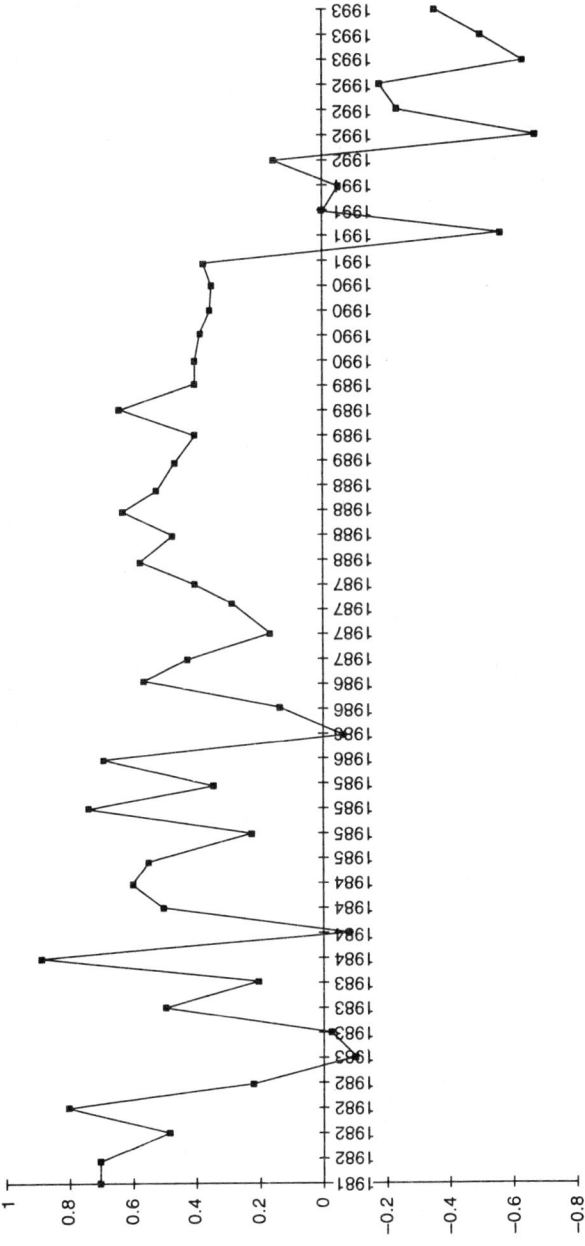

Figure 3.4 Evolution of ICCs' banking borrowing as a proportion of total external borrowing, 1981–93

The 1980s was a period of deregulation, structural change and enhanced competition in the financial system, and each contributed significantly to credit trends during the decade. The Bank of England (1990) notes: 'a massive increase in the availability of credit, whose roots can be traced back to the lifting of a series of restrictions on lending institutions in the early 1980s.' The 1980s was a decade during which competition in the financial system intensified substantially (Llewellyn, 1990b). There had been a discernible public policy shift towards recognising the benefits of competition in finance. The abandoning of cartels and restrictive practices in the financial system were both a cause and effect of increased competition. The change in the strategic objectives of financial institutions in favour of greater diversification also had the effect of intensifying competitive conditions in the financial sector: as financial institutions across the board diversified, the number of institutions in credit markets increased. In the 1970s, building societies operated in a cartelised, cohesive and semi-monopoly market environment but, as they confronted competition from banks during the 1980s, the building society sector became less cohesive.

Our central theme is that much of the increase in debt and lending during the 1980s represents in part a stock-adjustment phenomenon. During the 1980s several stock-adjustments were made which had the effect of generating a substantial demand and supply of credit to the personal and corporate sectors whilst the once-for-all adjustments were being made. In essence, the 1980s was a transitional period of adjustment from a *credit-constrained* to a *credit-liberalised* market regime. A substantial proportion of the rise in credit represented a once-for-all adjustment to a new environment. Several stock-adjustments operated during the 1980s, all of which worked in the direction of accelerating the pace of lending and borrowing:

The Financial System

- Abolition of hire purchase (HP) restrictions.
- Abolition of the building society cartel.
- Entry of building societies into wholesale funding markets: increasing their lending capacity.
- Changes in the capital structure of banks: allowing debt capital to be included in the capital base.
- The abolition of the Corset.
- Abolition of the reserve assets ratio requirement of banks.
- The tax treatment of gilt-edge securities transactions of building

societies which induced a once-for-all rise in the societies' liquidity ratio and switch towards mortgages.
• The change in the status of the TSB.

The Personal Sector

• A rise in the desired equilibrium debt–income ratio.
• A move towards the desired debt–income ratio after a previous constraint.
• Equity withdrawal from housing.
• The abolition of HP controls.
• A capital-gearing adjustment in the housing market.

These factors can be considered in terms of the basic framework of the banking firm in Figure 3.1. The sharp rise in lending to both the corporate, but most especially the personal, sector during the 1980s may be associated with:

1 A rise in the demand for credit: the demand curve shifts.
2 Reduced credit rationing due to increased competition and deregulation:
   • higher *risk thresholds* i.e., institutions being prepared to incur higher risk;
   • reduced *disequilibrium credit rationing* with the abolition of the building soceity cartel and the greater responsiveness of mortgage interest rates to market rates;
   • reduced *equilibrium credit rationing* as non-interest terms were adjusted.
3 Reduced perceptions of risk: lenders believed risks had been reduced.
4 Enhanced lending capacity associated, for instance, with changes in capital regulation of banks and wholesale funding of building societies.
5 Narrower lending margins: lower supply price of financial intermediation.

Stock Adjustment, Over-reaction and Risks

The immediate impact of deregulation is likely to be an initial stock-adjustment response by banks towards new steady-state sustainable balance sheet positions. *Stock-adjustment* factors represent the process through which financial institutions (or borrowers) adjust the structure and level of portfolios to new desired equilibrium positions following an identifiable shock. Financial institutions have a desired portfolio structure for a given set of market and regulatory conditions. If any of these conditions change, the desired portfolio changes and stock adjustments are made to achieve them. Such external shocks are frequently associated with policy changes. While the new portfolio equilibrium is being achieved through a finite once-for-all stock adjustment the volume of credit is substantially increased or decreased. As already noted, several measures of deregulation would have induced stock-adjustments to debt and lending during the 1980s. The IMF (1993) suggests a similar conclusion: 'The increase in borrowing was broadly based, suggesting that the debt accumulation reflected a backlog of unsatisfied demand for credit unleashed   after financial liberalisation.'

Figure 3.5 illustrates the nature of the stock-adjustment process which also incorporates an element of over-shooting. In the absence of constraining regulation banks might choose a trend growth of assets (*UU*). Regulation up to period *A* constraints balance sheets along *PQ*. Regulation is removed at time *A* which induces banks to make a finite adjustment (*QR*) in a relatively short period (*AB*) towards their chosen unconstrained position. In effect, banks adjust in a short period to a position they would have previously chosen had they not been constrained by regulation. An over-shooting effect (the possible reasons for which are outlined below) is represented by *RS*. This in turn is likely to induce a subsequent correction (*ST*) which might be characterised as either a 'credit crunch' (whereby banks reduce their lending because of their own capital constraints following the previous overexpansion) or because, following the deterioration in financial performance due to the risks absorbed during the *QS* phase, they become more risk averse. A similar model has been applied for an earlier period to bank lending to developing countries during the 1970s (Llewellyn, 1990b).

The stock-adjustment model outlined incorporates a phase of overreaction. There are several reasons why this might occur and it seems a relevant phenomenon in the case of British banks during the 1980s as balance sheet positions were taken beyond long-run sustainable positions. Reaction times in financial markets are short, adjustments can be made quickly, and the financial system is characterised by oligopolistic competition. As a result competitive pressures frequently force firms to move together: sometimes described as a 'herd instinct'. Such behaviour can be related to the competitive structure of the industry; if a stable equilibrium is disturbed by one firm this induces

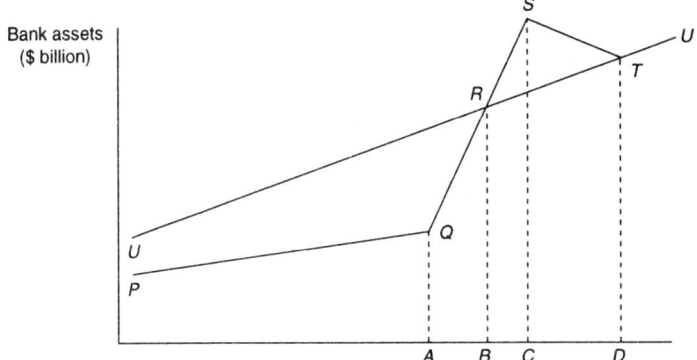

Figure 3.5   Response of banks to deregulation

others to follow. Some analysis has ascribed it to a property of the
incentive structure in that, in a world of uncertainty, the desire to avoid
personal blame for mismanagement is liable to make all risk-averse
bank managers subject to peer pressure to follow the same kind of
policy, and perhaps to assume that what is good for competitors is
equally good for them.

Major implications follow from this: when an initial equilibrium is
disturbed (perhaps by an act of deregulation), collective action is likely
to be substantial as all institutions and competitors move together. The
net result of collective change is likely to be substantial. At the same
time, the collective change can undermine the calculations made by
each firm individually because the force of the collective change changes
market conditions with each firm underestimating the response of competitors and hence the extent of the collective change.

Such behaviour has also been studied more formally and competing
explanations offered for similar behaviour between competitors. In
cohesion theory (Burt, 1987) competitive organisations maintain close
contact with each other and this induces them to behave in the same
way even if there is not explicit or implicit collusion. A second theoretical approach draws on the analysis of *competitive dynamics* (e.g.
Tirole, 1988) with firms copying the behaviour of others in order to
maintain market share. This merges with a third strand in the theoretical analysis which emphasises that, in the absence of knowledge about
how a new regime operates, firms maintain past behavioural patterns.
Thus bank strategies in a regulated regime were based on market share
objectives and this carried forward into the new deregulated market

environment. A study of the post-regulation environment in Norwegian banking gives strong support to the third approach (Reve *et al.*, 1992). In addition, the study offers support for the *structural equivalence* theory (Burt, 1987): firms occupying a similar network position face common external pressures and external expectations about what is required of them, and this induces similar behaviour.

The experience of both Scandinavian and UK banks during the 1980s suggests an element of over-reaction in the response to deregulation and increased competition. The factors indicating that a 'herd instinct' often prevails in banking behaviour have been examined in some detail as one of the contributory components in the over-reaction response to deregulation. A detailed study of the Norwegian banking system's responses to deregulation also identifies other behavioural characteristics which would induce an over-reaction:

- The establishment of asset growth and market share objectives by bank management and a momentum of growth once the process had begun.
- This was reinforced by the new (higher-risk) business appearing to be profitable in the short run.
- Weak internal control systems.
- Weak risk-assessment, monitoring and management systems partly because in the previous regime overall risks had been low due to credit rationing.
- Banks lacked experience of competition and inappropriately translated previous behaviour patterns to the new competitive environment.
- Banks attempted to expand rapidly in order to solve cost problems. In effect, regulation had the effect of sustaining a cost structure which was not viable in a competitive environment. Deregulation revealed this excess cost structure and induced, what turned out to be, a high-risk growth strategy as a solution to it.

In varying degrees these conclusions apply equally to the experience of the UK, and Cantor and Wenninger (1993) suggest an over-shooting phenomenon in US bank credit markets in the 1980s. The BIS (1992) suggests that this is a fairly universal phenomenon:

Competitive pressures encouraged greater acceptance of risk. Moreover, conscious risk-taking, underpinning an over-expansion, was fostered by the tendency to give priority to aggressive growth objectives over return on capital. The common practice of assessing performance in relation to the average and the fear of being 'left behind' helped to breed uniformity of judgement, potentially compounding individual error. Some of these elements are part and parcel of competition. But they are much more prominent in the transition from a protected to a competitive environment, from one where enterprises are confined to conducting business in familiar markets, following well-rehearsed operating rules, to one where new rules of the game apply.

Debt Positions

The sharp rise in borrowing by the personal and corporate sectors induced substantial rises in their respective capital and income gearing ratios. Figure 3.6 shows the personal sector debt–income ratio which rose from 57 per cent in 1989 to 115 per cent in 1989. Partly as a result of this, and the sharp rise in interest rates on floating rate debt during 1988 and 1989 (Figure 3.18), the personal sector's income gearing ratio rose from 6 per cent in the early 1980s to a record peak of 15 per cent in 1990 (Figure 3.6) although it subsequently declined sharply to 8 per cent by the beginning of 1993 in line with the fall in interest rates.

The gearing position of the corporate sector is given in Figures 3.7 and 3.8 and show a very sharp rise in aggregate corporate sector debt. However, although debt levels (in both real and nominal terms) reached very high levels (and similar to an earlier peak in 1970 – see Sargant, 1991), Young (1992, 1993) suggests that the levels were not as unprecedented when viewed in relation to the value of the corporate sector's capital, which is one measure of a company's ability to service debt. At the end of 1990, and because the market value of capital had risen relative to its replacement cost, the level of debt in relation to the market value of companies was around the average for the previous 20 years. Nevertheless, with such high debt levels the corporate sector was vulnerable to movements in interest rates and to any fall in equity prices. Although gearing levels were no higher in 1990 than in 1970, in the former period a considerably higher proportion was in the form of fixed-interest bond debt rather than the floating rate bank debt which was dominant in 1990.

Overall, such high gearing ratios of both the personal and company sectors made both sectors potentially vulnerable given that the bulk of debt is priced on a floating rate basis. High gearing ratios increase the default risk and may, therefore, adversely affect banks' perceptions of

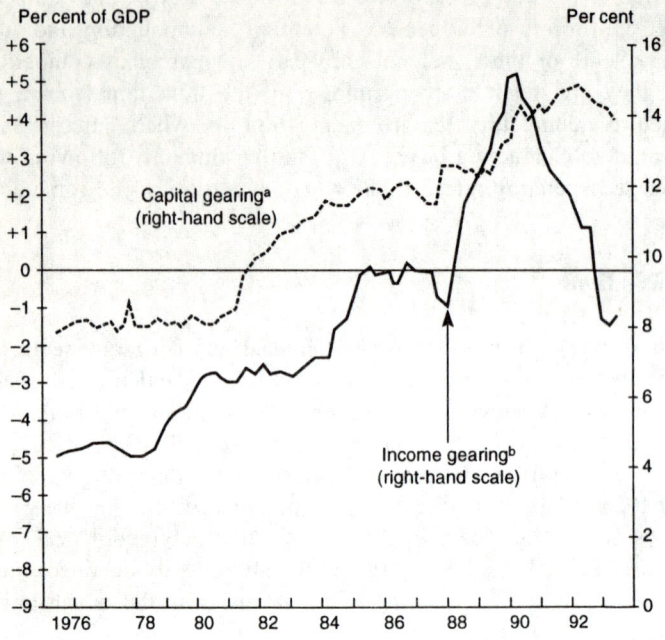

a Borrowing from banks and building societies as a proportion of net personal secto-financial and physical assets.
b Gross personal sector interest payments as a proportion of personal disposable income.

Source: Bank of England, *Inflation Report* (February 1994).

Figure 3.6   Personal sector gearing and financial deficit, 1976–92

credit-worthiness and hence the willingness to supply credit. To the extent that the high gearing ratios reflect an element of over-shooting by borrowers, the demand for credit would also be expected to decline at each level of income and interest rates. In terms of the framework given in Figure 3.5, the decline in borrowing (*ST*) is a reversal of the over-shooting (*RS*). Thus part of the explanation for the sharp decline in the pace of bank lending after 1990 is the unwinding of a previous over-shooting by both borrowers and lenders.

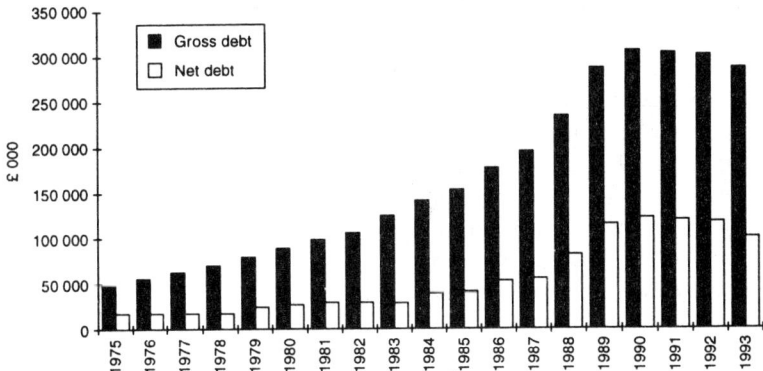

Figure 3.7   UK corporate debt, 1975–93

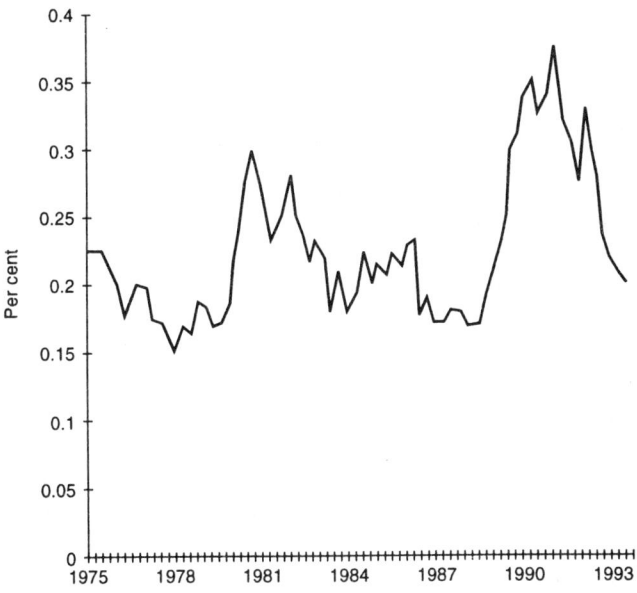

Figure 3.8   Income gearing of the corporate sector, 1975–93

BANKS' FINANCIAL PERFORMANCE: LOAN PROVISIONS

Factors internal to the banks which might induce a credit crunch – or supply-side impulse – focus ultimately upon capital, risks and profitability. Indications of recent trends in the financial performance of the four largest UK clearing banks are given in Tables 3.1–3.4. Table 3.1 derives the internal generation of bank capital (retentions) from profits, provisions for bad debt, taxation and dividend payments. Measured in terms of the internal generation of capital to support future balance sheet growth, there was a marked deterioration in financial performance after 1986. There was no overall internal capital generation in the period 1987–92 compared with £5.8 billion in the previous six years. However, this was not due to weak operating profits (net interest income *plus* other operating income *less* management costs) which rose in every year except one after 1975, including in 1991 and 1992 when the recession might have been expected to erode operating profits. In the period 1987–92 operating profits amounted to £31.4 billion and yet this generated no net capital. In the previous six years £5.8 billion of internal capital was generated on the basis of operating profits of £19.7 billion. As in other countries (e.g. Scandinavia) where financial performance of banks deteriorated sharply in the late 1980s and early 1990s, the reason for the absence of any internal generation of capital was the dramatic rise in provisions for bad debt. In the period 1987–92 provisions amounted to £26.4 billion (Table 3.1). Two phases are identified: 1987–9 when the bulk of provisions were against loans to developing countries, and post-1989 when provisions have been predominantly against domestic loans.

Figure 3.9 indicates the scale of provisions relative to operating profits and how this produced a volatile pattern in the internal generation of capital, being negative in four of the last six years to 1993. It is also the case that retentions were low, volatile and frequently negative after 1987 because dividends were maintained at high levels (though were reduced in 1991 and 1992) despite a declining trend in pre-tax profits. In all but one of the years 1987–92 dividend payments exceeded post-tax profits, and retentions (internal generation of capital) were negative in three years because of this: in effect, dividends were paid out of capital.

The key comparisons are summarised in Table 3.2 which shows provisions as a proportion of operating profits rising from less than 40 per cent in 1982–6 to over 70 per cent after 1987; dividends as a proportion of post-tax profits rose from 24.6 per cent to 94 per cent

Table 3.1 Profitability analysis of four UK clearing banks, 1975–93, £ million

Analysis	1975	1976	1977	1978	1979	1980	1981	1982	1983	1984	1985	1986	1987	1988	1989	1990	1991	1992	1993
Operating profit	469	699	865	1153	1691	1878	2065	2496	2995	3690	3998	4401	4640	5383	6294	5790	6648	7277	8055
– Normal provisions for bad debts	45	–	–20	69	120	405	394	972	1276	1761	1442	1361	993	940	1511	3867	5243	5849	4353
– Exceptional provisions	–	–	–	–	–	–	–	–	–	–	–	–	3357	–	4582	–	–	–	–
+ Other exceptional	–	–	–	–	–	–	–	–	–	–	–	–	–	–	–81	57	81	286	215
= Pre-tax profits	424	699	885	1084	1571	1473	1671	1524	1719	1929	2556	3040	290	4443	120	1866	1324	1142	3528
– Taxation	234	368	430	393	491	402	353	339	572	1110	1192	1069	335	1568	103	1024	560	578	1137
= Post-tax profits	190	331	454	690	1080	1071	1318	1185	1147	819	1364	1971	–45	2875	17	842	764	564	2391
– Minorities	8	15	16	17	21	28	46	71	67	–51	32	36	23	22	124	144	166	173	210
– Preference dividend	0.68	0.68	0.68	0.7	1	1	1	1	1	1	1	1	1	1	13	1	7	25	34
– Extraordinary items	–4	7	3	19	20	5	318	–5	4	14	–83	–52	–76	1	35	–491	–79	–19	–
– Ordinary dividends	58	71	83	102	141	166	201	235	269	296	364	457	549	737	874	879	858	764	1240
– Non-distributable reserves	–	–	–	–	–	–	–	–	–	–	–	–	–	–	–	–	–	–	–
= Retentions	127	237	350	550	897	871	752	883	806	559	1054	1529	–545	2088	–1088	259	–231	–421	859

Source: Banks' Annual Reports.

Table 3.2   Profitability and provisions of four UK banks, 1975–81 to 1987–92

Analysis	1975–81	1982–6	1987–92
Operating profits	8.8	17.6	36.0
− Provisions	1.0	6.8	26.4
= Pre-tax profits	7.8	10.8	9.2[1]
− Tax	2.7	4.3	4.2
= Post-tax profits	5.1	6.5	5.0
− Dividends	0.8	1.6	4.7
− Other adjustments	0.5	0.2	0.2
= Retentions	3.8	4.8	0.1
Provisions as per cent of operating profit	11.4	38.6	73.4
Dividends as per cent of post-tax profits	15.6	24.6	94.0
Retentions as per cent of operating profits	43.2	27.3	0.3

Note:
1. Includes − 0.5 of 'other exceptional' adjustments.

Source: See Table 3.1.

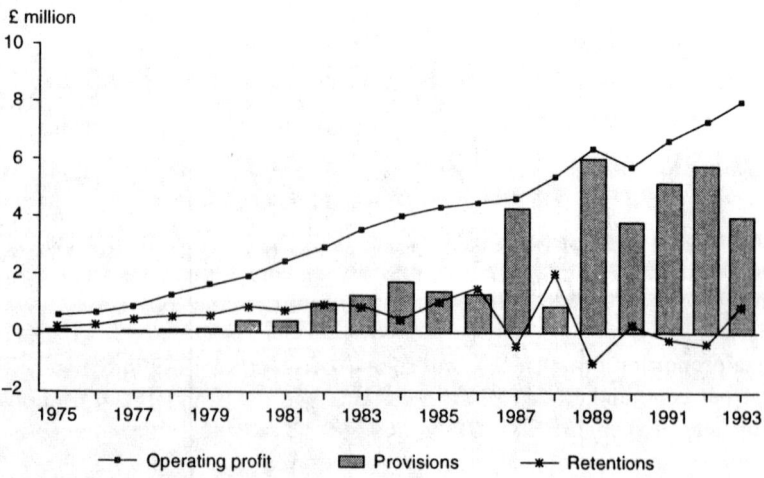

Figure 3.9   UK bank profitability, 1975–93

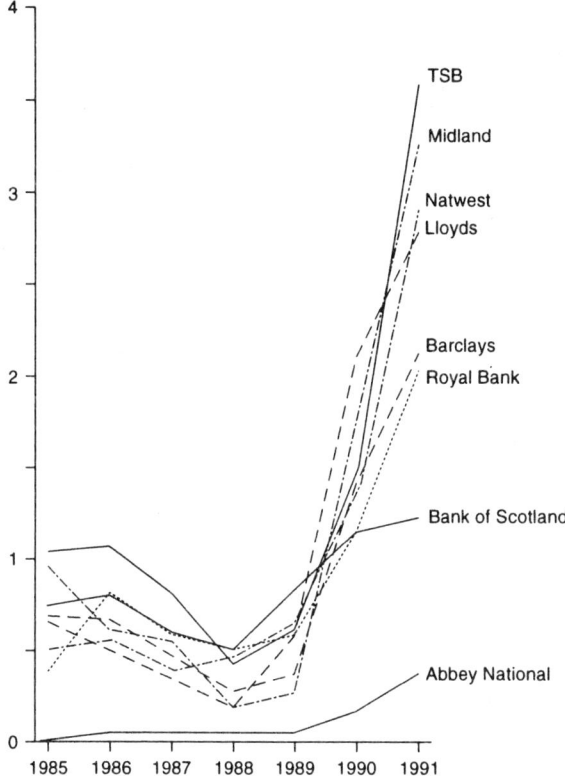

Figure 3.10   Domestic provisions charge/advances, 1985–91

and retentions as a proportion of operating profits slumped from 43 per cent (1975–81) to 27 per cent (1982–6) and further to 0.3 per cent in the period 1987–92. Figure 3.10 also indicates that provisions have risen relative to loans. In the recession of the early 1980s, bad debts as a proportion of advances peaked at 1 per cent; in 1989 they reached 2.4 per cent, and Budd (1990) notes that bad debts have been proportionately greater than in previous recessions. In 1992 outstanding provisions as a proportion of total loan assets were at a record high level.

The pattern and size of banks loan losses between 1987 and 1992 indicate that the risks in bank lending had risen. However, the interpretation is ambiguous as the risk profile in banks' balance sheet positions may rise for one of five reasons:

1 Banks choose to take more risks by changing their behaviour (e.g. by reducing credit-rationing behaviour as part of their competitive strategy).

2 The same micro behaviour becomes more risky because of *systemic* changes in the banking industry that may emerge in a less regulated and more competitive environment; examples of this would include all banks simultaneously expanding substantially; an erosion of 'relationship banking'; the 'fallacy of composition' (behaviour viable for a single bank acting alone being less viable when all firms behave in the same way); borrowers raising gearing ratios, etc.

3 Risks rise either because more risky projects are put to banks, or because the economy itself has become unexpectedly more risky which in turn increases the risk in bank portfolios (Kling, 1986).

4 Banks change their behaviour (e.g. diversify) in the mistaken belief that new areas are not more risky than current business.

5 Banks, in the process of asset growth, develop a high-risk concentrated portfolio by an excessive concentration of new loans in a particular sector of the economy. Individual loans to the same sector may appear to have the same risk characteristics (and hence the banks are unable to discriminate between them) but the overall portfolio becomes more risky because it is excessively concentrated. In the UK, as in Scandinavia and the USA, loans to the construction sector and to property companies rose sharply over the 1980s. Loans to the construction sector rose seven-fold over the decade and to property companies by a multiple of 17 (Table 3.3). As a result, the share of total banking lending to the two sectors rose from 6.9 per cent in 1983 to 12.5 per cent in 1990.

A major issue is whether competition induced banks knowingly to take more risk, or whether unanticipated changes in either the banking or economic environment made given bank portfolios and strategies inherently more risky.

It is likely that each of these factors has been operating in the UK. In the more intense competitive environment, banks did reduce credit rationing, and absorbed what must have been known to be more risky business even if the full extent of the greater risks were underestimated. The new competitive environment, and induced over-reaction, also had the effect of making banking systematically a more risky business. The BIS (1992) also notes that problems were compounded in many countries (notably the UK) by a lax monetary policy (which induced an over-extension by both lenders and borrowers). It is evi-

Table 3.3   UK bank lending to property companies and construction sector, 1980–93, £ million

Year	Construction sector	As per cent of total lending	Property companies	As per cent of total lending	Total bank lending
1980	2369	–	2242	–	N/A
1981	2565	–	2710	–	N/A
1982	3491	–	3523	–	N/A
1983	3968	3.23	4448	3.62	122732
1984	4609	3.10	5420	3.65	148605
1985	5074	3.02	7109	4.22	168280
1986	5675	2.79	9349	4.60	203069
1987	7203	2.97	13360	5.50	242899
1988	10751	3.52	21348	7.00	304996
1989	15135	3.66	31963	7.73	413663
1990	17335	3.84	38996	8.63	451611
1991	16411	3.44	39670	8.32	476677
1992	15488	3.31	37944	8.11	467653
1993[1]	13893	2.94	35040	7.42	472186

Notes:
1. 1993 figures to end of August.
N/A not available.

Source: *Financial Statistics.*

dent that the unexpected depth of the recession was a significant factor in the higher level of provisions and loan losses. It is also clear that banks developed an excessive exposure to the property market with a substantial rise in bank lending to real estate projects based on the expectation that property values would continue to rise. Given the banks' exposure to the property sector, the subsequent fall in property values adversely affected banks in three ways: it undermined the assumptions upon which some of the lending of the 1980s had been based; it made some borrowers particularly vulnerable; and it eroded the value of loan collateral. Asset-growth and market-share strategies also had the effect of increasing the average risk profile of banks' portfolios. All of this was compounded by inadequate risk identification and analysis systems in the new deregulated and competitive environment. The scenario was not unique to the UK (Llewellyn, 1992a).

Following a decade of economic expansion an economic downturn began in 1990. It was to prove to be a substantial and prolonged recession. Banks always face difficult pressures in a recession via reduced demand for voluntary credit; increased demand for 'distress'

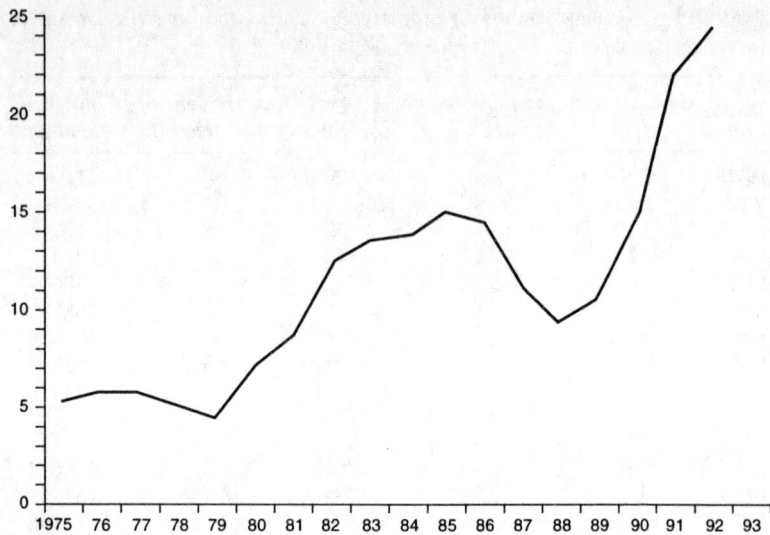

Source: CSO.

Figure 3.11   UK company liquidations, actual value, 1975–93

borrowing; therefore a rise in the average risk on the loan portfolio; lower asset values; a general rise in lending risks; and the need to make higher provisions. The recession in the UK was particularly difficult for banks for several reasons: the unprecedented financial and debt position of both the corporate and personal sectors following a decade of sharp increases in borrowing – their high income and capital gearing position had made them especially vulnerable at a time of high interest rates; the sharp fall in property prices; insolvencies occurring earlier in the cyclical downswing due to the 1986 Insolvency Act making it more hazardous for companies to trade wrongfully; and an unprecedentedly high level of real interest rates at a time of deep recession. Figure 3.11 shows the sharp rise (to unprecedented levels) in the number of company liquidations.

Banks suffered badly due to the combined impact of the economic downturn, the precipitous fall in property prices, and the fall in the general rate of inflation. The impact of these factors was made worse by the evident earlier over-expansion in bank lending and higher-risk profile banks absorbed in their response to competition and deregulation. The massive provisions made in 1987 also reflect past over-lending to developing countries, and this may also reflect similar responses to increased competition in international banking during the 1970s.

Banks' Capital Position

These trends are also reflected in the banks' generation of capital. Table 3.4 gives for the same four banks' changes in their BIS capital and its components for the period 1976–93. In the period 1988–92, capital resources (defined as Tier 1 *plus* Tier 2 capital) were increased by £3.6 billion which (at an annual rate of £903 million) represented a sharp decline from the two earlier periods identified (£3.2 billion, 1983–88; £1.6 billion, 1976–83). There were also substantial differences in the sources of capital. In particular, the internal generation of capital (qualifying Tier 1 Reserves) was negative (£1.6 billion) having contributed 26 per cent and 53 per cent of the total increase in capital in the two earlier periods. Property revaluation reserves were also sharply negative due to the decline in property prices in the period 1988–92. On the other hand, General Provisions (allowable within limits in Tier 2 capital) contributed 24 per cent of total capital in 1988–92 compared with less than 2 per cent in the period 1976–88.

Notwithstanding the negative contribution of the internal generation of capital, the banks were able to increase their capital base by the issue of subordinated debt. In the period 1988–92 Tier 2 capital contributed 61 per cent of the total. However, this can necessarily only be a finite stock-adjustment given that Tier 2 capital cannot exceed 50 per cent of the total capital base. In aggregate for the four banks, the proportion of the capital base represented by Tier 2 capital rose from 45.8 per cent in 1988 to 47.6 per cent in 1992, and by 1992 the ratio for the individual banks ranged between 43.4 per cent and 50.9 per cent. Thus there is a finite regulatory limit to the extent that capital can be injected in the absence of the generation of Tier 1 capital, and the market will impose a limit on the extent to which new equity issues can be made in the absence of an internal generation of capital.

Table 3.4 shows a significant improvement in the generation of capital in 1993 when £2.2 billion was added; in particular, the improved profits position enabled an internal generation of capital to contribute over 40 per cent of the total increase and qualifying reserves rose by 9 per cent. Table 3.5 gives two sets of capital ratios for each of the four banks. The risk asset ratio fell for each of the banks between 1988 and 1990 (as did the Tier 1 capital ratio for two of the banks). There has, however, been a significant rise in capital ratios since 1990 though

Table 3.4 Changes in BIS capital of the four major UK clearing banks, 1976–83 to 1993

Change in:	1976–83		1983–8		1988–92		1993	
	£million	per cent of change in total capital	£million	per cent of change in total capital	£million	per cent of change in total capital	£million	per cent of change in total capital
Ordinary share capital	266	2.4	2 251	17.2	2 069	57.3	43	2.0
Qualifying minority interests	739	6.6	–345	–2.6	57	1.6	4	–
Qualifying tier 1 reserves	5 838	52.5	3 332	25.5	–1 622	–44.9	882	40.3
Preference capital	–	–	–	–	923	25.6	188	8.6
Tier 1 capital	6 843	61.5	5 238	40.1	1 427	39.5	1 117	50.9
Asset revaluation reserves	635	5.7	2 050	15.7	–2 552	–70.7	–81	–3.7
General provisions	856	7.7	–279	–2.1	853	23.6	109	5.0
Preference capital	14	–	–	–	–	–	–	–
Perpetual subordinated debt	–	–	4 208	32.2	1 665	46.1	1 192	54.4
Term subordinated debt	2 780	25.0	1 847	14.1	2 218	61.4	–146	–6.6
Minority interests	–	–	–	–	–	–	–	–
Tier 2 capital	4 285	38.5	7 826	59.9	2 183	60.5	1 074	49.0
Tier 1 and Tier 2 capital	11 128	100	13 064	100	3 610	100	2 191	100

Source: Banks' Annual Reports.

Table 3.5 Capital ratios, per cent

	Barclays	Lloyds	Midland	Natwest
Tier 1 capital ratio (core capital ratio)				
1986	N/A	5.7	N/A	N/A
1987	N/A	4.8	N/A	N/A
1988	6.0	5.6	6.5	5.5
1989	5.7	4.4	5.4	5.3
1990	5.8	5.2	5.4	5.2
1991	5.9	6.2	5.5	5.5
1992	5.5	6.0	5.7	5.2
1993	6.0	6.6	6.5	5.7
Risk asset ratio (total capital ratio)				
1986	N/A	10.7	N/A	N/A
1987	N/A	9.1	N/A	N/A
1988	9.3	10.1	11.8	9.8
1989	9.0	7.4	10.0	9.2
1990	8.3	8.5	9.8	9.1
1991	8.7	9.7	10.3	9.6
1992	9.1	9.8	10.7	9.8
1993	9.8	10.6	11.3	10.8

Note: N/A not available.

Source: Banks' *Annual Reports*.

this partly reflects the very slow pace of bank lending. Each bank was significantly above the international minimum of 8 per cent for the risk asset ratio (and hence this might be interpreted as banks having no immediate capital constraint).

However, *ex post* capital ratios do not in themselves indicate measures of capital ease. First, although the internationally agreed minimum risk asset ratio is 8 per cent, the Bank of England sets strictly confidential target risk asset ratios individually for each bank. Thus although each bank has capital in excess of 8 per cent, the relevant benchmark is the target risk asset ratio and this must be equal to or higher than 8 per cent. In the absence of knowledge about target ratios, published ratios do not indicate the strength of capital ease. Secondly, if the Bank of England had raised the targets, rises in actual risk asset ratios would indicate deliberate measures designed to tighten *ex ante* capital constraints.

A third reservation is that banks would rationally choose to operate with capital ratios above the target minimum so as to maintain room for manoeuvre and it is possible that, in a recession, banks might choose to widen the excess to reflect increased risks.

The major reservation, however, is that the data show *ex post* capital positions and do not indicate what actions have been taken to achieve the outcome. Thus a bank which raises its capital ratio by contracting the balance sheet (perhaps because of an *ex ante* capital constraint) cannot be described as being in a capital ease position. Given that the volume of capital was rising (albeit very modestly) in the period during which bank lending was comparatively weak, an *ex post* rise in capital ratios does not in itself indicate that banks were not capital constrained. The banks' capital positions have been improved through a series of measures: securitising a proportion of loan portfolios (a process often motivated by a desire to ease a capital constraint); a shift towards low risk-weight assets (e.g. mortgages and government securities); a cut in dividends by two banks (Midland in 1990 and Barclays in 1992) and a series of business disposals (e.g. withdrawing from US and other foreign sales of subsidiaries, etc.). As noted in an earlier section, these are each symptoms of actual or *ex ante* capital constraint and each would have the effect of raising *ex post* capital ratios. The evident switch from high to low risk-weighted assets is demonstrated in Figure 3.12 by comparing the relative movements of the banks' capital–asset ratios (capital as a proportion of total assets) and their risk–asset ratios (capital as a proportion of the sum of risk-adjusted assets). For three of the banks the risk–assets capital ratio rose in 1991 and 1992, while capital ratios were either constant or declined.

Overall, degrees of capital ease or constraint cannot be inferred from *ex post* movements in banks' capital ratios. The data in Table 3.1 also indicate that recent contributions to the capital base from retained (post-provisions) profits have been too low to support significant balance sheet expansion, and it is evident that banks cannot rely on external capital injections if internal contributions are weak either because of low underlying profitability or because continued large provisions are required. Capital components are not perfectly substitutable and banks may be as much concerned at the *quality* of the capital base as its total; banks may appear to have sufficient capital but be constrained by its quality. Tier 1 (predominantly equity capital) is superior to Tier 2 (in that it is available to finance asset write-offs) and Figure 3.13 indicates that for two of the banks the proportion of Tier 1 capital fell between 1990 and 1992. Figure 3.14 indicates that equity–asset ratios have declined.

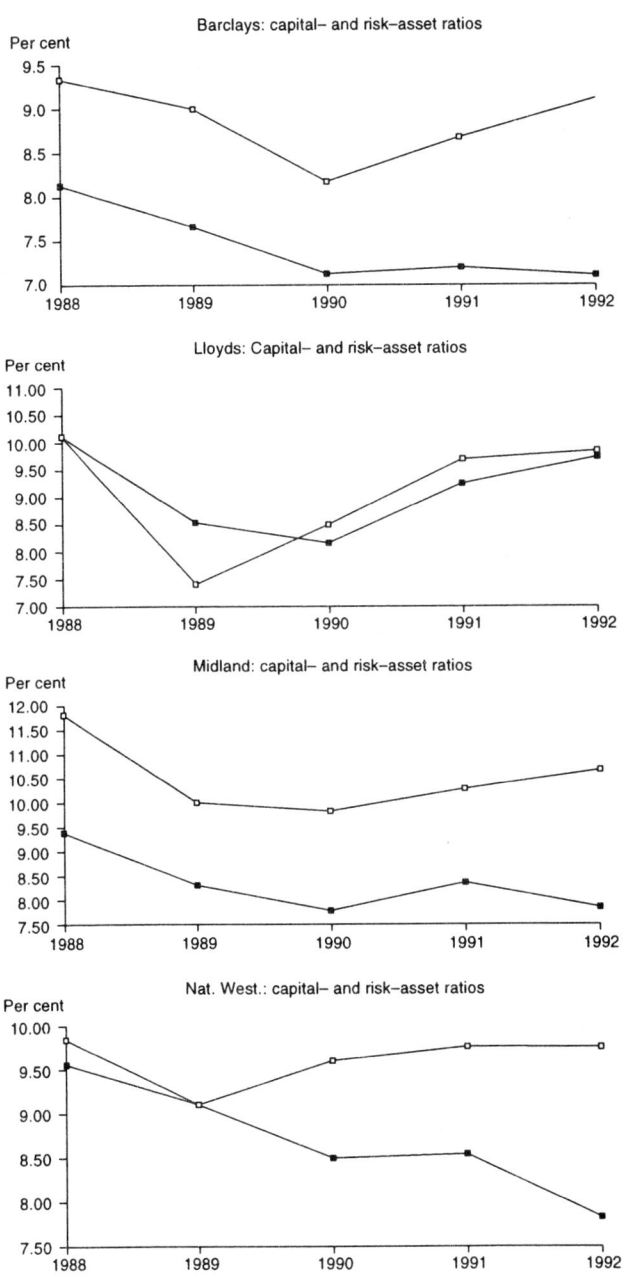

Figure 3.12   Relative movements of the banks' capital–asset ratios, 1988–92

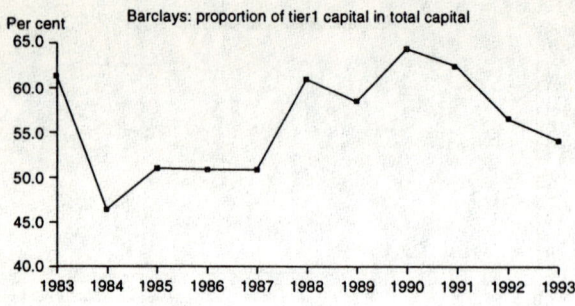

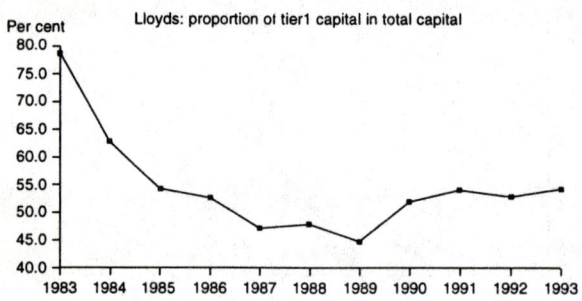

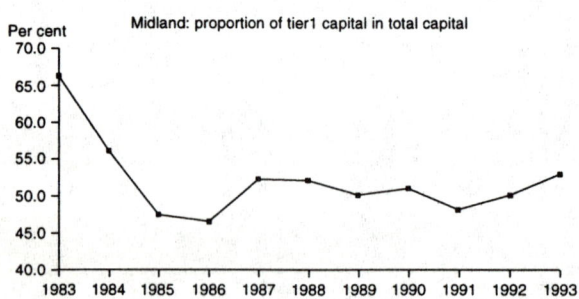

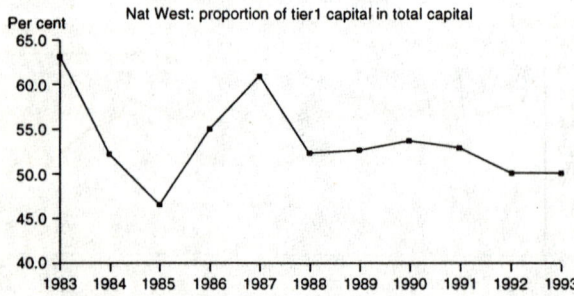

Figure 3.13 Banks' proportion of Tier 1 capital in total capital, 1983–93

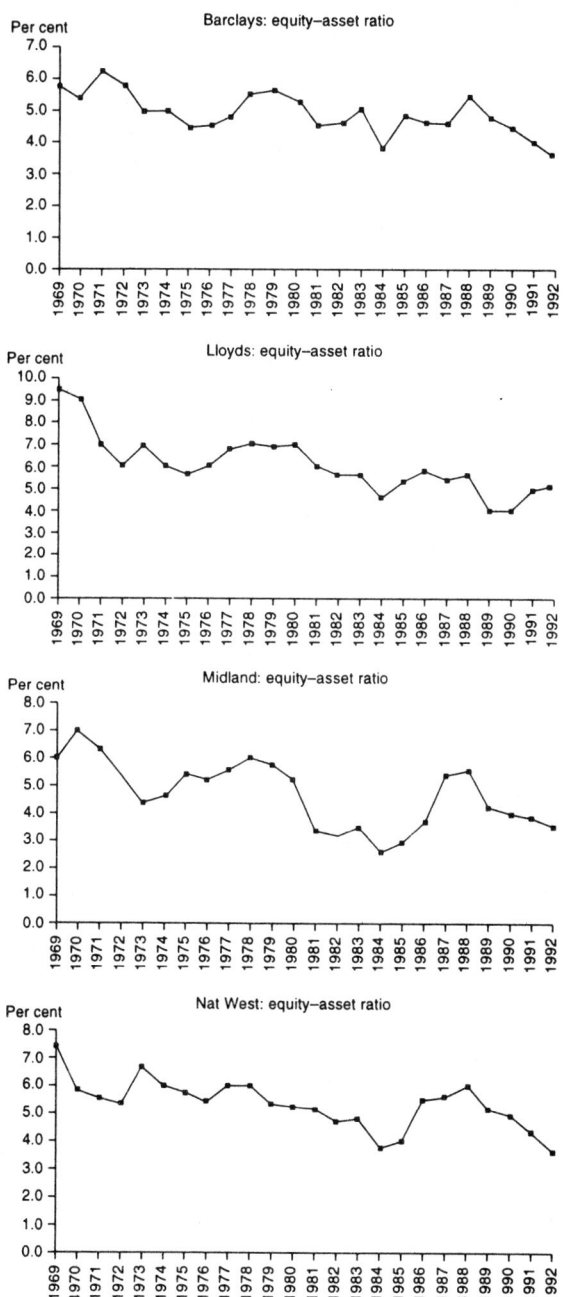

Figure 3.14   Banks' equity–asset ratios, 1969–92

On the face of it, with a perfectly efficient capital market, one-off reductions in capital due to exceptional loan losses which, because of the special circumstances that gave rise to them, are not expected to be repeated need not present a capital problem. In such circumstances a rational response is to seek a recapitalisation by seeking new external capital. In practice, this may be too sanguine a view: the capital market might not be convinced that full provisions had been made; the shock of past losses might adversely affect expectations about future profitability, and confidence in bank management might have been impaired to the extent that, while past mistakes may not be repeated, different errors could be made in the future. The experience of too many 'special' losses creates doubt about the behavioural characteristics of banks operating in a highly competitive environment.

REASONS FOR A DECLINE IN BANK LENDING

As borrowing from banks is a subset of the total demand for finance by the corporate sector, the demand for bank finance changes because of changes in the total demand for finance (internal and external), because borrowers switch between internal and external sources, or because substitutions are made between different forms of external finance (e.g. bank borrowing and capital market issues). Supply and demand for bank finance interact over the cycle. In general, and other things being equal, the demand for voluntary bank finance rises in the upswing of the cycle and banks are willing to meet it, but decreases in the downswing. The involuntary demand for finance rises in the downswing of the cycle with banks sometimes prepared to accommodate it, but only in the early stages. The demand for different types of external finance reflects the relative costs and characteristics of different forms of finance, portfolio choices by borrowers, but also constraints in the supply of particular forms. If, for instance, companies increase their borrowing from the capital market this may reflect either an explicit portfolio choice or an unwillingness or inability of banks to lend. Similarly, a decline in bank lending may reflect a decline in the demand for finance, a lower demand for bank finance within a constant total, or supply constraint faced by banks. It is difficult in practice to identify *ex ante* preferences from *ex post* data and to distinguish between shifts in the demand for bank finance and changes in the supply conditions imposed by the banks themselves. The two may also interact: the demand curve may shift because borrowers perceive that the probability of success in the demand for a loan has been reduced, and an autonomous shift in the supply of finance impacts on income and expenditure which in turn affects the demand for loans.

The willingness of banks to lend is determined by several factors: their perception of the credit-worthiness of borrowers and the credit standards they impose, actual or anticipated cash flow by borrowers, borrowers' balance sheet positions and in particular gearing ratios, general perceptions of risk, the banks' degree of risk aversion, the availability of acceptable collateral offered by borrowers, and the banks' capital position. It is therefore difficult to isolate autonomous and endogenous supply and demand shifts over the cycle.

The framework offered by Kliesen and Tatom (1992) (relating only the supply and demand for bank loans to the rate of interest) is unsatisfactory as it does not consider the economics of the banking firm and the factors which influence the supply price of financial intermediation as considered in Figure 3.1. In terms of the analytical framework of the banking firm, the factors that induce a decline in bank lending may be divided between those that: shift the demand curve for total external finance, shift the demand curve for bank loans within a given total, shift the supply curve of loans and deposits, shift the supply curve of loans relative to that of deposits, and those which induce *disequilibrium* or *risk-threshold* credit monitoring. The alternative scenarios are summarised as follows.

Autonomous Shift in Total Demand for Credit

- cyclical effects;
- increased uncertainty regarding expected rates of return;
- increased risk aversion by borrowers;
- balance sheet constraints: reduced demand for credit following the emergence of disequilibrium; income or capital gearing ratios.

Autonomous Shift in Demand for Bank Credit Relative to the Total

- relative cost and terms of bank finance and alternative funding options;
- interest rate cycle: increased demand for fixed interest (capital market) funds at low points in the interest rate cycle;
- financial innovation in the capital market widening the range of capital market instruments ('spectrum filling', see Llewellyn, 1992d);

- a desire to diversify the structure of liabilities following a period of substantial bank borrowing;
- increased *equilibrium* credit rationing: banks demand more onerous non-interest terms (e.g. collateral requirements).

Endogenous Shift in Demand Curve

- Fewer projects are put to banks because of a perception of a lower probability of success. If banks signal an increased risk aversion, firms may choose to save transactions costs by not seeking bank finance for projects that previously would have been put to their bankers.
- The demand curve shifts as a result of a shift in the supply curve of loans as borrowers perceive that wider margins are temporary.

Shift in Supply Curve of Deposits and Loans

- rise in general level of interest rates;
- increased attractiveness of alternatives to bank deposits (e.g. mutual funds, etc.), which shifts to the left the exogenous supply curve of deposits and hence also the endogenous supply curve of loans;
- increased perceptions of bank risk by depositors.

Shift in Supply Curve of Loans Relative to Deposits

- increased bank costs;
- a target to increase post-tax/provisions profits to generate internal capital;
- increased risk of loans;
- increased risk aversion by banks;
- capital constraint: higher price of capital or requirement (portfolio or regulation induced) to hold more capital relative to deposits;
- tightening of credit standards;
- decline in the value of collateral, e.g. asset prices;
- shift in business strategy from balance sheet growth to rate of return on equity;
- offsetting of a previous over-shooting of loan portfolios;
- deterioration in balance sheet position of borrowers.

Credit Rationing

• Increased *risk-threshold, equilibrium*, and *disequilibrium* credit rationing (see Figure 3.2).

In practice, the impact of these supply and demand factors is difficult to isolate, most especially during a period of structural change in behaviour patterns of banks and borrowers. However, in general if demand is the dominant influence then, other things being equal, the demand for all forms of external finance is likely to decline and there is no obvious reason to expect significant changes in the share of alternative financing options. It would also be expected that banks' lending margins would either fall or remain constant as suggested by Cantor and Wenninger (1993). However, this is an ambiguous outcome because if the reduced demand for credit is a reflection of a recession, lending risks are likely to rise and banks would rationally widen spreads in order to incorporate larger risk premia in loan interest rates. This indicates the difficulty of separating supply and demand impulses.

Conversely, if the impulses derive from a leftward shift in the supply curve of loans relative to that of deposits, the unambiguous expectation is that the banks' lending margins would widen. A hardening of non-interest terms on loan contracts would also be expected. If this shift reflected constraints (e.g. capital) operating on the banks rather than a rise in the risk of borrowers, a decline in bank lending would be accompanied by an increase in alternative borrowing such as through capital market issues. While bank and capital market funds are less than perfect substitutes for all borrowers (and for some are not substitutable at all) there is a sufficient cohort of corporate borrowers which can substitute capital market funds when bank financing becomes less available. With reference to US experience, Cantor and Wenninger (1993) suggest that wider spreads between banks' lending rates and funding costs indicate a reduced willingness to lend. While not conclusive, in general widening spreads are more likely to be associated with supply-side impulses than shifts in demand.

Detecting a Credit Crunch

Having assessed the possible causes of a credit crunch in UK bank lending, the purpose of this section is to attempt to identify possible periods during the recent recession when bank lending behaviour was symptomatic of a credit crunch. In doing this, it is important to distinguish (as far as is possible) between periods of declining bank lending which are attributable to the usual cyclical declines in demand during recessions, and periods where the supply of bank lending is declining sharply *relative* to demand. It is the latter which represents a genuine credit crunch and which we attempt to isolate in this section. In doing this we face a fundamental identification problem in the sense that what we observe in respect of bank lending volume and interest rate data is generally the outcome of the interaction of supply and demand factors. Hence, it is inherently difficult to identify periods of genuine supply-side credit crunch. In order to alleviate this problem, an econometric model has been developed of the demand for bank lending by Industrial and Commercial Companies (ICCs) which can be used to identify periods when the real volume of bank lending to this sector declined more sharply than the real demand for bank lending.

The formal econometric model is discussed in more detail subsequently and in the Appendix. Before using the model of bank loan demand, however, it is useful to first identify some key indicators which might point to the existence of a supply-side credit crunch. First, as our simple model of bank intermediation illustrates (Figure 3.1), a period during which there was a significant decline in the supply of bank lending would be expected to coincide with a period in which the interest spread on bank lending was increasing significantly. In contrast, a period characterised by a decline in the demand for bank lending would be expected to be accompanied by constant or possibly declining interest spreads. It is clear from Figure 3.5, that bank lending to companies had been declining from late 1989/early 1990. As we can see from Figure 3.15 during 1990 this was accompanied by a falling interest spread in terms of the average weighted spreads over LIBOR for syndicated credits to ICCs. This is consistent with a demand-driven decline in bank lending. From the first quarter of 1991, however, this spread increased very sharply before moderating again from 1991:4. The same pattern is evident for margins on all bank lending to the corporate sector in Figure 3.16 which is taken from the *Bank of England Quarterly Bulletin*. This evidence suggests that a credit crunch is most likely to have occurred during 1991. While arguing that: 'it is difficult to conclude from the evidence so far available that there is or will be a credit crunch [in the UK] which will seriously worsen the recession', Budd (1990) notes that wider spreads and a tightening of lending criteria are usually caused by a deteriorating financial position of banks and especially loan-loss experience. It is also the case that, as noted by Kliesen and Tatom (1992), periods when credit crunches

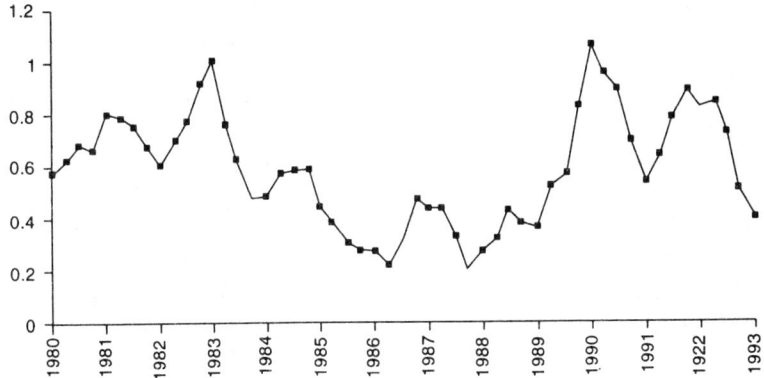

Figure 3.15 Average weighted spreads over LIBOR for syndicated credits to ICCs, 1980–93

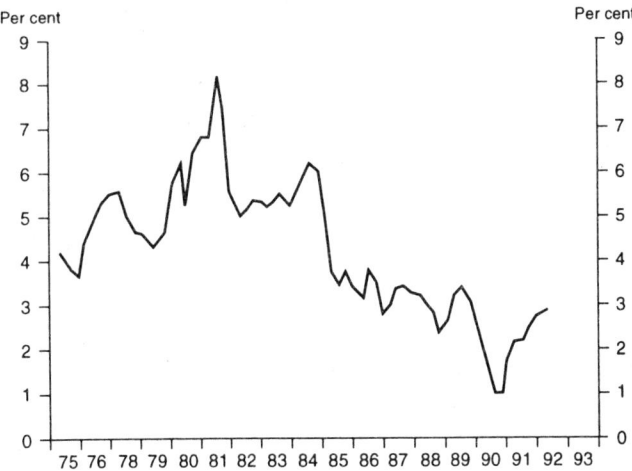

Figure 3.16 Margin on bank lending to corporate sector, 1976–93

are believed to occur also tend to be periods of recession when bank-ruptcy and default rates on loans rise. Thus, a widening spread is a rational response to compensate for these higher risks.

The second indicator which we might look to as an indication of a possible supply-side credit crunch is a decline in bank lending to the corporate sector relative to that sector's real requirements. Figure 3.17 plots bank lending to ICCs as a proportion of Gross Domestic Fixed Capital Formation (GDFCF) and Increase in Book Value of Stocks. This proportion appears to have been on a modest trend decline from 1988 and may be associated with the emergence of an inverted yield curve over this period (Figure 3.18) which would tend to make capital market financing relatively more attractive than bank lending linked to short term interest rates. It is quite clear from Figure 3.17, however, that this proportion declined dramatically from the early part of 1991, particularly during the second quarter. Indeed, the emergence of a negative proportion implies some net repayment of bank lending by the company sector. This is clearly consistent with the evidence provided by bank interest spreads in the context of an emerging credit crunch during 1991, although the evidence from Figure 3.17 does suggest that the credit crunch, if it did exist, was somewhat less significant during the latter part of 1991.

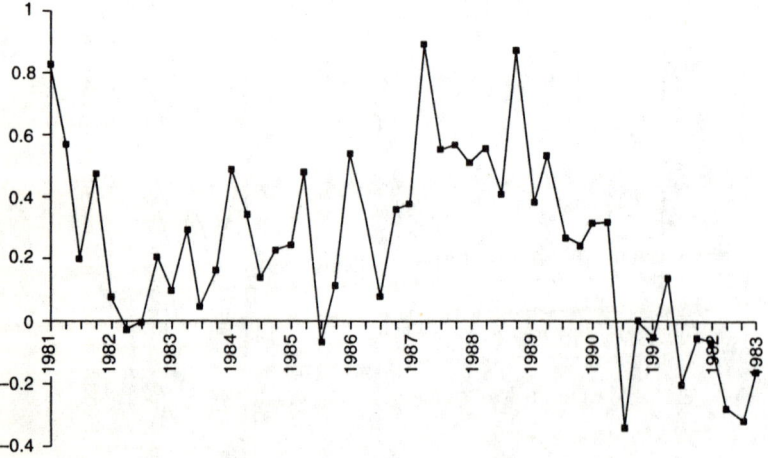

Figure 3.17   Bank lending as a proportion of gross domestic fixed capital formation and increase in book value stocks, 1981–93

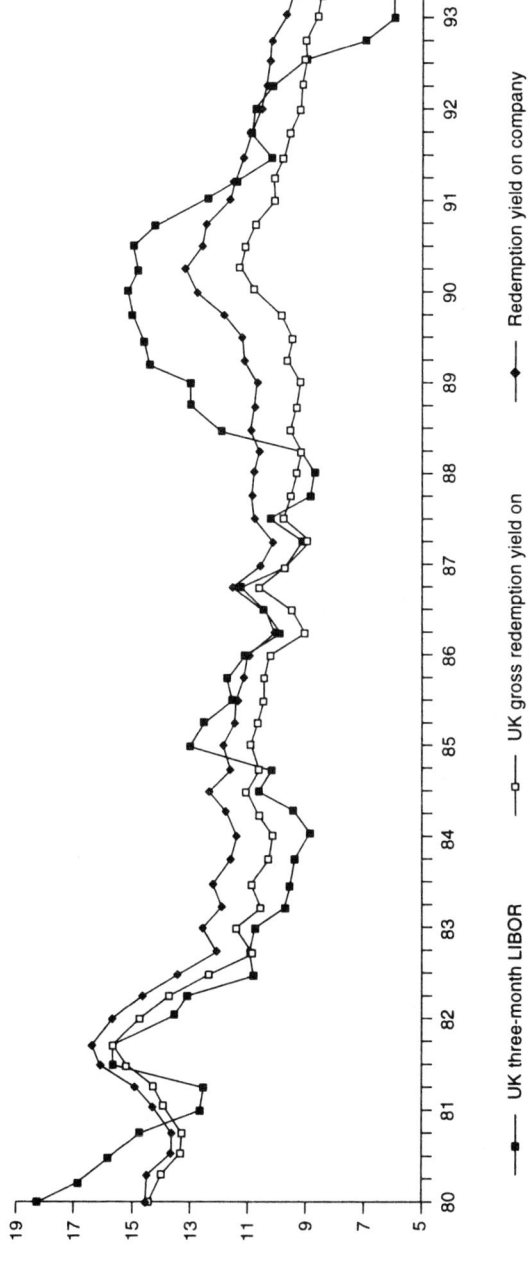

Figure 3.18 Evolution of the three-month LIBOR and of government and corporate securities redemption yield, 1980–93

UK three-month LIBOR

UK gross redemption yield on 20-year gilts

Redemption yield on company debenture and loan stocks

In terms of interpreting this second piece of evidence, it is clearly possible that the decline in bank lending relative to the real funding requirements of the company sector in 1991 was due solely to a change in portfolio preferences on the part of ICCs. In other words, companies may simply have sought to finance their external borrowing requirements from sources outside the banking sector for reasons such as relative costs, etc. This explanation does seem at odds with the previous experience, however, which suggested a steady trend decline in the proportion of bank lending relative to GDFCF as a consequence of evolving portfolio preferences on the part of ICCs. This is echoed in the moderate trend decline in the proportion of ICCs' bank borrowing relative to total external borrowing between 1988 and early 1991 (Figure 3.4). The sudden and dramatic decline in bank lending to ICCs relative to total external borrowing and investment requirements, combined with an unprecedented sustained period where both these latter proportions remained negative, seems more consistent with a supply-side contraction in bank lending than a demand-induced decline.

As mentioned previously, explaining the very sharp contraction in the share of bank lending to companies during 1991 in terms of a decline in demand brought about by a shift in the portfolio preferences of the company sector seems at odds with the very sharp increase in lending spreads on bank lending to ICCs during 1991. Of course, it could be argued that the causation runs from rising spreads on bank lending to a decline in demand for bank lending and an increase in the demand by ICCs for other sources of external finance. This argument, however, does not explain the initial rise in bank lending spreads. The only two possibilities for the sudden widening of bank lending spreads would seem to be a supply-side contraction of bank lending, as outlined earlier, or a significant increase in the risks on corporate lending (or at least an increase in banks' perceptions of this risk). Clearly, the latter would also be reflected in the bond market in terms of an increase in the yield gap between corporate bond yields and Government bond yields. As can be seen from Figure 3.19, however, the yield gap reached a peak in early 1990 and subsequently declined. This suggests that at the time of the hypothesised credit crunch in early 1991 lending to the company sector was viewed as being considerably less risky than it had been during 1989 and 1990. Default risk is likely to increase as gearing ratios rise (Davis, 1990), and it is significant that the income-gearing of the corporate sector peaked in late 1990 and thereafter declined (Figure 3.8). This would suggest that the financial position of companies became less rather than more pre-

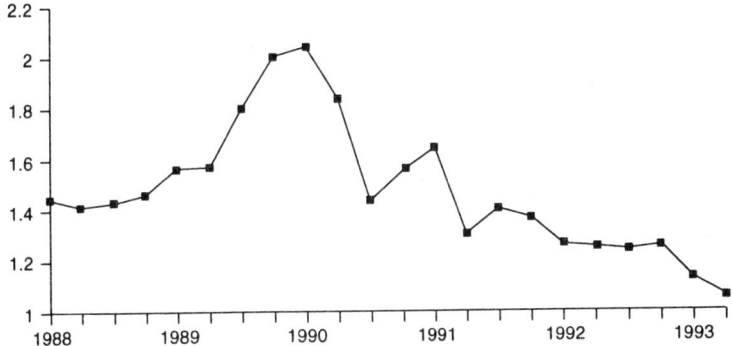

Figure 3.19   Evolution of the differential between corporate and government redemption yield on securities, 1988–93

carious during 1991. However, a note of caution is entered about the interpretation of yield differentials as a measure of the markets' judgement about default risk; Lund (1990) suggests that structural weaknesses in the UK bond market may distort credit spreads. Nevertheless, Davis (1987) indicates that, in general (but with qualifications), there is a fairly strong correlation between spreads and defaults but that risks may not be altogether accurately priced in the UK bond market (Davis, 1990).

Finally, Figures 3.20 and 3.21 illustrate that other sources of funding (such as ordinary share issues and capital issues) increased sharply as a percentage of ICCs external funding from early 1991, and thereafter mirrored the movements of bank lending as a proportion of the latter. While this is to be expected, it is important to note that for most companies these alternative sources of finance will not be perfect substitutes for bank lending. Hence, if the sharp decline in bank lending in early 1991 can be characterised as a genuine supply-side credit crunch it seems likely that some firms will be able to substitute into alternative sources of funding, while other firms will find themselves credit constrained in the sense of having to reduce their capital investment expenditures, etc. below planned levels.

Having analysed the evidence from some key indicators *vis-à-vis* the emergence of a credit crunch in early 1991, we can with some confidence dismiss the notion that the decline in bank lending simply reflected a decline in the demand for external funding associated with the course of the business cycle. While this is a plausible explanation for the sharp decline in bank lending during 1989 and 1990, it does

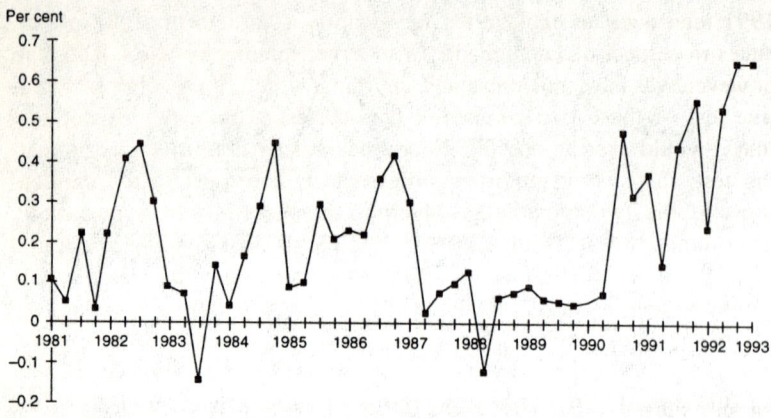

Figure 3.20   Ordinary shares as a proportion of external funds, 1981–93

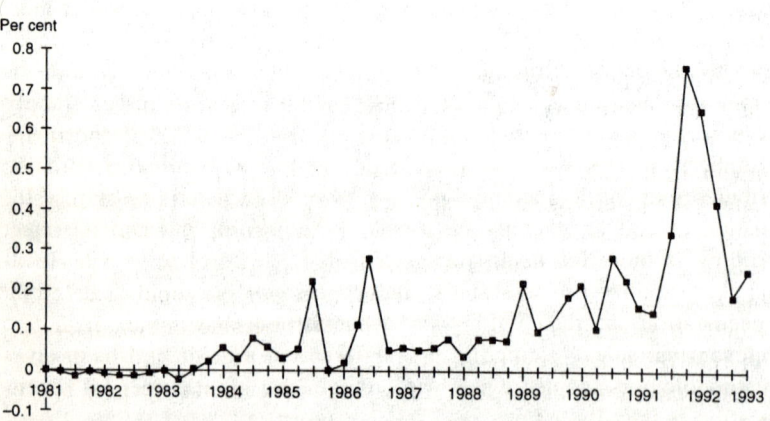

Figure 3.21   Other capital issues as a proportion of external funds, 1981–93

not seem appropriate for the 1991 experience. Evidence has also been presented which suggests that a supply-side contraction provides a more plausible explanation for the sharp downturn in bank lending in early 1991 than does an explanation based upon a shift in portfolio preferences in respect of the demand for external finance by ICCs. Thus far, however, we have not presented anything which approaches a definitive test of these two competing hypotheses. Although it is unlikely that it would ever be possible to produce a truly definitive discriminating test, there is an important difference with respect to the implications of the two hypotheses which forms the basis of a potentially discriminating test. In the case of a decline in bank lending associated with a shift in portfolio preferences, the company sector as a whole would be able to satisfy its demand for bank finance. If, however, the decline in bank lending were associated with a supply-side contraction, we would expect that at least some portion of the company sector (those least able to substitute into other forms of borrowing) would be credit constrained. Hence, the notional demand for bank lending would be greater than the available supply of credit.

One way of discriminating between the two competing hypotheses outlined above, therefore, is to construct an econometric model of the demand for bank lending by ICCs and to ascertain whether periods which seem to exhibit characteristics consistent with a credit crunch are also periods where the notional demand for bank lending (as forecast by the econometric model) is in excess of actual bank lending. In order to construct a model of the demand for bank lending (in real terms) we have developed a model similar to that developed by Cuthbertson (1985). Whereas the latter adopted an Autoregressive Distributed Lag (ADL) methodology, we have adopted the two-stage estimation procedure whereby the long-run equilibrium demand for bank lending is modelled using Johansen's (1988) cointegration technique on the variables in levels. The lagged residuals from this long-run specification are then fed into a dynamic short-run model with the relevant variables specified in first differences. The general-to-specific methodology is adopted whereby a very general higher order lag specification is initially adopted and this is sequentially tested down to arrive at a parsimonious short run specification.

Further details on the econometric methodology and results are provided in the Appendix and will not be discussed here in great detail. It is worth noting, however, that the main variables specified in the demand model are: GDP; the rate of interest on bank lending to corporates which, following Cuthbertson (1985), is proxied as base rate plus 1 per cent; the real demand by ICCs for external finance, and a domestic relative interest rate term. The latter is measured as the differential between the bank lending rate and the three-month Local Authority rate and is included to pick up the choice which companies have between bank borrowing and running down existing liquid assets. All the coefficients on these variables have the expected signs and are of reasonable magnitudes. Furthermore, the short-run dynamic model passes the standard battery of diagnostic tests and has an R^2 of around 0.6. This is reasonable for an error correction model of this type especially given the fact that in periods of supply-side constraint we would expect a divergence between supply and notional demand with the short side (namely supply) being the observed outcome.

Clearly, in order to estimate a model of the demand for bank lending by ICCs from observed bank lending data without also simultaneously considering the supply-side specification, we are implicitly assuming that for the most part the corporate sector is not credit constrained and hence notional demand is satisfied by the available supply. Having estimated such a model we can now proceed to compare the model forecasts for bank loan demand against actual bank lending. Given that our previous evidence suggests that any credit crunch was likely to be at its most severe in 1991:2, we chose to estimate the error correction model up to 1990:2 and to use this estimated model to obtain forecasts for bank lending demand for the subsequent four quarters. It can be seen from Figure 3.22 that the decline in bank lending which occurred during 1991:2 was far in excess of the decline in bank lending demand as forecast from the model. This clearly provides tentative support for the hypothesis that there was a severe supply-side credit crunch emerging at this time at least in respect of bank lending to the corporate sector.

It should be recognised, however, that the evidence provided in Figure 3.22 could be misleading in the context of the credit-crunch hypothesis. If, for example, the sharp downturn in bank lending in early 1991 was wholly attributable to a decline in the demand for bank lending, *and* the model of the demand for bank lending was providing poor out-of-sample forecasts (predicted demand above actual), we would obtain the result observed in Figure 3.22. Clearly, if this were the case, the evidence would be giving the erroneous impression of supporting the credit-crunch hypothesis. It was noted above, however, that after 1991:2 bank lending (as a proportion of their external borrowing) exhibited something of a modest recovery. Hence any credit crunch would be expected to be less significant over this period. Similarly, a

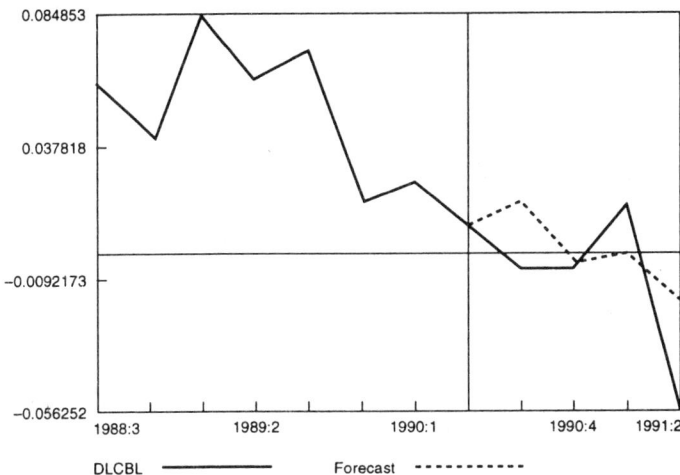

Figure 3.22   Plot of actual and static forecast(s), 1988:3–1991:2

reasonable model of the demand for bank lending would be expected to forecast actual bank lending more accurately over the latter period than the former given that discrepancies between notional demand and supply would be expected to be smaller in the latter period. Conversely, if the model was genuinely characterised by poor forecasting ability, it would be expected to continue to forecast poorly in the latter period.

For the reasons outlined above, therefore, the short-run dynamic error correction model was also estimated up to 1991:2 and used to provide demand forecasts for the subsequent four quarters. As can be seen from Figure 3.23, the demand model forecasts the changes in actual bank lending extremely accurately during this subsequent period, suggesting that the previous evidence of a significant decline in bank lending relative to demand during the second quarter of 1991 was more attributable to a genuine supply-side credit crunch than to forecasting errors on the part of the demand-side model.

Finally, it is worth noting that although the demand-side model seems to suggest that the observed period of credit crunch was essentially transitory with no evidence of demand in excess of supply in the second period of analysis (1991:3–1992:2), this is probably an erroneous conclusion to draw. The reason is that a severe contraction of bank lending such as occurred in early 1991 would be expected to have knock-on effects in subsequent periods. Those firms which could not find alternative finance elsewhere would undoubtedly cut back on

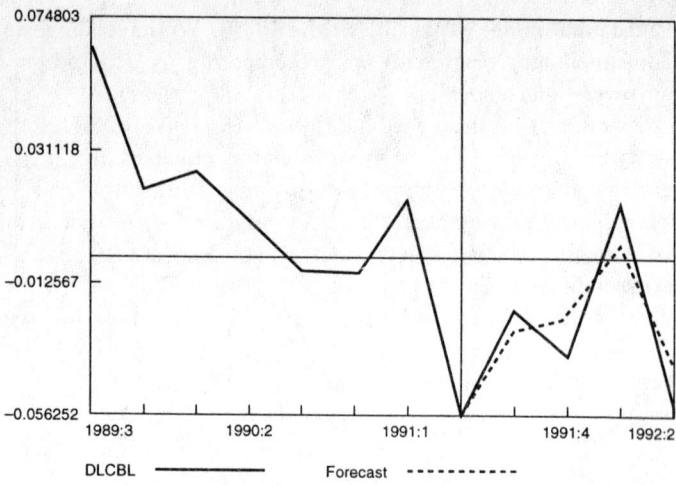

Figure 3.23 Plot of actual and static forecast(s), 1989:3–1992:2

expenditure plans and hence reduce their demands for future bank finance. On the other hand, firms who were able to seek alternative
sources of finance would do so, and would be further encouraged to
do so by the rising spreads on bank lending. Both these factors would
imply that in subsequent periods the demand for bank lending by ICCs
could be brought back into line with the available supply. That is not
to say, however, that the credit crunch ceases to be a problem and
ceases to generate economic and social costs. In reality, what may
have happened is that the company sector was forced, via an initial
contraction in bank lending, to adopt a much lower level of bank borrowing than it would otherwise have chosen to adopt. Clearly, it would
be expected that significant economic costs would be generated in this
transition to the new lower level/proportion of bank borrowing.

ASSESSMENT AND CONCLUSIONS

A period of unprecedented expansion in bank lending and rise in gearing ratios in the 1980s has been followed by a sharp decline in bank
lending since 1989. These trends have been considered within a simple framework of the banking firm. In both episodes, supply and demand impulses have interacted. There can be little doubt that supply
factors (induced by deregulation and increased competition) were powerful

in the substantial credit expansion of the 1980s. We have suggested a stock-adjustment approach with an over-shooting as a paradigm for both borrowers and lenders.

The sharp deceleration in lending since 1989 is likely, therefore, to at least partly reflect attempts to unwind the effect of the previous over-reaction: borrowers attempting to lower gearing ratios and lenders evolving a more sustainable portfolio of risks. From the vantage point of a major clearing bank, Budd (1990) also argues that: '[the decline in lending] can partly be seen as an inevitable consequence of the nature of the previous boom.' In addition, the recession would normally induce a weaker trend in the demand for credit.

However, we have also been concerned to identify exogenous supply-side impulses from the banks, i.e. elements of 'hard' (inability to lend) or 'soft' (unwillingness to lend) credit crunch. The analisis has been conducted at three levels: first, it seems hardly credible that the banks' experience of under-estimating and under-pricing risks, massive loan-loss provisions, and the virtual zero internal generation of capital between 1987 and 1992 would not have induced a change towards more restrictive behaviour. In this sense it would be a mirror image of changes in behaviour during the 1980s. This would imply an element of both soft and hard credit crunch: increased risk aversion, and a potential capital constraint. Banks have undoubtedly become more conscious of risk, and credit standards have tightened. A Bank of England survey in 1991 indicated that:

> The banks are certainly more cautious in their lending and are adhering more rigidly to existing lending criteria . . . There has been something of a return to 'relationship banking' with banks generally supportive of existing customers but very wary of taking on new ones in current circumstances.

The second level of analysis has been to observe different aspects of bank behaviour: asset sales, securitisation, cuts in dividends, and business disposals. Each of these is at least consistent with an actual or incipient capital constraint. A key argument is that *ex post* capital ratios above regulatory minima do not indicate capital ease. The Bank of England report noted above argued that: 'UK banks by and large do not have a problem in meeting BIS capital adequacy guidelines.' Nevertheless, it also commented: 'But they are conscious of the need to husband their capital and of the need to improve profitability.' It is still necessary to consider how banks have achieved their capital ratios.

The third strand of the analysis has been to apply econometric tests. Here we find decisive evidence of supply-side impulses, most especially in 1991: spread behaviour, a decline in the share of bank lending, the sudden and dramatic decline in bank lending relative to total external borrowing and investment requirements, and clear econometric evidence based upon a model of the demand for bank credit that there has been excess demand for bank credit.

While not arguing that the decline in bank credit has nothing to do with demand conditions, we can with some confidence dismiss the notion that the decline in bank lending simply reflected a decline in the demand for external funding associated with the course of the business cycle.

Appendix

The variables specified in the long-run cointegrating relationship are listed below:

$LCBL$: Bank lending to ICCs in real log terms.
LY : Log of real GDP.
RBL : Bank lending rate (bank base rate + 1%).
DRI : Domestic relative interest rate (RBL-RLA), where RLA is the three-month Local Authority rate.
CDF : ICCs demand for finance in real terms.
CD : Dummy variable reflecting the imposition and removal of the Corset.

The sample period is 1975: 1–1993: 2.

Prior to embarking upon the cointegration analysis, the order of integration of the variables was checked using the Dickey Fuller (DF) and Augmented Dickey Fuller (ADF) test statistics. With the obvious exception of the dummy variable CD, all the variables were found to be integrated of order 1, $I(1)$. That is, all variables were found to be stationary in first difference terms and hence are all appropriate variables to be specified in the long-run cointegrating relationship.

The cointegration analysis was conducted using Johansen's multivariate maximum likelihood procedure (Johansen, 1988). As can be seen from Table A3.1, using a standard lag length of 4 in the VAR, the Trace Test indicates that there are two possible cointegrating vectors. Of these, one vector forms a sensible long-run relationship for the demand for bank lending in term of *a priori* signs, etc.

The chosen cointegrating vector, together with the normalised coefficients is given in Table A3.2.

Although the coefficient on CDF appears to be very small, the appropriate χ^2 (2) test statistic indicates that the null hypothesis that the coefficient on CDF is zero can be rejected at the 5 per cent level (χ^2 (2) = 14.336).

Having estimated the long-run cointegrating relationship, the lagged residuals from this estimation are then used in the derivation of a standard short-run dynamic error correction model. Following the general-to-specific methodology, a general higher order lag specification of order 4 is initially utilised and this is then sequentially tested down to arrive at a parsimonious short-run model. The preferred specification is detailed below:

$$\Delta LCBL = 0.254 \; \Delta_1 LCBL + 0.336 \; \Delta_4 LCBL + 0.224 \; \Delta LY - 0.099 \; \Delta_3 DRI$$
$$ (0.10) (0.093) (0.089) (0.0053)$$

$$+ \; 0.0000058 \; \Delta CDF + 0.0000015 \; \Delta_2 CDF - 0.0913 \; LRES + 0.00738$$
$$(0.00000107) (0.00000106) (0.0218) (0.00337)$$

where $LRES$ = lagged residuals from the cointegrating regression and standard errors are in brackets.

157

Table A3.1 Trace test

Null	Alternative	Statistic	Critical value
$r = 0$	$r = 1$	125.82	76.07
$r \leq 1$	$r = 2$	57.27	53.11
$r \leq 2$	$r \geq 3$	31.36	34.91

Table A3.2 Cointegrating vector and normalised coefficients

Variable	Coefficients (normalised in brackets)
LCBL	2.0731 (−1.000)
LY	−4.979 (2.4018)
RBL	0.105 (−0.051)
DRI	0.419 (−0.202)
CDF	−0.000015 (0.000073)
INTERCEPT	32.3280 (−15.59)

$R^2 = 0.5999$ $DW = 2.21$ SE of regression $= 0.02$
$\chi^2(4) = 3.602$ $\chi^2_1(1) = 0.019$ $\chi^2(2) = 1.849$ $\chi^2_2(1) = 0.294$.

The preferred error correction model seems sensible in respect of the signs of the estimated coefficients and has a reasonable fit in terms of the R^2 statistic. Furthermore, the model passes the standard battery of diagnostic tests including tests for 4th order serial correlation ($\chi^2(4)$), functional form ($\chi^2_1(1)$), normality ($\chi^2_\chi(2)$) and heteroskedasticity ($\chi^2_2(1)$)

Note

1. We are greatly indebted to Sophie Haincourt and Nitesh Patel for computational assistance in the preparation of this paper.

References

Baer, H. and J. McElravey (1993) 'Capital Shocks and Bank Growth: 1973–1991', Federal Reserve Bank of Chicago, *Working Paper*.

Bank of England (1990) 'Banking Act Report for 1989/90', *Quarterly Bulletin*.

Bernanke, B. (1993) 'Credit in the Macroeconomy', Federal Reserve Bank of New York, *Quarterly Review* (Spring).

Bernanke, B. and C. Lown (1991) 'The Credit Crunch', *Brookings Papers on Economic Activity*, 2.

Bank for International Settlements (BIS) (1989) *Annual Report* (Basle: BIS).

Bank for International Settlements (BIS) (1992) *Annual Report* (Basle: BIS).

Budd, A. (1990) 'Credit Crunch: Causes and Consequences', *Barclays Bank Review* (November).

Burt, R. (1987) 'Social Contagion and Innovation: Cohesion *v.* Structural Equivalence', *American Journal of Sociology*, 92.

Cantor, R. and J. Wenninger (1993) 'Perspectives on the Credit Slowdown', Federal Reserve Bank of New York, *Quarterly Review* (Spring).

Clair, R. and K. Yeats (1991) 'Bank Capital and its Relationship to the Credit Shortage in Texas', mimeo.

Congdon, T. (1992) 'The Condition of the British Financial System', *Gerrard and National, Economic Review* (October).

Cuthbertson, K. (1985) 'Sterling Bank Lending to UK Industrial and Commercial Companies', *Oxford Bulletin*, 47(2) (May).

Davis, E. (1987) 'Rising Sectoral Debt–Income Ratios: A Cause for Concern?', BIS, *Economic Papers*, 20 (Basle: BIS).

Davis, E. (1990) 'Credit Quality Spreads, Bond Market Efficiency and Financial Fragility', LSE Financial Markets Group, *Discussion Paper*, 97.

Friedman, B. (1989) 'Changing Effects of Monetary Policy on Real Economic Activity', in B. Friedman, *Monetary Policy Issues in the 1990s* (Kansas City: Federal Reserve Bank of Kansas City).

Friedman, B. (1993) 'Comment on Cantor and Wenninger (1993)', Federal Reserve Bank of New York, *Quarterly Review* (Spring).

IMF (1993) 'Boom and Bust in Asset Markets in the 1980s: Causes and Consequences', *Staff Studies for the World Economic Outlook* (December).

Johansen, S. (1988) 'Statistical Analysis of Cointegration Vectors', *Journal of Economic Dynamics and Control*. 12, 231–54.

Jones, D. (1933) 'Comment on Bernanke, B., "Credit in the Macroeconomy"', Federal Reserve Bank of New York, *Quarterly Review* (Spring).

Kent, R.J. (1980) 'Credit Rationing and the Home Mortgage Market', *Journal of Money, Credit and Banking*, 12.

Kliesen, K. and J. Tatom (1992) 'The Recent Credit Crunch: The Neglected Dimensions', Federal Reserve Bank of St Louis, *Review* (September/October) 18–36.

Kling, A. (1986) 'The Banking Crisis from a Macroeconomic Perspective', Working Paper, Board of Governors of Federal Reserve System.

Llewellyn, D.T. (1990a) 'The International Capital Transfer Process: A Critique of the 1970s', in G. Bird (ed.), *International Financial Regime* (Guildford: Surrey University Press).

Llewellyn, D.T. (1990b) 'Competition and Structural Change in the British

Financial System', in E. Gardener (ed.) *The Future of Financial Systems and Services* (London: Macmillan).

Llewellyn, D.T. (1992a) 'Secular Pressures on Banking in Developed Financial Systems: Is Traditional Banking an Industry in Secular Decline?', in D. Fair and R. Raymond *The New Europe: Evolving Economic and Financial Systems in East and West* (Dordrecht, Kluwer Academic).

Llewellyn, D.T. (1992b) 'The Performance of Banks in the UK and Scandinavia', Sveriges Riksbank, *Quarterly Review*, 3.

Llewellyn, D.T. (1992c) 'Is There a Credit Crunch?', *Banking World* (January).

Llewellyn, D.T. (1992d) 'Financial Innovation: A Basic Analysis', in H. Cavanna (ed.) *Financial Innovation* (London: Routledge).

Llewellyn, D.T. and M. Holmes (1992) *Competition or Credit Controls?* (London: Institute of Economic Affairs).

Lund, T. (1990) 'Sterling Spreads: What Is To Be Done?', *CSFB Research* (London: Credit Suisse First Boston).

Myers, S. and N. Majluf (1984) 'Corporate Financing and Investment Decisions When Firms Have Information That Investors Do Not Have', *Journal of Financial Economics* 521–9.

Nellis, J. and R. Thom (1983) 'The Demand for Mortgage Finance in the UK', *Applied Economics*, 15.

Owens, R. and S. Shraft (1991) 'Survey Evidence of Tighter Credit Conditions: What Does It Mean?', *Federal Reserve Bank of Richmond, Economic Review* (March).

Oztas, J. and F. Zahn (1975) 'Interest and Non-Interest Credit Rationing in the Mortgage Market', *Journal of Monetary Economics*, 1.

Reve, T. *et al.* (1992) *Bankkrisen*, Norge, Socialokonomisk Institutt (University of Oslo, Norway).

Sargant, J.R. (1991) 'Deregulation, Debt and Downturn in the UK Economy', National Institute of Economic and Social Research, *Review* (August).

Stiglitz, J. and A. Weiss (1981) 'Credit Rationing in Markets with Imperfect Information', *American Economic Review*, 71, 3 (June), 393–410.

Syron, R. (1991) 'Are We Experiencing a Credit Crunch?', *New England Economic Review* (July).

Tirole, J. (1988) *Theory of Industrial Organisation* (Cambridge, Mass., MIT Press).

US Council of Economic Advisers (1992) *Economic Report of the President* (Washington, DC).

Young, G. (1992) 'Corporate Debt', National Institute of Economic and Social Research, *Review* (February).

Young, G. (1993) 'Debt Deflation and the Company Sector: the Economic Effects of Balance Sheet Adjustment', National Institute of Economic and Social Research. *Review* (May).

Comment

Roger Bootle

Chapter 3 is extremely interesting, written with admirable clarity and shot through with insights into the workings of the British banking system. Moreover, I generally concur with most of its judgements. I offer four diverse comments below: (1) a theoretical quibble; (2) some remarks on the treatment of banks in economic theory; (3) a perspective on banking practice; and (4) a comment on the implications for macroeconomic policy.

A THEORETICAL QUIBBLE

It has long been evident that the *IS–LM* curve paradigm does not easily cope with the banking system. The paradigm portrays a world in which there are only two assets – money and government bonds. But the money, though explicitly acknowledged as the liabilities of the banking system, does not appear to have any asset counterpart on the other side of the bank balance sheet. Meanwhile, it is left unclear how the investment spending which is the subject of the *IS* curve is financed.

Although this paradigm has been of immense value in the teaching of macroeconomics, it can often be a barrier to the understanding of finance. There is often no convenient way of presenting a financial issue within this framework. Nevertheless, Llewellyn and Drake try to put credit crunch into this framework. They say:

> Thus an exogenous reduction in the banks' willingness to lend either severely constrains bank dependent borrowers entirely or, where substitutions can be made, forces borrowers to employ more costly forms of credit. In terms of the standard *IS–LM* paradigm, the effect is to shift the *IS* curve to the left.

You can see why the authors describe credit crunch in this way. The effect is to constrain the amount of investment spending and lower income. But this characterisation seems to me to be misleading. In the standard *IS–LM* model the effect of a leftward shift of the *IS* curve would be to reduce the rate of interest. By contrast, the effect of a reduced supply of credit (inflicted by a credit crunch) would be to *raise* credit interest rates or to increase credit rationing, a surrogate for higher rates. This is much better conveyed in the *IS–LM* curve framework by a leftward shift of the *LM* curve. That produces a rise in interest rates which then brings a shift *along* a given *IS* curve to result in lower investment spending. (Even this involves some convolution, of course, because the rise in interest rates, implicitly or explicitly produced by a credit crunch, is a rise in relative rates – lending rates relative to deposit rates – whereas the rise in rates described in the *IS–LM* curve model is a rise in bond rates.)

BANKING IN ECONOMIC THEORY

It has long been an extraordinary feature of the economic theory of banking that it has placed so much emphasis on liquidity aspects and so little on capital aspects. In the British system, this has been particularly odd since that has always operated such that the authorities would supply whatever quantity of cash was required by the system. They have sought to operate monetary policy solely by dictating the short-term rate of interest. Thus, not only have individual banks not felt themselves subject to a cash constraint, but such a restraint has not even applied to the system as a whole.

By contrast, shortage of capital has applied quite clearly at the level of the individual bank. Moreover, there has been no way of 'borrowing' capital from the parts of the system which might have too much. Accordingly, the idea of the system consisting of 'representative banks' does some violence to reality – the distribution of the demand for banking facilities in relation to the distribution of capital between banks plays a major role.

Why did the economic theory of banking miss the significance of capital for so long? I can only suppose that this was a by-product of the emphasis on the 'unique' quality of banks and the search for 'moneyness', as opposed to the recognition of banks as businesses, aided and abetted by the effects of banking regulation, which meant that banking was not an ordinary business.

Although the authors do not explicitly make this connection, there is a close analytical similarity between the effects of a credit crunch imposed, say, for reasons of capital shortage, and the old style of lending restrictions operated by the banking system at the behest of the monetary authorities. The reasons for the restrictions in lending are different in the two cases, but the way the banks respond to the shortage of lending capacity, the effects on the economy, and the way of representing the change in theoretical models may all be similar. Thus literature on modern British credit crunch connects closely with the older tradition of monetary analysis of lending controls, credit ceilings and the like.

BOOM AND BUST

Llewellyn and Drake are rightly concerned to try to distinguish (credit-crunch) supply factors from the demand for finance. What makes this so difficult in practice is that the two tend to change simultaneously in the same direction and for the same reasons. There has recently been a tendency to blame the banks for subsequent debt problems because they over-extended credit in a wave of lending euphoria at the end of the 1980s. Doubtless some blame can be attached to the banks.

But it must be recognised that it was not only the banks who were overtaken by this euphoria. It was a national mood which affected the man in the street, companies, politicians, the monetary authorities, commentators, newspapers, borrowers and, of course, lenders. With the benefit of hindsight, the banks should have been more restrained and resistant to this mood. They should have been able to stand back from it.

In practice, though, their own internal structure makes this difficult. In virtually all banks, the lending function tends to be in the ascendant and the credit function subsidiary. Indeed the credit officers are often seen as killjoys, holding back the business of the bank. Moreover, this function may be ill-equipped to stand up against the macroeconomic risks, as opposed to individual credit risks, to which a bank may be exposed in a period of over-lending.

The institutional difficulties of dealing with these problems are similar to the difficulties of the safety officer inspecting a transport vehicle – airline, coach or cross-channel ferry. The checks seem boring, excessive, bureaucratic, an unnecessary burden, potentially restricting business and profit. Accordingly, the institution is in danger of finding ways of downplaying them or merely going through the motions – until something goes wrong.

In banking, the 'something going wrong' is a series of major defaults and debt write-downs. For a while, when this occurs, it gives status back to those in the institution who say 'no'. But it will then not be long before a spell of continued 'success' starts the cycle again.

MACROECONOMIC POLICY

Llewellyn and Drake suggest that the recent history of bank lending
growth can be seen to reflect a stock-adjustment mechanism, with over-
shooting. This may well be right. If so, it could have effects on the
significance of the banking numbers for macroeconomic policy.

Most monetarists see the rapid growth of the monetary aggregates
in Britain in the 1980s as accurately predicting the rapid growth and
inflation of the Lawson boom at the end of the decade. In fact broad
money over- and pre-predicted it, for monetary growth was very strong
throughout the decade. The reason, probably, was the stock-adjustment
process which the authors describe. This led to an increase in the ratio
of bank assets and liabilities to GDP, much of which reflected purely
financial factors (the degree of bank intermediation) with little or no
significance for GDP or inflation.

The early 1990s saw this pattern reversed. For all the reasons Llewellyn
and Drake describe, banks were fairly conservative in their lending
policies. Meanwhile, bank customers continued to be wary of bank
indebtedness. The result was a period when the ratio of bank assets
and liabilities to GDP fell. In that case, reliance on the broad money
numbers as a guide to the growth of nominal GDP could have led to
under-prediction. But by 1996, bank balance sheets were expanding
fast again. Had the cycle turned already?

Comment

Alan Budd[1]

I enjoyed Chapter 3 and I congratulate Llewellyn and Drake on a thorough and careful piece of work. In my comments I shall concentrate on two questions – first, do the authors convincingly demonstrate that there has been a credit crunch in the UK? Second, has financial deregulation changed the nature of the business cycle because it has changed the credit cycle?

First, has there been a credit crunch? This obviously requires two stages. First we need a satisfactory definition of 'credit crunch', and then we need to examine the data to see whether it corresponds to that definition. An analogy would be asking whether there has been global warming. We would first define what we mean by 'global warming', and then look at the measurements to see whether it has occurred.

The authors devote some space to the possible meaning of credit crunch in Chapter 3, though I do not think that they ever settle for one precise definition. That may be fair enough since the expression does have a variety of possible meanings. I think that for much of the time they adopt a very wide definition which is: 'any independent change in the conditions under which banks supply loans relative to the terms on which they acquire funds'. In their simple model of the banking firm, as illustrated in Figure 3.1, a credit crunch would involve:

- any widening of the spread over the cost of deposits;
- any increase in credit rationing.

It is important to note what a very general definition that is.

The alternative world (in which credit crunches do not occur) would be one in which bank lending is entirely demand-determined at the current market rate of interest *plus* some constant spread. In such a world, banks would simply be a frictionless tube down which funds flowed from depositors to borrowers. Once we knew the (constant) spread we would have no further interest in banks at all.

It may often be convenient to assume that banks were like that and it may have been close enough to the truth. But we should surely not be surprised if banks have some supply behaviour of their own: and if a credit crunch simply means that banks have some independent effect on the supply of bank credit relative to demand then it is puzzling:

1 that we have a special expression to describe this phenomenon – 'credit crunch'; and
2 that people have been so concerned to deny that there has been a credit crunch; it would appear that such behaviour would be quite normal and not require special comment.

I would willingly admit, without even considering the evidence, that we do have credit crunches from time to time and that there was one in the UK in 1991. We might easily guess how banks would behave over the cycle. Like other firms, banks become more optimistic in the boom. They revise upwards their view about sustainable growth. They perceive less risk. They are impressed by the increases in asset values of their customers (which they assume are permanent). They gain capital through retained profits and find it easy to raise capital on the market.

All this goes into reverse in the recession. So the supply of advances rises relative to demand during a boom and falls during a recession. When banks were more than usually unpopular during 1991 it was said that the cyclical behaviour of spreads was evidence of uncompetitive behaviour. In a competitive market, it was said, spreads would have risen in the boom and fallen in the recession; but the reverse happened.

However this behaviour is quite consistent with competitive behaviour if we recognise:

• that risk premia fall in the boom;
• that profit margins rise considerably, as a result of high fixed costs, when the volume of lending rises.

Profit margins – as opposed to spreads – did rise in the boom and fall in the recession).

Since there is a 'credit-crunch industry' we must assume that some people, at least, mean more by a credit crunch than a move in supply relative to demand. I suggest that we could distinguish between a weak and strong credit crunch. (This is not quite the same as the distinction between 'hard' and 'soft' credit crunches referred to on p. 000 of Chapter 3.) A weak credit crunch could refer to the' type of story I have just described. We could, in principle, construct a model of the banking sector which would include normal responses to cyclical changes in risk perceptions, etc. (Identification would clearly be difficult in practice.)

A strong credit crunch would involve behaviour which departed from previous experience.

Since I have only just suggested this distinction I can hardly complain if the authors did not make it themselves, though it would be interesting to know whether they are referring to a credit crunch in this strong sense. As far as the evidence is concerned there does seem to have been an exceptional fall in advances in 1991, but we must also accept that it was an exceptionally deep recession.

There is one additional development which strengthens their case. They point out that bank lending fell as a share of total lending during the recession. One might argue that under normal circumstances the share of bank lending would actually rise since companies might wish to preserve their relationship with banks during a recession.

As far as the econometric results are concerned I am not sure how far they advance the case. I have two difficulties. The first is that it is surprising that Llewellyn and Drake found a function for the demand for bank advances which covered a period in which there was a sharp change in regime, because of financial deregulation. The second is that I am not sure to what extent their method allows for changes in spread. (I assume that in the UK it does so, since base rate tends to be fairly close to a market rate while the banks vary the margin over base.)

There are two other points I would like to make about the credit boom that preceded the recession. The first is that I believe that an important part of the credit expansion was the battle between Barclays and NatWest for the leadership of the UK banking market. Barclays Bank wanted to become No. 1 by 1991 and they achieved this partly through a very large rights issue (almost precisely at the peak of the cycle) in 1988. That may have been sensible long-run profit-maximising behaviour but it obviously greatly increased the vulnerability of the banks to an unexpectedly severe recession.

My second point is that the authors comment that increased competition led banks to take on extra risks. This is a comment that is often made and Llewellyn has made it elsewhere in relation to capital requirements. I often wonder whether this is rational behaviour. To me it is rather like the following. We observe that someone's income has fallen and notice that he has increased the amount that he bets on the pools. We would normally regard this as irrational behaviour and it is surprising to think that banks or any other types of company behave in this way. It is as if they try to maintain the expected returns from their activities at the cost of higher risk. I would find it difficult to find the utility function into which this behaviour fitted.

Let me move on to my general point about the cycle. It is very similar to the point that Roger Bootle's Comment has made about the *IS–LM* analysis (p. 161). The story here is that the growth of credit during the boom can be partly explained by financial deregulation. That seems quite clear enough, and it is also quite possible that there was some over-shooting so that the slowdown has partly been a response to that over-shooting. (That might be another example of a credit crunch.) But we ought to consider the possibility that the cyclical behaviour of bank lending has changed because of financial deregulation.

As I have described earlier, in the boom the increased demand for loans will be matched be an increased willingness of banks to lend, and in the recession there will be a reverse process. In other words there is at least a weak credit crunch in the downturn.

Before we had deregulation, banks were behaving in a way that suggested that they were irrelevant to the process of credit creation and did in fact allow loans to be demand-determined. Now this is no longer the case and we shall therefore have a much stronger credit cycle during the normal economic cycle. It will not necessarily be as severe as the process in the late 1980s and early 1990s since that period included a once-for-all adjustment to deregulation. As the authors suggest, there may also have been some over-shooting on the way up and some over-correction on the way down.

That would lead me to ask three questions:

- First, is this a correct analysis?
- Second, does it matter? and
- Third, what implications does it have for the conduct of monetary policy?

It would be interesting to gain some answers from future research by Llewellyn and Drake, or by others.

Note

1. These comments are the personal views of the author; they are not necessarily those of the Treasury.

4 Leverage as a State Variable for Employment, Inventory Accumulation and Fixed Investment

Charles W. Calomiris, Athanasios Orphanides and Steven A. Sharpe[1]

INTRODUCTION

'Debt-deflation' refers to one of the ways in which the cumulative past of the economy matters for its future evolution. In a debt-deflation, existing debt contracts become a burden on producers. consumers, or intermediaries, and prevent them from achieving levels of activity that they otherwise would have achieved had their earlier contracting decisions been different. Adverse shocks to real income or a lower than anticipated price level effectively raise the burden or value of debt relative to equity, and the amount of debt payments relative to cash flow, which in turn reduce agents' credit-worthiness and force them to limit their activities. As Keynes (1931) and Fisher (1933) argued, debt-deflations that constrain expenditures of firms and individuals, as well as lending by intermediaries, can produce debt-deflation spirals of ever-worsening economic conditions. Much research on the Great Depression and other historical depressions has focused on debt-deflation as one of the ways in which shocks to demand produced persistent declines in aggregate economic activity by undermining the credit-worthiness of borrowers and banks (Mishkin, 1978; Hunter, 1982; Bernanke, 1983; Eichengreen and Sachs, 1985, 1986; Calomiris and Hubbard, 1989; Temin, 1989; Bernanke and James, 1991; Calomiris, 1993).

Banks that choose to increase their loan–asset or debt–capital ratios prior to the onset of a recession, for example, will incur the greatest proportional losses of capital and will experience more extreme increases in their debt–capital ratios relative to banks that had been less aggressive prior to the recession. As the riskiness of uninsured liabilities of such banks rises during debt-deflations, they will have to limit new lending, accumulate capital by retaining more earnings or issuing stock, or pay higher interest rates on uninsured liabilities than their rivals. They also may be subject to runs on uninsured liabilities. If such runs occur on an economy-wide basis, they can create large externalities for banks and their borrowers (Calomiris and Gorton, 1991).[2] In today's environment of deposit insurance and government capital regulation, banks are most likely to be forced to contract lending or pay the costs of issuing new stock under conditions of high uncertainty about the value of their portfolios (high lemons premia). Some researchers refer to this as a 'capital crunch', and argue that it has been an important impediment to expansion in bank lending in recent years (Syron, 1991; Bernanke and Lown, 1992; Peek and Rosengren, 1992; Baer and McElravey, 1992).

Consumers who expand their debt during a boom run the risk of being burdened by high debt-service–income ratios and illiquidity of assets. If conditions worsen, they will have to tighten their discretionary expenditures relative to other consumers during subsequent lean years. Consumers that expanded debt to purchase illiquid consumer durables will be especially constrained, since many of their assets are not saleable (Mishkin, 1976).

Farm owner–operators are also vulnerable to adverse income and wealth shocks because of their reliance on debt to finance their farm operations, and because agency considerations require that their net worth be invested in a highly undiversified portfolio of farm land, which is subject to substantial price change (Calomiris, Hubbard and Stock, 1986; Hubbard and Kashyap, 1992; Calomiris and Himmelberg, 1994). During the US farm bust of the early 1980s, the run-up in farm leverage during the 1970s forced many farmers and their bankers into insolvency, and limited aggregate farming activity by more than the initial shock to demand.

In general, firms that use debt to expand operations aggressively during booms are likely to be among the least credit-worthy if a recession strikes, and may be forced to contract activity more than their rivals. Many economists expressed concern during the boom of the 1980s about the potentially destabilising consequences of the growing debt burdens of industrial borrowers (Friedman, 1986, 1989; Bernanke and Campbell, 1988).

Industrial firms' susceptibility to problems of debt-deflation is exacerbated by four factors. First, firms with the greatest potential for long-term expansion may be the ones most dependent on debt. Models of contracting suggest that debt may be desirable because it limits adverse selection, moral hazard, and monitoring costs under asymmetric information (Jensen and Meckling, 1976; Townsend, 1979; Myers and Majluf, 1984; De Meza and Webb, 1987; Jensen, 1986). Thus the firms most likely to rely on debt may be relatively unseasoned credit risks for which problems of asymmetric information are most pronounced. High-growth firms in new industries – those on which the future growth of the economy may be most dependent – are particularly subject to problems of financial instability.[3]

Second, theoretical models of optimal investment strategies suggest that there are advantages to rapid expansion which encourage firms to invest quickly, rather than slowly as would be required if firms wished to eschew a reliance on outside funds (and hence debt). This literature emphasises advantages of investing during periods of high aggregate economic activity (Murphy, Shleifer and Vishny, 1989).

Third, corporations may not properly anticipate how aggregate economic circumstances affect the liquidity of their assets, and thus may be excessively optimistic regarding their ability to avoid costly financial distress. This, in turn, may lead to excessive leveraging. Shleifer and Vishny (1992) argue that during the boom of the 1980s, the liquidity of industrial assets was high, and hence the potential cost of financial distress was presumed to be low. Firms may have been surprised to find the liquidity of their assets decline (and hence their exposure to financial distress increase) with the recession of 1989–91.

Fourth, tax considerations (particularly in the USA) have motivated excessive reliance by firms on debt. Gertler and Hubbard (1990) argue that the contracting benefits of debt cannot plausibly explain the debt buildup in the USA of the 1970s and 1980s.[4] Interest relative to corporate earnings rose from under 10 per cent in 1946 to roughly 20 per cent during the early 1960s. From 1966 to 1986, the debt-service ratio rose to 60 per cent. The double taxation of dividends and the increasing burden of corporate taxation in recent decades can explain the rising use of debt. The cost of this tax policy is the reduced economic activity produced by high leverage ratios during times of declining demand, and the physical costs of debt renegotiation and bankruptcy.

Recent commentators, both within academia and the popular press, have argued that the worst fears about the excesses of leverage in the 1980s have come true in the aftermath of the recession of 1989–91. The proportion of debt in default in 1991 was double its previous peak (Remolona *et al.*, 1992). Some researchers have argued that renegotiation and bankruptcy costs on defaulted debt also have risen in the 1980s, due to the increasing proportion of debt in the form of 'arm's length'

Leverage as a State Variable

bonds, rather than loans from intermediaries. Renegotiations of bond issues entail larger costs due to problems of coordination among bondholders, and greater asymmetry of information between firms and their lenders (Gilson, John and Lang, 1990; Brown, James and Mooradian, 1991; Asquith, Gertner and Scharfstein, 1992).

The slow recovery from the recession in 1991 and 1992 has been attributed by some to a 'debt overhang' problem in the major industrialised nations. For example, in an article entitled 'Recovery Hits the Wall', the *Economist* (16 January 1993, 77) argues that declines in the value of commercial property in the USA, Britain, and Japan weakened the credit-worthiness of corporations, and limited their potential to expand during the recovery. In Britain, commercial property has declined by 45 per cent from its peak. A study by McWilliams (1992), cited by the *Economist*, argues that low commercial property values, through their effect on debt: equity ratios, have constrained the availability of commercial loans to corporations.

In a similar vein, Bernanke and Lown (1992) found that loan growth in the USA during 1991 and 1992 was slower than during other postwar recoveries. Bernanke and Lown (1992) and Bernanke (1993) claim that neither the recession, nor the protracted recovery of lending in 1991–2, can be attributed to tight monetary policy. Bernanke (1993) argues that '1990–1991 might be the only recession since the 1950s in which tight money was *not* a significant factor in the slowdown of lending'. Rather, these authors attribute slow loan growth to the deterioration in the credit quality of borrowers, due to high debt service burdens and the collapse of real estate values (see also Perry and Schultze, 1993). Other evidence supports a link between declining credit-worthiness and slow growth in recent years. Gertler and Gilchrist (1993) – who attach greater weight to tight monetary policy in explaining the recession – point to the relative decline of small manufacturing firms (relatively unseasoned credit risks) during the recent recession as further evidence that credit-worthiness has been an important constraint on investment. Apparently, financial planners at American corporations agree that debt overhang presented a burden during the recession, as evidence by the significant 'deleveraging' of corporate balance sheets in recent years (Frydl, 1991, 1992; Remolona *et al.*, 1992).

Leverage effects on corporate activity can be hard to identify convincingly using aggregate time-series analysis, for three reasons. First, aggregate debt relative to aggregate assets may not be a good indicator of the representative debt–asset ratio of firms. Second, leverage may be a more important constraining influence on cyclically sensitive firms, and thus important leverage effects may not be visible in aggregate data. Third, post-war aggregate data provide too few observations of variation in economic activity (six major recessions for the USA). Using panel data expands observations by examining links between leverage and behavior cross-sectionally as well as across time.

Microeconomic analysis of the effects of leverage has produced mixed findings. Studies of financial distress find important effects on investment, employment, and sales from leverage. In a panel study of Compustat firms, Whited (1991) found that during recession phases of the business cycle, firms reduced investment in order to accumulate working capital (to strenghen their balance sheets). Brown, James and Ryngaert (1992) find that, among firms experiencing financial distress, those with higher leverage suffered the largest declines in investment and employment. Opler and Titman (1994) examine *industries* in which financial distress is occurring, and find that higher-leveraged firms experienced greater declines in sales. On the other hand, sceptics stress that leverage is an endogenous variable that may serve as a proxy for other effects. One study of fixed capital investment (Kopcke and Howrey, 1994) argues that if one properly controls for lags of sales, investment, capital, and cash flow, balance sheet effects are not important for fixed capital investment.

The approach Kopcke and Howrey (1994) take to measuring leverage effects on investment, however, may be flawed in an important respect. They consider the role of balance sheet variables as separate regressors in the investment equation. But they do not consider whether balance sheet measures are important as 'state variables' that condition the effects of *other* variables on investment. For example, a firm that expands capital during a sales boom and finances that expansion with debt may increase its vulnerability to a subsequent decline in sales. The average effect of leverage *per se* on investment may be small, but it may increase the responsiveness of investment to a *contraction* in sales. Indeed, Cantor (1990) finds that employment and capital expenditures at more highly-leveraged firms are more responsive to earnings, and Sharpe (1994) finds that employment of more highly-leveraged firms is more sensitive to sales.

Once one begins to focus on leverage as a state variable, it becomes important to consider asymmetries in the effects from leverage. As Calomiris and Hubbard (1990) show theoretically, and as Hubbard and Kashyap (1992) demonstrate empirically in their study of aggregate US farm investment, leverage constraints on growth are asymmetric. The role of leverage as a conditioning variable for the effect of sales growth on investment should depend on whether sales are growing or shrinking. A firm that builds up leverage, but experiences continuing growth in sales, may show a relatively stable continuing relationship between sales and capital expenditures because capacity constraints do not bind. If anything, one might expect high leverage to dampen the effect of positive changes in sales on future investment. On the other hand, a highly leveraged firm that experiences a contraction in sales may contract investment more in response to declining sales, as debt capacity becomes a problem. Sharpe (1994) finds some evidence of such an asymmetry in the role of leverage as a conditioning variable for employment. He finds that leverage increases the sales sensitivity of employment more during business cycle contractions than during business cycle expansions.

In this chapter, we examine the effect of leverage as an asymmetric conditioning variable for fixed capital investment, inventory investment and employment. We analyse panel data on US durable-goods manufacturers from the 'R&D Master File' constructed by Hall *et al.* (1988) for 1959–85. We chose durable-goods manufacturers because of the cyclicality of their sales, which makes the identification of leverage effects more likely.

Our results are similar for investment, inventories, and employment. In all three cases, leverage acts as an important conditioning variable for changes in sales, and in all three cases, leverage matters much more as a conditioning variable during episodes in which sales are declining. These results provide evidence in favour of the importance of 'debt overhang' problems for manufacturing firms, and lend credence to macroeconomic models of debt-deflation. The next section describes our data and methodology and presents our results. In the third section, we consider limitations of our findings for measuring the magnitude of debt-deflation effects.

METHODOLOGY AND FINDINGS

We construct a panel data set of durable-goods manufacturers for the period 1959–85 (see the Data Appendix for a detailed description of the data). Our endogenous variables are the log difference of employment, the log difference of inventories, and the difference of the ratio of gross fixed capital investment to the initial stock of fixed capital. Examining differences removes firm-specific effects that might otherwise bias our results. The specification of inventories as a log difference, regressed on the log difference of sales, is consistent with assuming a long-run target inventories–sales ratio and lagged adjustment. The specification of fixed capital investment as the difference of the ratio of investment to capital, regressed on the ratio of sales to capital, is consistent with the standard neoclassical model of constant returns to scale and quadratic adjustment costs (for example, Hayashi, 1982; Fazzari, Hubbard and Petersen, 1988; Calomiris and Hubbard, 1995). After screening for outliers (observations and lags in which a firm tripled in size by assets, sales, or employment, or made an acquisition whose value exceeded 20 per cent of its own value), our sample retains 10 883 observations.

Our interest is in examining the potential importance of leverage as a conditioning variable in models that gauge the effects of changes in sales (demand) on employment, inventories, and fixed investment. Because the role of leverage as a conditioning variable may be different depending on whether the economy is expanding or contracting, we construct the indicator variables P and N. P takes a value of one during NBER recoveries and expansions, and zero during recessions; N takes a value of one during recessions and zero otherwise. Each of our regressions allows the dependent variable to depend on current and lagged sales, the lagged dependent variable, firm size (fixed capital), leverage, the interaction between sales and firm size, and the interaction between leverage and sales. Some specifications also allow regressors, including the interaction of leverage and sales growth, to enter asymmetrically – that is, interacted with either P or N. To avoid problems of simultaneity, leverage is defined with a lag of two years (the year before the date of the earliest observation on any other regressor). We report results for simple OLS regressions, as well as for instrumental-variables (IV) regressions, which use macroeconomic indicators and lagged variables as instruments for sales. To the extent that sales changes are themselves responding within the year to changes in employment, inventory investment, and fixed capital investment, endogeneity of sales may weaken the estimated effect of the leverage–sales interaction if leverage measures the ability of firms to respond to changes in demand. Our instrumental variables estimates provide a way around that problem.

Table 4.1 provides data on the means and standard deviations of each of the variables included in our analysis.

Tables 4.2a and 4.2b report the results for the employment specifications, with and without the P and N interactions. Here and elsewhere OLS regressions are reported in panel a, while instrumented results are reported in panel b. In all regressions, standard errors are

Table 4.1   Summary statistics

Variables	Mean	Std Dev.	Observ.
Sales growth	0.027	0.204	10 883
Sales–capital	3.719	3.175	10 883
Capital	4.729	1.814	10 883
Gross invest.–K	0.196	0.180	10 883
Employment growth	0.016	0.190	10 883
Inventory growth	0.035	0.248	10 883
Debt–assets	0.104	0.207	10 883
Working capital–Capital	0.442	0.679	10 883

corrected for heteroscedasticity. In many cases, this had the effect of doubling or tripling the size of estimated standard errors. Equations are estimated after removing the means from the conditioning variables in all results reported below, to facilitate interpretation of the interaction effects. We report versions of the regressions with contemporaneous and lagged sales change, as well as versions that combine the current and lagged data on sales growth into a single two-year window.

To gauge the total effect of sales growth on employment growth for a firm of given size and leverage, and for a given state of the economy, one sums the relevant coefficients from the regressions, each multiplied by the difference between the average value of the regressors and those of the firm. For example, according to equation (2a), the effect of a 1 per cent decline in sales growth during the first year of a recession for a firm of average size with a leverage ratio of 0.5 is employment growth of -0.35 per cent (-0.35 = -0.29 + [-0.14] × [0.5 − 0.1]).

Regressions (1a) and (1b) for employment growth confirm Sharpe's (1994) finding of a positive and significant coefficient on the interaction between leverage and lagged sales growth. Regressions (2a) and (2b) decompose that effect according to whether the economy is expanding or contracting. The effect of sales on employment is more affected by leverage during recessions, and such effects are much larger in the instrumented regressions. As shown in regressions (4a) and (4b), which collapse the two years of sales into a single period, the interactive effect is much larger during negative sales growth episodes, and is not statistically significant during positive growth episodes, and again, the difference is larger in the instrumented regression. This provides confirmation for the asymmetric effect of leverage posited by the debt-deflation hypothesis.

Table 4.2 Employment regressions
(OLS – standard errors corrected for heteroscedasticity);
log difference of employment (*DLEMP*); (standard errors in parentheses)

(a) Variables	(1a)	(2a)	Variables	(3a)	(4a)
Constant	−0.010	−0.010	Constant	−0.009	−0.007
	(0.002)	(0.002)		(0.002)	(0.002)
$DLEMP_{-1}$	−0.108	−0.108	$DLEMP_{-1}$	−0.035	−0.035
	(0.017)	(0.017)		(0.014)	(0.014)
LEV	−0.043	−0.044	LEV	−0.037	−0.035
	(0.010)	(0.011)		(0.010)	(0.011)
SIZE	−0.036	−0.034	SIZE	−0.037	−0.035
	(0.009)	(0.010)		(0.009)	(0.010)
DLS	0.224		DLS(−1,0)	0.400	
	(0.012)			(0.010)	
PDLS		0.203	PDLS(−1,0)		0.385
		(0.014)			(0.011)
NDLS		0.290	NDLS(−1,0)		0.446
		(0.020)			(0.017)
DLS_{-1}	0.601				
	(0.014)				
$PDLS_{-1}$		0.604			
		(0.017)			
$NDLS_{-1}$		0.605			
		(0.023)			
DLS × LEV	0.015		DLS(−1,0) × LEV	0.037	
	(0.078)			(0.061)	
PDLS × LEV		−0.009	PDLS(−1,0) × LEV		0.020
		(0.088)			(0.074)
NDLS × LEV		0.141	NDLS(−1,0) × LEV		0.112
		(0.129)			(0.079)
DLS_{-1} × LEV	0.071				
	(0.081)				
$PDLS_{-1}$ × LEV		0.098			
		(0.104)			
$NDLS_{-1}$ × LEV		−0.010			
		(0.101)			
DLS × SIZE	−0.123		DLS(−1,0) × SIZE	−0.072	
	(0.064)			(0.047)	
PDLS × SIZE		−0.125	PDLS(−1,0) × SIZE		−0.089
		(0.068)			(0.053)
NDLS × SIZE		−0.133	NDLS(−1,0) × SIZE		−0.022
		(0.142)			(0.094)
DLS_{-1} × SIZE	−0.060				
	(0.086)				
$PDLS_{-1}$ × SIZE		−0.052			
		(0.108)			
$NDLS_{-1}$ × SIZE		−0.045			
		(0.124)			
Adj. R^2	0.492	0.494		0.432	0.433

Table 4.2 Employment regressions
(instrumental variables – standard errors corrected for heteroscedasticity);
log difference of employment (*DLEMP*); (standard errors in parentheses)

(b) Variables	(1b)	(2b)	Variables	(3b)	(4b)
Constant	−0.014 (0.002)	−0.012 (0.002)	Constant	−0.012 (0.002)	−0.011 (0.002)
$DLEMP_{-1}$	0.037 (0.021)	0.048 (0.022)	$DLEMP_{-1}$	0.117 (0.020)	0.111 (0.020)
LEV	−0.022 (0.011)	−0.019 (0.103)	LEV	−0.021 (0.011)	−0.011 (0.012)
SIZE	−0.024 (0.010)	−0.008 (0.012)	SIZE	−0.030 (0.010)	−0.011 (0.011)
DLS	0.265 (0.018)		DLS(−1,0)	0.386 (0.012)	
PDLS		0.266 (0.031)	PDLS(−1,0)		0.398 (0.016)
NDLS		0.312 (0.025)	NDLS(−1,0)		0.417 (0.022)
DLS_{-1}	0.571 (0.020)				
$PDLS_{-1}$		0.534 (0.029)			
$NDLS_{-1}$		0.588 (0.040)			
DLS × LEV	0.292 (0.146)		DLS(−1,0) × LEV	0.057 (0.077)	
PDLS × LEV		0.227 (0.186)	PDLS(−1,0) × LEV		−0.045 (0.092)
NDLS × LEV		0.524 (0.171)	NDLS(−1,0) × LEV		0.443 (0.173)
DLS_{-1} × LEV	−0.125 (0.103)				
$PDLS_{-1}$ × LEV		−0.155 (0.155)			
$NDLS_{-1}$ × LEV		0.005 (0.248)			
DLS × SIZE	−0.721 (0.107)		DLS(−1,0) × SIZE	−0.049 (0.063)	
PDLS × SIZE		−0.615 (0.164)	PDLS(−1,0) × SIZE		−0.275 (0.078)
NDLS × SIZE		−0.378 (0.198)	NDLS(−1,0) × SIZE		0.601 (0.191)
DLS_{-1} × SIZE	0.267 (0.108)				
$PDLS_{-1}$ × SIZE		−0.048 (0.162)			
$NDLS_{-1}$ × SIZE		0.884 (0.238)			
Adj. R^2	0.213	0.212		0.191	0.191

Note:
DLEMP is the log difference (growth rate) of employment. LEV is the ratio of the book value of debt (less cash assets) divided by the book value of assets. SIZE is total tangible capital (plant, equipment, and inventories). P and N prefixes denote interactions with zero-one indicator variables (N for recession phases, P for non-recession phases). DLS is the log difference of sales (sales growth). Lagged variables are denoted by a subscript of −1. Variables are annual with the exception of sales in some regressions, where they are defined over a two-year period. The notation (−1,0) applied to sales growth denotes a two-year growth rate over the period of the lagged year and the current year.

Table 4.3 provides analogous results to those of Table 4.2, but for the log difference of inventories. As before, the interaction between leverage and sales is larger and more statistically significant for the recession episodes, and the instrumented coefficients are much larger. Moreover, in regression (8b) the coefficient on the leverage–sales interaction is negative and significant for expansion periods. These findings are consistent with the proposition that as firms reach their debt capacity they are more vulnerable to bad news, and (possibly) are less able to expand in response to good news.

Table 4.4 presents results for fixed capital investment (the simple difference of the ratio of investment to capital). The results on the asymmetry of the role of leverage as a conditioning variable are similar to those of Tables 4.2 and 4.3 in the sense that recession episodes show positive and more significant leverage conditioning effects, expansion phases show negative coefficients on the leverage–sales interaction, and both effects are strengthened by instrumenting.

Our findings of significant, asymmetric conditioning effects for leverage in employment, inventory accumulation, and fixed investment are surprisingly strong when one considers that, cross-sectionally, leverage ratios could be positively associated with greater creditworthiness. That is, our interpretation of leverage has implicitly assumed that debt capacity is the same across firms, and therefore, that leverage ratios of different firms are comparable measures of 'distance from debt capacity'. If, however, some firms have higher leverage *because* they have higher debt capacity, one could find that leverage acts as an indicator of greater potential access to funds, not less. In theory, this effect could reduce – and possibly change the sign of – the sales–leverage interaction effect. Our inclusion of a size–sales interaction effect removes some of this problem by controlling for differences in debt capacity correlated with size, but that is not likely to control fully for debt–capacity differences.[5] Thus our findings for leverage likely understate the true 'within-firm' effect from increasing debt relative to capacity, because we have not

Table 4.3   Inventory regressions
(OLS – standard errors corrected for heteroscedasticity);
log difference of inventories (*DLVNT*); (standard errors in parentheses)

(a) Variables	(5a)	(6a)	Variables	(7a)	(8a)
Constant	0.009	0.010	Constant	0.011	0.010
	(0.002)	(0.003)		(0.002)	(0.003)
$DLVNT_{-1}$	−0.055	−0.052	$DLVNT_{-1}$	−0.016	−0.014
	(0.015)	(0.015)		(0.015)	(0.015)
LEV	−0.109	−0.116	LEV	−0.103	−0.098
	(0.015)	(0.017)		(0.016)	(0.018)
SIZE	−0.038	−0.040	SIZE	−0.041	−0.039
	(0.014)	(0.015)		(0.014)	(0.015)
DLS	0.086		DLS(−1,0)	0.390	
	(0.014)			(0.015)	
PDLS		0.137	PDLS(−1,0)		0.396
		(0.017)			(0.017)
NDLS		−0.050	NDLS(−1,0)		0.370
		(0.024)			(0.029)
DLS_{-1}	0.709				
	(0.022)				
$PDLS_{-1}$		0.682			
		(0.026)			
$NDLS_{-1}$		0.747			
		(0.042)			
DLS × LEV	0.014		DLS(−1,0) × LEV	0.051	
	(0.078)			(0.107)	
PDLS × LEV		−0.134	PDLS(−1,0) × LEV		−0.009
		(0.087)			(0.134)
NDLS × LEV		0.418	NDLS(−1,0) × LEV		0.252
		(0.149)			(0.124)
DLS_{-1} × LEV	0.107				
	(0.148)				
$PDLS_{-1}$ × LEV		0.204			
		(0.184)			
$NDLS_{-1}$ × LEV		−0.106			
		(0.189)			
DLS × SIZE	−0.320		DLS(−1,0) × SIZE	0.034	
	(0.116)			(0.085)	
PDLS × SIZE		−0.291	PDLS(−1,0) × SIZE		0.005
		(0.135)			(0.101)
NDLS × SIZE		−0.373	NDLS(−1,0) × SIZE		0.103
		(0.189)			(0.144)
DLS_{-1} × SIZE	0.349				
	(0.108)				
$PDLS_{-1}$ × SIZE		0.335			
		(0.134)			
$NDLS_{-1}$ × SIZE		0.259			
		(0.185)			
Adj. R^2	0.347	0.353		0.250	0.251

Table 4.3   Inventory regressions
(Instrumental variables – standard errors corrected for heteroscedasticity);
log difference of inventories (*DLVNT*); (standard errors in parentheses)

(b) Variables	(5b)	(6b)	Variables	(7b)	(8b)
Constant	−0.012	−0.004	Constant	0.002	−0.006
	(0.003)	(0.003)		(0.003)	(0.003)
$DLVNT_{-1}$	0.135	0.141	$DLVNT_{-1}$	0.173	0.203
	(0.020)	(0.020)		(0.019)	(0.020)
LEV	−0.036	−0.044	LEV	−0.063	−0.014
	(0.017)	(0.020)		(0.017)	(0.021)
SIZE	0.010	0.027	SIZE	−0.040	0.001
	(0.017)	(0.021)		(0.015)	(0.018)
DLS	−0.086		DLS(−1,0)	0.393	
	(0.025)			(0.016)	
PDLS		−0.036	PDLS(−1,0)		0.512
		(0.039)			(0.023)
NDLS		−0.099	NDLS(−1,0)		0.327
		(0.042)			(0.037)
DLS_{-1}	1.111				
	(0.028)				
$PDLS_{-1}$		0.964			
		(0.041)			
$NDLS_{-1}$		1.275			
		(0.058)			
DLS × LEV	0.382		DLS(−1,0) × LEV	0.069	
	(0.166)			(0.126)	
PDLS × LEV		0.013	PDLS(−1,0) × LEV		−0.326
		(0.172)			(0.148)
NDLS × LEV		1.318	NDLS(−1,0) × LEV		1.515
		(0.295)			(0.347)
DLS_{-1} × LEV	−0.263				
	(0.160)				
$PDLS_{-1}$ × LEV		−0.054			
		(0.222)			
$NDLS_{-1}$ × LEV		−0.262			
		(0.465)			
DLS × SIZE	−0.616		DLS(−1,0) × SIZE	0.163	
	(0.203)			(0.115)	
PDLS × SIZE		0.031	PDLS(−1,0) × SIZE		−0.381
		(0.265)			(0.158)
NDLS × SIZE		−1.143	NDLS(−1,0) × SIZE		1.071
		(0.362)			(0.323)
DLS_{-1} × SIZE	−0.192				
	(0.208)				
$PDLS_{-1}$ × SIZE		−0.838			
		(0.310)			
$NDLS_{-1}$ × SIZE		0.203			
		(0.477)			
Adj. R^2	0.174	0.177		0.110	0.118

(continued on page 182)

Note:
DLVNT is the log difference (growth rate) of inventories. *LEV* is the ratio of the book value of debt (less cash assets) divided by the book value of assets. *SIZE* is total tangible capital (plant, equipment, and inventories). *P* and *N* prefixes denote interactions with zero-one indicator variables (*N* for recession phases, *P* for non-recession phases). *DLS* is the log difference of sales (sales growth). Lagged variables are denoted by a subscript of −1. Variables are annual with the exception of sales in some regressions, where they are defined over a two-year period. The notation (−1,0) applied to sales growth denotes a two-year growth rate over the period of the lagged year and the current year.

controlled for cross-sectional variation in firms' debt capacities. This should be a promising avenue of future research.

Our regressions also include firm size interactions with sales change, and we allow these to vary according to whether sales growth is positive or negative. As with the coefficients on leverage, we find that asymmetries are important in size–sales interactions, as well, although the interpretation of these coefficients is not straightforward. In employment regressions, the sensitivity to sales growth is largest for small firms, and this effect is largely attributable to small firms' employment sensitivity to positive sales shocks, as shown most clearly in regressions (4a) and (4b). In the case of inventories, there is no clear average size–sales interaction (see regressions (7a) and (7b)), but we do find that moments of positive sales growth see a greater sensitivity of inventories to sales growth for small firms, and the opposite size effect for episodes of sales contractions. In fixed investment regressions, larger firms appear to be more sensitive to sales growth, and this effect does not depend on whether sales are expanding or contracting. Thus, there is no consistent size-related asymmetry of sales sensitivity across our three sets of regressions. Future work should address the question of why firm size–sales interaction effects are so different across the three sets of regressions.[6]

In addition to leverage's significance as a conditioning variable for sales, leverage also enters significantly as a regressor by itself, but it enters with a positive sign in the fixed capital regressions and a negative sign in the employment and inventory regressions. This illustrates the difficulty of interpreting the information content of leverage as an intercept variable, as discussed above. Observed differences may reflect firm fixed effects. For example, if leverage is correlated with fixed capital intensity, then (holding sales effects constant) firms with higher leverage may be more likely to invest in fixed capital and less likely to increase inventories or employment.

Our regression results for leverage suggest that other balance sheet variables may also prove useful as state variables for sales effects on

Table 4.4 Fixed investment regressions
(OLS – standard errors corrected for heteroscedasticity);
difference of investment–capital (*DI–K*); (standard errors in parentheses)

(a) Variables	(9a)	(10a)	Variables	(11a)	(12a)
Constant	−0.002 (0.002)	−0.002 (0.002)	Constant	−0.003 (0.002)	−0.002 (0.002)
$DI–K_{-1}$	−0.365 (0.021)	−0.366 (0.021)	$DI–K_{-1}$	−0.406 (0.018)	−0.405 (0.018)
LEV	0.018 (0.010)	0.021 (0.010)	LEV	0.019 (0.010)	0.021 (0.010)
SIZE	−0.017 (0.010)	−0.015 (0.010)	SIZE	−0.016 (0.010)	−0.016 (0.010)
DS–K	0.056 (0.003)		DS–K(−1,0)	0.046 (0.002)	
PDS–K		0.057 (0.003)	PDS–K(−1,0)		0.046 (0.002)
NDS–K		0.057 (0.006)	NDS–K(−1,0)		0.049 (0.005)
$DS–K_{-1}$	0.035 (0.003)				
$PDS–K_{-1}$		0.034 (0.003)			
$NDS–K_{-1}$		0.043 (0.007)			
DS–K × LEV	0.012 (0.012)		DS–K(−1,0) × LEV	0.005 (0.010)	
PDS–K × LEV		0.006 (0.014)	PDS–K(−1,0) × LEV		−0.005 (0.010)
NDS–K × LEV		0.027 (0.020)	NDS–K(−1,0) × LEV		0.019 (0.012)
$DS–K_{-1}$ × LEV	−0.008 (0.012)				
$PDS–K_{-1}$ × LEV		−0.022 (0.010)			
$NDS–K_{-1}$ × LEV		0.002 (0.022)			
DS–K × SIZE	0.078 (0.018)		DS–K(−1,0) × SIZE	0.064 (0.012)	
PDS–K × SIZE		0.075 (0.021)	PDS–K(−1,0) × SIZE		0.057 (0.013)
NDS–K × SIZE		0.080 (0.035)	NDS–K(−1,0) × SIZE		0.084 (0.023)
$DS–K_{-1}$ × SIZE	0.052 (0.015)				
$PDS–K_{-1}$ × SIZE		0.038 (0.015)			
$NDS–K_{-1}$ × SIZE		0.105 (0.047)			
Adj. R^2	0.300	0.304		0.293	0.296

Table 4.4　Fixed investment regressions
(instrumental variables – standard errors corrected for heteroscedasticity);
difference of investment ($DI–K$); (standard errors in parentheses)

(b) Variables	(9b)	(10b)	Variables	(11b)	(12b)
Constant	−0.002	−0.001	Constant	−0.002	−0.001
	(0.002)	(0.002)		(0.002)	(0.002)
$DI–K_{-1}$	0.122	0.123	$DI–K_{-1}$	0.041	0.047
	(0.062)	(0.063)		(0.035)	(0.034)
LEV	0.019	0.015	LEV	0.021	0.024
	(0.012)	(0.012)		(0.012)	(0.012)
$SIZE$	−0.007	0.002	$SIZE$	−0.006	−0.005
	(0.012)	(0.012)		(0.012)	(0.011)
$DS–K$	0.065		$DS–K(-1,0)$	0.034	
	(0.006)			(0.004)	
$PDS–K$		0.065	$PDS–K(-1,0)$		0.031
		(0.009)			(0.004)
$NDS–K$		0.071	$NDS–K(-1,0)$		0.044
		(0.010)			(0.009)
$DS–K_{-1}$	0.002				
	(0.010)				
$PDS–K_{-1}$		0.000			
		(0.009)			
$NDS–K_{-1}$		0.011			
		(0.018)			
$DS–K \times LEV$	0.017		$DS–K(-1,0) \times LEV$	0.010	
	(0.016)			(0.012)	
$PDS–K \times LEV$		−0.018	$PDS–K(-1,0) \times LEV$		−0.024
		(0.021)			(0.015)
$NDS–K \times LEV$		0.082	$NDS–K(-1,0) \times LEV$		0.028
		(0.039)			(0.017)
$DS–K_{-1} \times LEV$	−0.004				
	(0.019)				
$PDS–K_{-1} \times LEV$		−0.035			
		(0.026)			
$NDS–K_{-1} \times LEV$		−0.052			
		(0.044)			
$DS–K \times SIZE$	0.124		$DS–K(-1,0) \times SIZE$	0.043	
	(0.031)			(0.020)	
$PDS–K \times SIZE$		0.178	$PDS–K(-1,0) \times SIZE$		0.066
		(0.038)			(0.025)
$NDS–K \times SIZE$		0.078	$NDS–K(-1,0) \times SIZE$		0.062
		(0.085)			(0.040)
$DS–K_{-1} \times SIZE$	−0.027				
	(0.030)				
$PDS–K_{-1} \times SIZE$		−0.021			
		(0.035)			
$NDS–K_{-1} \times SIZE$		0.081			
		(0.069)			
Adj. R^2	0.048	0.050		0.043	0.045

Note:
DI–K is the difference of the investment-to-capital ratio. *LEV* is the ratio of the book
value of debt (less cash assets) divided by the book value of assets. *SIZE* is total
tangible capital (plant, equipment, and inventories). *P* and *N* prefixes denote interactions
with zero-one indicator variables (*N* for recession phases, *P* for non-recession phases).
DS–K is the log difference of sales-to-capital ratio. Lagged variables are denoted by a
subscript of –1. Variables are annual with the exception of sales in some regressions,
where they are defined over a two-year period. The notation (–1,0) applied to sales
ratios denotes a two-year change over the period of the lagged year and the current
year.

investment. Indeed, recent theoretical and empirical work has suggested
that working capital stocks may be important in reducing the
responsiveness of fixed investment to changes in income. Whited (1991),
Fazzari and Petersen (1993), Carpenter, Fazzari, and Petersen (1993),
Calomiris and Hubbard (1995), and Calomiris, Himmelberg, and Wachtel
(1994) argue that firms accumulate working capital, in part, as a self-
insuring buffer, which can be drawn down during low-earnings episodes
to maintain fixed capital investment. This implies that working capital
should counteract, in part, the effect of declines in sales on fixed
investment. Firms with high working capital will not be as susceptible
to declines in sales.

We ran regressions (not reported here) for employment and fixed
investment similar to those in Tables 4.2–4.4, in which working capital
takes the place of leverage as a conditioning variable for sales. As
before, the effect is significant and asymmetric. Consistent with the
above-mentioned arguments about working capital as a buffer for fixed
investment, higher working capital stocks reduce the response of fixed
capital investment and employment to sales growth only during episodes
of declining sales.

Finally, in regressions not reported here, we investigated whether
leverage constraints had different effects on firms with different investment
opportunities. Some researchers have argued that debt can be an effective
device for constraining the investment of firm managers with negative
net present value investment opportunities. If, consistent with that
argument, the leverage effects we describe here were traceable only to
firms with poor investment opportunities, then leverage constraints might
be viewed as beneficial, since they would only limit undesirable
investments. To investigate this we split our sample in two, dividing
observations according to firms' ratios of market-to-book values of equity.
Interestingly, contrary to the view that leverage constraints efficiently
limit investment by wasteful firm managers, we found that firms with
higher market-to-book value of equity exhibited much larger effects

from leverage constraints. In other words, our results appear to reflect the behaviour of firms with relatively favourable investment opportunities.

CONCLUSIONS

The results from our panel data study suggest that leverage may act as an important propagator of shocks during business cycles – especially during downturns – and this lends credence to the potential importance of 'debt overhang' effects. Despite the advantages of panel data for qualitatively identifying balance sheet effects, they may not be as useful for measuring the importance of those effects for the business cycle. In general, our coefficient estimates will understate the macroeconomic importance of balance sheet effects for two reasons. First, microeconomic analysis of investment takes the macroeconomic environment as given. In particular, if aggregate sales are themselves affected by aggregate investment, then leverage effects will produce declines in sales, as well as contractions in investment in response to declines in sales. Second, as we argued above, our coefficients on the sales–leverage interaction effect probably understate the effect of leverage because they do not control for cross-sectional variation in firms' debt capacities.

The remaining challenges for measuring the importance of leverage in the business cycle include the estimation of firm-specific debt capacities and the construction of a general equilibrium model that allows sales to respond endogenously to other changes in the economy (including leverage). Future work should also explore whether cross-sectional differences in the composition of debt or cross-time changes in the laws governing bankruptcy affect the magnitude of leverage's effect as a conditioning variable. Finally, we have only estimated linear models of leverage interaction effects. If the effect of leverage on the responsiveness of investment, inventories and employment to sales growth are larger for larger leverage ratios, however, then one would expect to find non-linear conditioning effects of leverage.

Data Appendix

Firm-level data are drawn from the R&D Master File (documented in Hall, *et al.*, 1988), which is constructed from Standard & Poors Compustat files and has annual observations on manufacturing firms dating from 1959 to 1985. The panel contains firms that enter and exit in various years; our sample retains this characteristic. After discarding observations because of missing data and dropping five observations per firm in order to create lags and a lead, our sample contains 22 298 observations

The sample is then spit into two sets of two-digit industries, one in which the average covariance of sales growth of sample firms in the two-digit industry with GNP is high, and the other where the average covariance with GNP is low (using the dichotomy of Sharpe, 1994). One might expect that if there is any effect of leverage or size on the responsiveness of endogenous variables to increases in demand, it should be most distinguishable among firms in industries where cyclical fluctuations are a more dominant feature of the dynamics. The more cyclical subsample of industries fairly closely corresponds to the durables industries. These include firms that fall into the following two-digit industries: 24, 25, 30 and 33–37, which includes all durables industries except Stone, Glass and Clay (32) and Instruments (38), and includes a non-durables industry (Rubber and Miscellaneous Plastic Products (30)). In addition, we exclude firms in 4-digit industries where at least 10 per cent of employment observations were footnoted (in the firm *Annual Statements*) as containing a 'substantial' number of seasonal workers. 'Substantial' is defined by Compustat as 'at least 10 per cent of the labor force.'

After discarding observations because of missing data and the creation of lags, the data were screened for outliers – observations and lags in which a firm tripled in size by assets, sales or employment, or made an acquisition whose value exceeded 20 per cent of its own value. The screen eliminates 6 per cent of the observations, leaving 10 883 for our analysis.

CONSTRUCTION OF VARIABLES

The three dependent variables are constructed as follows. Employment growth is the log difference of employment, where the number of employees is an annual figure reported at the end of the firm's fiscal year. This is reported by some firms as an average number of employees and by some as the number at the year-end. If both were given on the *Annual Report*, Compustat uses the year-end figure. They make no attempt to distinguish between the two in their data; in the analysis below, we treat this as a year-end figure. Growth in inventories is equal to the log difference in the inflation-adjusted level of inventories, which is converted into real inventory growth by subtracting the growth (year-end over year-end) in the producer price index (PPI). Investment is measured as investment in PPE divided by the lag of the inflation-adjusted net capital stock. (See Hall *et al.*, 1988, for a detailed description of the procedure for adjusting PPE and inventories for inflation.) In our regressions we use the difference of the investment rate as our dependent variable.

For the employment and inventory regressions, sales growth is measured as the log difference in sales *less* the log difference in the PPI. For the investment regressions, sales growth is measured as the first difference of normalised sales, where sales is normalised by the lag of the inflation-adjusted net capital stock. We use 'current' and 'lagged' sales growth as independent variables. In the case of the investment specifications, this is straightforward, since both investment and sales are measured as flows over the year. Since employment and inventories are measured at year-end, we compute 'current sales' growth in these cases as the log of sales in the year just beginning *minus* the log of sales over the year just ended.

The primary measure of financial leverage is called the 'net leverage' ratio. This ratio is computed as the book value of total debt over book value of assets, with net short-term assets subtracted from both numerator and denominator. Net short-term assets includes cash *plus* short-term investments *plus* receivables *less* payables. Netting out short-term liquid assets is meant to produce a comprehensive measure of overall 'tightness' of the firm's balance sheet. In order to eliminate outliers – anomalies in our leverage measures that tend to arise when book equity is negative (yielding extremely high leverage), we truncate book value equity at zero. Book equity value is favoured because it is more stable than market value and presumably provides a measure of the firm choice of balance sheet leverage that is not highly sensitive to the market's current assessments.

Firm size is measured as the log of total inflation-adjusted tangible capital value, the sum of inflation-adjusted net plant and equipment and inflation-adjusted inventories. We use lagged values of our leverage and size measures to avoid endogeneity problems. In the employment and inventory regressions, we use the second lag, while the third lags are used in the investment regressions. (With respect to current sales growth, leverage and size characteristics are measured with a lag of three periods.)

The indicator variable used to characterise whether the economy is expanding or contracting takes on a value of one during NBER recoveries and expansions, and zero during recessions. This variable is observed at monthly frequency, and thus the timing of its observation can be gauged relative to the last month of the firm's fiscal year. We use the value of this indicator at the mid-point of the period during which lagged sales growth is measured. Thus, relative to when firm employment and inventory are observed, we use the 12-month lag of the recession indicator; relative to the end of the year during which investment is carried out, we employ the two-year lag of this indicator.

INSTRUMENTS

Included in the set of instruments are our (lagged) balance sheet measures of firm leverage, working capital, and size, as well as the second lags of endogenous variables – sales growth, employment growth, inventory growth and the change in investment. Interactions between the firm balance sheet characteristics and the second lags of the endogenous variables are also included.

Macroeconomic series to be used as instruments are matched up to the micro data firm by firm, taking into account that different firms' fiscal year-ends fall in different months. In our sample, 57 per cent of the observations are firms with fiscal years ending in December. Another 10 per cent have fiscal years ending in June, with the rest scattered across the remaining 10 months. Because of variation in reporting dates, our data contain more variation in the time dimension than does standard annual data. To exploit the fiscal year-end variation, and to enable a finer analysis on the timing issues, we use a mixed-frequency approach to matching the data. Generally, macroeconomic instruments are computed at a semi-annual frequency and matched up to the annual firm-level data in accordance with the following schematic:

$$E_{t-2} \qquad\qquad E_{t-1} \qquad\qquad E_t$$
$$z6 \quad z5 \quad z4 \quad z3 \quad z2 \quad z1$$

where E is firm i's employment at the end of fiscal year t and $z(s)$ is the value of the macro variable z averaged over a six-month period which is centered at $(s-1)/2$ years prior to the firm's fiscal year-end. Macro growth rates or changes are thus calculated at a semi-annual frequency as well: $Dz1 = z1 - z2$. Four variables are used to proxy for the business cycle: growth in industrial production, the CPI inflation rate, changes in the ratio of wholesale inventories: sales, and changes in the real Federal funds rate.

We exclude the first two semi-annual lags of our macro instruments because they are potentially correlated with the error term. Thus we include the third ($Dz3$) through the sixth ($Dz6$) lag of the growth of industrial production, the change in the real Fed funds rate, the change in the ratio of wholesale inventories to wholesale sales of durable goods, and the CPI inflation rate. First and second order interactions between firm leverage, working capital, and size with each of the macro instruments are also included. These interactions allow predicted firm sales growth to vary in response to macro variables according to differences across firms associated with size and leverage. Finally, we double the size of our instrument set by including interactions between the recession indicator variable and all of the other instruments.

Notes

1. The authors thank participants at City University Debt-Deflation Conference (London, April 1994) for helpful comments. Opinions expressed are those of the authors and do not necessarily reflect those of the Federal Reserve Board or the Federal Reserve System.
2. It is worth noting that runs are not restricted to banks. For example, in

1970, in the wake of the failure of a large commercial paper issuer (Penn Central), the commercial paper market experienced a run for several weeks (Calomiris, 1994). Similar concerns about exposure to systemic financial instability motivate expressions of concerns about the growing markets in financial derivatives.

3. Calomiris and Hubbard (1995) find that, during the mid-1930s, firms with the largest estimated shadow costs of external finance (which often were small firms in new industries) had roughly twice the debt-equity ratios of firms with low costs of external finance (large firms in established industries). The cost of external finance can be measured in 1936–37 because of the existence of the surtax on undistributed profits, which set rising marginal surtax rates on retained earnings. By examining a firm's surtax margin, Calomiris and Hubbard (1995) estimate the shadow cost of external finance, and examine differences in the behavior of high- and low-surtax margin firms.

4. Gertler and Hubbard (1990) argue that there are alternative means of contracting (essentially debt contracts indexed to aggregate business cycle conditions in simple ways) which would provide all the incentive advantages of debt without the costs of potential destabilisation through debt-deflation. But the tax code would not recognise such contracts as debt, and therefore, firms avoid them. The increasing importance of bonds relative to loans from intermediaries also suggests that debt is motivated by tax considerations. Incentive advantages of debt contracting related to asymmetric information suggest that debt would largely take the form of intermediated debt. Bond financing does not involve the concentration of debt holding or the design and enforcement of complicated covenants that characterise borrowing from financial intermediaries. But much of the runup in debt has taken the form of widely-held bond issues of large, highly seasoned credit risks.

5. The reason the sales-size interaction controls for debt capacity differences correlated with size is that the coefficient on the triple product of size, leverage, and sales can be approximated linearly by the sales-leverage and sales–size effects.

6. Recent research on the links between fixed capital investment and working capital investment may shed some light on this phenomenon. One possibility is that small firms (which face greater financing constraints and tend to be more dependent on internally generated funds) may use working capital (including inventories) as a self-insuring buffer to keep fixed investment smooth. Evidence for this proposition is presented in Fazzari and Petersen (1993), Calomiris and Hubbard (1995), and Calomiris, Himmelberg and Wachtel (1994). This may explain why small firms' fixed capital investments are less sensitive to sales (since they build up stocks of working capital as well as fixed capital whenever they see an increase in sales). It also may explain why inventories are more sensitive to sales during an episode of increasing sales. But this story does not explain why small firms should show less sensitivity of inventories to sales during episodes of declining sales. During times of shrinking sales, small firms should sell off inventories to keep fixed capital investment smooth in the face of declining earnings. One possibility is that unin-

tended increases in inventories during sales declines are more important for small firms, but the rationale for such an effect is unclear.

References

Asquith, P., R. Gertner and D. Scharfstein (1992) 'Anatomy of Financial Distress: An Examination of Junk Bond Issuers', *Working paper*, MIT.

Baer, H.L. and J.N. McElravey (1993) 'Capital Shocks and Bank Growth', Federal Reserve Bank of Chicago, *Economic Perspectives* (July–August).

Bernanke, B.S. (1983) 'Non-Monetary Effects of the Financial Crisis in the Propagation of the Great Depression', *American Economic Review*, 73 (June), 257–76.

Bernanke, B.S. (1993) 'Credit in the Macroeconomy', Federal Reserve Bank of New York, *Quarterly Review* (Spring), 50–70.

Bernanke, B.S. and J.Y. Campbell (1988) 'Is There a Corporate Debt Crisis?', *Brookings Papers on Economic Activity*, 1, 83–125.

Bernanke, B. and H. James (1991) 'The Gold Standard, Deflation, and Financial Crisis in the Great Depression: An Historical Comparison', in R.G. Hubbard (ed.), *Financial Markets and Financial Crises* (Chicago: The University of Chicago Press), 33–68.

Bernanke, B. and C. Lown (1992) 'The Credit Crunch', *Brookings Papers on Economic Activity*, 2, 205–39.

Brown, D.T., C. James and R. M. Mooradian (1991) 'The Information Content of Exchange Offers Made by Distressed Firms', *Working Paper*, University of Florida.

Brown, D.T., C. James and M. Ryngaert (1992) 'The Effects of Leverage on Operating Performance: An Analysis of Firms' Responses to Poor Performance', *Working paper*, University of Florida.

Calomiris, C.W. (1993) 'Financial Factors in the Great Depression', *Journal of Economic Perspectives*, 7 (Spring), 61–85.

Calomiris, C.W. (1994) 'Is the Discount Window Necessary? A Penn-Central Perspective', Federal Reserve Bank of St Louis, *Review* (May/June), 31–55.

Calomiris, C.W. and G. Gorton (1991) 'The Origins of Banking Panics: Models, Facts, and Bank Regulation', R.G. Hubbard (ed.), in *Financial Markets and Financial Crises* (Chicago: The University of Chicago Press), 109–73.

Calomiris, C.W. and C.P. Himmelberg (1994) 'Directed Credit Programs for Agriculture and Industry: Arguments from Theory and Fact', *Proceedings of the World Bank Annual Conference on Development Economics 1993*, (113–38).

Calomiris, C.W. and R.G. Hubbard (1989) 'Price Flexibility, Credit Availability, and Economic Fluctuations', *Quarterly Journal of Economics*, 104 (August), 429–52.

Calomiris, C.W. and R.G. Hubbard (1990) 'Firm Heterogeneity, Internal Finance, and Credit Rationing', *Economic Journal*, 100 (March), 90–104.

Calomiris, C.W. and R.G. Hubbard (1995) 'Internal Finance and Investment: Evidence from the Undistributed Profits Tax of 1936–1937', Journal of Business, 68 (October) 443–82.

Calomiris, C.W., C.P. Himmelberg and P. Wachtel (1994) 'Commercial Paper and Corporate Finance: A Microeconomic Perspective', *Carnegie-Rochester Series on Public Policy* (forthcoming).

Calomiris, C.W., R.G. Hubbard and J. Stock (1986) 'The Farm Debt Crisis and Public Policy', *Brookings Papers on Economic Activity*, 2, 441–85.

Cantor, R. (1990) 'Effects of Leverage on Corporate Investment and Hiring Decisions', Federal Reserve Bank of New York, *Quarterly Review*, 31–41.

Carpenter, R.E., S.M. Fazzari and B.C. Petersen (1993) 'Inventory (Dis)Investment, Internal Finance Fluctuations, and the Business Cycle', *Working Paper*, Washington University in St Louis.

De Meza, D., and D.C. Webb (1987) 'Too Much Investment: A Problem of Asymmetric Information', *Quarterly Journal of Economics* (May) 281–92.

Eichengreen, B., and J. Sachs (1985) 'Exchange Rates and Economic Recovery in the 1930s', *Journal of Economic History*, 45, 925–46.

Eichengreen, B., and J. Sachs (1986) 'Competitive Devaluation in the Great Depression: A Theoretical Reassessment', *Economic Letters*, 22, 67–71.

Fazzari, S.M. and B.C. Petersen (1993) 'Investment Smoothing with Working Capital: New Evidence on Financing Constraints', *Rand Journal of Economics* (Autumn), 328–42.

Fazzari, S., R.G. Hubbard and B.C. Petersen (1988) 'Financing Constraints and Corporate Investment', *Brookings Papers on Economic Activity*, 1141–95.

Fisher, I. (1933) 'The Debt-Deflation Theory of Great Depressions', *Econometrica* 1 (October), 337–57.

Friedman, B.M. (1986) 'Increasing Indebtedness and Financial Instability in the United States', in B.M. Friedman, *Debt, Financial Stability, and Public Policy* (Kansas City: Federal Reserve Bank of Kansas City).

Friedman, B.M. (1989) 'View on the Likelihood of Financial Crisis', in M. Feidstein (ed.), *Reducing the Risk of Economic Crisis* (Chicago: The University of Chicago Press).

Frydl, E.J. (1992) 'Overhangs and Hangover: Coping with the Imbalances of the 1980s', Federal Reserve Bank of New York, *Annual Report*.

Frydl, E.J. (ed.) (1991) *Studies on Corporate Leveraging*, Federal Reserve Bank of New York (September).

Gertler, M. and S. Gilchrist (1993) 'Monetary Policy, Business Cycles, and the Behavior of Small Manufacturing Firms', *Working Paper*, New York University.

Gertler, M. and R.G. Hubbard (1990) 'Taxation, Corporate Capital Structure, and Financial Distress', *Tax Policy and the Economy*, 4, 43–71.

Gilson, S.C., K. John and L.H.P. Lang (1990) 'Troubled Debt Restructurings', *Journal of Financial Economics*, 27, 315–53.

Hall, B.H., C. Cummins, E.S. Laderman and J. Mundy (1988) 'The R&D Master File Documentation', NBER, *Technical Working Paper*, 72.

Hayashi, F. (1982) 'Tobin's Marginal q and Average q: A Neoclassical Interpretation', *Econometrica*, 50 (January), 213–24.

Hubbard, R.G., and A. Kashyap (1992) 'Internal Net Worth and the Investment Process: An Application to US Agriculture', *Journal of Political Economy*, 100, 506–34.

Hunter, H.M. (1982) 'The Role of Business Liquidity During the Great Depression and Afterwards: Differences Between Large and Small Firms', *Journal of Economic History*, 42, 883–902.

Jensen, M.C. (1986) 'Agency Costs of Free Cash Flow, Corporate Finance, and Takeovers', *American Economic Review*, 76 (May), 323–30.

Jensen, M.C. and W.H. Meckling (1976) 'Theory of the Firm: Managerial Behavior, Agency Costs and Ownership Structure', *Journal of Financial Economics*, 3, 305–60.

Keynes, J.M. (1931) 'The Consequences to the Banks of the Collapse of Money Values', in J.M. Keynes, *Essays in Persuasion* (London: Macmillan; New York: W.W. Norton, 1963).

Kopcke, R.W. and M.M. Howrey (1994) 'A Panel Study of Investment: Sales, Cash Flow, the Cost of Capital, and Leverage', Federal Reserve Bank of Boston, *New England Economic Review* (January–February), 9–30.

McWilliams, D. (1992) 'Commercial Property and Company Borrowing', Royal Institution of Chartered Surveyors (November).

Mishkin, F.S. (1976) 'Illiquidity, Consumer Durable Expenditure, and Monetary Policy', *American Economic Review*, 66, 642–54.

Mishkin, F.S. (1976) 'The Household Balance Sheet and the Great Depression', *Journal of Economic History*, 38, 918–37.

Murphy, K.M., A. Shleifer and R.W. Vishny (1989) 'Industrialization and the Big Push', *Journal of Political Economy*, 97 (October), 1003–26.

Myers, S.C. and N. Majluf (1984) 'Corporate Financing and Investment Decisions When Firms Have Information That Investors Do Not Have', *Journal of Financial Economics*, 13, 187–221.

Opler, T.C. and S. Titman (1994) 'Financial Distress and Corporate Performance,' *Journal of Finance*, 49 (July), 1015–40.

Peek, J. and E. Rosengren (1992) 'The Capital Crunch in New England', Federal Reserve Bank of Boston, *New England Economic Review* (May–June), 21–31.

Perry, G.L. and C.L. Schultze (1993) 'Was This Recession Different? Are They All Different?', *Brookings Papers on Economic Activity*, 1, 145–211.

Remolona, E., R.N. McCauley, J.S. Ruud and F. Iacono (1992) 'Corporate Refinancing in the 1990s', Federal Reserve Bank of New York, *Quarterly Review* (Winter), 1–27.

Sharpe, S.A. (1994) 'Financial Market Imperfections, Firm Leverage, and the Cyclicality of Employment', *American Economic Review*, 84, 1060–74.

Shleifer, A. and R.W. Vishny (1992) 'Liquidation Values and Debt Capacity: A Market Equilibrium Approach', *Journal of Finance* (September), 1343–66.

Syron, R. (1991) 'Are We Experiencing a Credit Crunch?' Federal Reserve Bank of Boston, *New England Economic Review* (July–August), 3–10.

Temin, P. (1989) *Lessons from the Great Depression* (Cambridge, Mass.: MIT Press).

Townsend, R. (1979) 'Optimal Contracts and Competitive Markets with Costly State Verification', *Journal of Economic Theory* (October), 265–93.

Whited, T.M. (1991) 'Investment and Financial Asset Accumulation', *Journal of Financial Intermediation*, 1, 307–34.

Comment

Leslie Hannah

Leslie Hannah's comments made at the conference have been incorporated by the authors in the revised version of Chapter 4. We would therefore like to acknowledge Professor Leslie Hannah's contribution to the chapter.

Comment

Terence C. Mills

Calomiris *et al.*'s Chapter 4 is an interesting look at whether the investment decisions of firms are influenced by their existing financial condition, particularly leverage. This is investigated by analysing a large and very rich panel data set. The econometric techniques used are worthy of discussion and I shall make two substantial points on them.

Although the authors claim that they are using a panel data set, this would appear to be somewhat misleading. A 'complete' panel would contain $N \times T$ observations on N firms observed over T years (perhaps, as here, after creating the required number of leads and lags). In the Data Appendix, it is stated that observations were also discarded because of missing data and through eliminating outliers, before attention was concentrated on the subsample of durable-goods manufacturers. This leaves $N \times T = 10890$ observations, but it is not clear that N (the number of firms) or T (the number of years) actually are: presumably T is (at most) 21, but are all firms observed over the entire time span, i.e. is the panel data set incomplete?

Assuming that it is incomplete leads to some interesting econometric problems in itself, but Calomiris *et al.* avoid these by fitting single regressions to the entire set of $N \times T$ observations, i.e. by implicitly assuming that the N intercepts are the same and the $N \times K$ slope coefficients of the K regressors are themselves identical. As Hsiao (1986, 11) states, 'if this assumption is not valid, . . . the pooled least squares estimates may lead to false inferences'. Since Calomiris *et al.*, make heavy use of coefficient estimates and associated standard errors, it might be have been desirable to have provided a test statistic for this implicit null hypothesis, given that it can be constructed, under the assumption that the errors are independently normally distributed with zero mean and constant variance, as a standard F-statistic (Hsiao, 1986, 15).

This distributional assumption made about the error leads me to my second point. All the inferences made in Chapter 4 rely on the assumption of an independently normally distributed error having constant variance (as does the F-test mentioned above), yet no diagnostic tests are provided to allow us to assess whether this assumption is valid. Indeed, no tests of model misspecification are provided at all, even though they are now standard output from typical econometric regression packages. The impact and consequences of heteroscedasticity, for example, are well known, but I am particularly thinking here of the possible presence of non-normality and non-linearity. The former, particularly the 'fat-tailed' variety, can have severe effects on the robustness of OLS, thus calling into question any inferences drawn from coefficients so estimated, while the latter can seriously bias the responses observed.

Readers might be more convinced by the empirical evidence presented here – which, after all, lies at the core of the chapter – if such information were provided. Moreover, if it is found that serious misspecification of these forms does exist, then alternative estimation methods would be required: robust techniques should be used if non-normality is found, non-parametric estimation if non-linearity is uncovered.

Reference

Hsiao, C. (1986) *Analysis of Panel Data* (Cambridge: Cambridge University Press).

5 Debt-Deflation: Theory and Evidence

Mervyn King[1]

Be not made a beggar by banqueting upon borrowing.
(Ecclesiasticus 18: 33)

INTRODUCTION

Over the years 1989–92 many of the major industrialised countries have experienced protracted periods of below-trend growth, and some the longest recession since the 1930s. And the most severe recessions occurred in those countries which had experienced the largest increases in private debt burdens. Figure 5.1 illustrates this correlation for ten major countries, the G7 countries together with Australia, Norway and Sweden. It plots the *difference* between the actual annual growth rate between 1989 and 1992 and the trend growth rate (measured by the average growth rate of GDP between 1974 and 1989), against the *change* in the ratio of household debt to GDP from 1984 to the end of 1988.[2] The larger the increase in debt over the preceding five years, the greater the shortfall in output relative to its trend level. It is not surprising, therefore, that the phrase 'debt-deflation', coined by Irving Fisher some 60 years ago, has been rediscovered by the economics profession. Is the coincidence of a rise in debt burdens and the prolonged nature of the recent recession an accident of history, or does it reflect deeper forces affecting the behaviour of market economies?

In this chapter I shall assess the relevance of debt-deflation to aggregate economic fluctuations. Let me start by posing four questions about the phenomenon of debt-deflation:

1 First, why should an increase in purely inside, or internal, debt affect the behaviour of the economy? Does not the Modigliani–Miller theorem tell us that real variables such as output and employment are invariant to the debt–equity ratio of the corporate sector? I shall argue that debt-deflation is not necessarily inconsistent

197

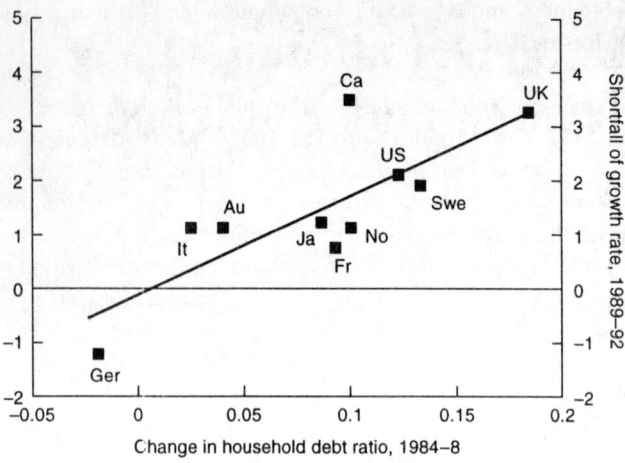

Sources: OECD (1992); own calculations.

Figure 5.1   Debt and the 1990s' recession: 10 major countries

with the Modigliani–Miller theorem, and can result from behaviour in the household sector.

2   Second, what was Fisher's model of debt-deflaion, and why was it largely ignored by our profession both at the time and subsequently? Why did Keynes, in particular, pay virtually no attention to Fisher's contribution? I shall suggest that the principal reason for this neglect is that debt-deflation is best thought of as a real business cycle, and not a monetary, phenomenon.

3   Third, is it possible to construct a simple model of debt-deflation that captures at least some of its main features? I shall show that recent contributions to the literature on consumption provide components of a formal analysis of Fisher's mechanism. The key is to examine debt-deflation in a model of purely distributional shocks with no aggregate uncertainty at all. Although I have described debt-deflation as a real business cycle phenomenon, it cannot be analysed within the conventional RBC framework with a representative consumer. Distributional shocks are the essence of the model.

4   Fourth, what is the evidence for the proposition that debt-deflation contributed to the length and depth of the recent recession? I shall present some preliminary results on the importance of debt ratios in explaining the pattern of consumption growth during the recession in ten major countries and on the link between the distribution of

indebtedness and aggregate consumption growth using household data for the UK.

Irving Fisher put forward his thesis in his book *Booms and Depressions* in 1932. Comparisons with the 1930s have a perennial fascination for economists. During the summer of 1992, those with a sense of history were very conscious that the date of the French referendum on the Maastricht treaty, Sunday 20 September, was not only a key time for the ERM but was also the very date in 1931 when Britain left the gold standard. And the last major country to abandon the gold standard was, of course, France, in 1936. The similarities with recent events are self-evident. More relevant to my concern here is a comparison of the behaviour of consumption in the 1930s and the 1990s. I shall return to this later. But I want, first, to discuss the link between the theory of business cycles and the concept of debt-deflation. A theory of business cycles has three elements. First, a model of the initial shock hitting the economy. Second, a propagation mechanism which magnifies the initial shock and describes its impact (both magnitude and duration) on aggregation demand. Third, an explanation of why changes in aggregate demand affect output rather than prices. Debt-deflation is not a complete theory of the business cycle in two respects. First, it is concerned only with the way in which an initial shock is transmitted through the economy and not how that shock itself comes about. Debt-deflation concerns the propagation mechanism which determines the depth and duration of the recession. Fisher's story is relevant because it explains why aggregate demand responds to an initial shock by more than would be predicted by a representative consumer model. Distributional effects are an important part of the transmission mechanism of both monetary and real shocks.

Second, Fisher's theory does not provide a convincing explanation of why changes in aggregate demand should lead to changes in output rather than prices. With flexible prices, and especially interest rates, short-run changes in output reflect supply shocks and equilibrium responses of factors, such as labour supply, to changes in prices. Much of the debate on the causes of the Great Depression – among them Friedman and Schwartz (1963), Temin (1976, 1993), and, more recently, Eichengreen (1992) – has focused on the responsibility of domestic monetary policy, the gold standard, or other shocks for the contraction in prices and output. But, as Bernanke (1993) points out in his review article of Eichengreen's (1992) book, one of the important puzzles of that period 'why did the declines in *nominal* income of the early 1930s lead to such deep and protracted falls in *real* variables such as output and employment?' The magnitude and duration of the monetary non-neutrality remains to be explained. This is a question about the supply side of the economy, and I shall return to it at the end of the chapter. But for the most part I shall concentrate on the role of debt-deflation as a propagation mechanism from an initial shock to aggregate demand.

Before turning to a discussion of debt-deflation in the 1930s and the 1990s, I want to mention two aspects which have been the focus of discussion of debt-deflation in the post-war literature, but on which I shall not dwell. The first concerns the role of the aggregate price level. In the 1930s the absolute price level fell – from 1929 to 1933 the average fall in producer prices in the 10 countries shown in Figure 5.1 was 27 per cent. In the 1990s the price level rose – by an average of 6 per cent from 1989 to 1992 in the ten countries. But a falling absolute price level is not a necessary condition for debt-deflation. What matters is the fluctuation of *asset* values relative to the unit of account in which debts are denominated. A falling price level exacerbates the problem, in part because it is often associated with a rise in the real interest rate. But this reinforces the point that in essence debt-deflation is a real not a monetary phenomenon, and is concerned with changes in relative prices. It is the change in the distribution of net worth from debtors to creditors which leads to a fall in demand and output.

A second line of enquiry which I shall not pursue in this chapter is the rise in the effective, or 'virtual', cost of capital resulting from the impact of a downturn in activity on the cost of financial intermediation. This argument – based on the role of asymmetric information – stresses the distinction between 'insiders' and 'outsiders' in the supply of finance to the corporate sector. Banks or other financial intermediaries with a continuing relationship with a firm can supply funds at a lower cost than 'outsiders' because of their superior information about the firm's management and prospects. The unobservable cost of financial intermediation drives a wedge between the cost of capital and the observable rate of interest. Moreover, this unobservable component of the cost of capital varies both across countries and over time as result of differences and changes in the distribution of wealth between insiders and outsiders. As a dimension of the process of economic development the story is convincing, but whether such changes in the technology of providing credit can explain business cycle fluctuations in output is still open to question, not least because of the difficulty in measuring the unobservable marginal cost of financial intermediation. In using this approach to explain the depth of the Great Depression in the USA in terms of a loss of informational capital following the collapse of an unprecedentedly large number of banks, Bernanke (1983) used changes in the net worth of firms and banks as an explanatory variable for future changes in output. Since news about the future is rapidly assimilated by financial markets, correlations between changes in net worth and subsequent changes in output are open to a number of interpretations of which an adverse shift in the technology of supplying credit is only one. Nevertheless, this line of enquiry has been a fruitful source of ideas on financial intermediation.[3]

In the remainder of this chapter I shall discuss, first, some common patterns in the experience of the major industrial countries during the recession; second, Fisher's model of debt-deflation and its reception by his contemporaries; third, a model of certain aspects of debt-deflation that seem to me most germane to our recent experience; and, finally, some fragments of empirical evidence relevant to the ideas I shall be discussing.

DEBTS AND CONSUMPTION: THE RECENT EXPERIENCE

I want to start by presenting three 'stylised facts' about debt and its impact on the major industrialised countries.

Internal Debt Burden

The first 'stylised fact' concerns the increase in internal debt burdens which have, in recent years, grown enormously in both the USA and UK. In his book Fisher (1932) presented a table showing the estimated change in total debts in the USA from 1929 to 1932, both at nominal prices and deflated by a price index of wholesale commodities or, as Fisher termed it, the 'businessman's dollar'. Table 5.1 shows Fisher's numbers and the equivalent figures for the USA and UK over the period 1989–92. In nominal terms debt – both private and total – rose more rapidly between 1989 and 1992 than between 1929 and 1932, but the fall in the price level led to a much sharper proportionate (though a similar absolute) increase in the real burden of debt in the earlier period. Nevertheless, the disinflationary policies of the early 1990s meant that by 1992 inflation was no longer the means by which the real burden of debt could be steadily reduced.

Table 5.1   Debts – then and now, 1929–32 and 1989–92 (USA), 1989–92 (UK)

| | 1929–32 USA | | | 1989–92 USA | | 1989–92 UK | |
	$ billion current	$ billion 1989	per cent	$ billion	per cent	£ billion	per cent
Nominal							
Private	−41	−278	−21.1	876	12.7	284	23.8
Total	−37	−251	−15.7	1799	18.4	339	24.6
Real[1]							
Private	40	271	20.7	265	3.8	81	6.8
Total	68	461	29.1	893	9.2	102	7.4

Note:
1. Deflated by the 'businessman's dollar' (index of wholesale commodity prices).

Sources: Fisher (1932, Table 2, p. 109); OECD (1992).

Character of the Recession

The second 'stylised fact' concerns the character of the recession which has been rather different from earlier post-war recessions. In both the UK and USA output peaked in 1990:2 and recovery has been abnormally slow since output reached its trough – in 1991:1 in the USA and 1992:1 in the UK.[4] Can we identify the causes of the recession in the early 1990s? Recent studies by Olivier Blanchard, Robert Hall, and George Perry and Charles Schultze, throw light on the US experience. Blanchard (1993) concludes that 'By far, the main proximate cause of the recession was a consumption shock'; Hall (1993) argues that 'changes in consumption not associated with changes in disposable income may be an important part of a bigger story about the late 1980s and early 1990s'; and Perry and Schultze (1993) conclude that 'spending by consumers has not only been weak during this recovery, . . . but [was] substantially overpredicted relative to earlier recessions' by equations estimated on post-war data. In the UK, too, falls in consumption were larger than in previous recessions – aggregate consumption fell for seven consecutive quarters and by 3.5 per cent from peak to trough, a period in which real disposable income rose by 1.1 per cent.[5] An illuminating way to illustrate the different nature of the recent recession is shown in Figure 5.2. It shows the behaviour of consumption relative to an estimated trend level of GDP over the eight quarters both preceding and following the trough in output. Figure 5.2 shows

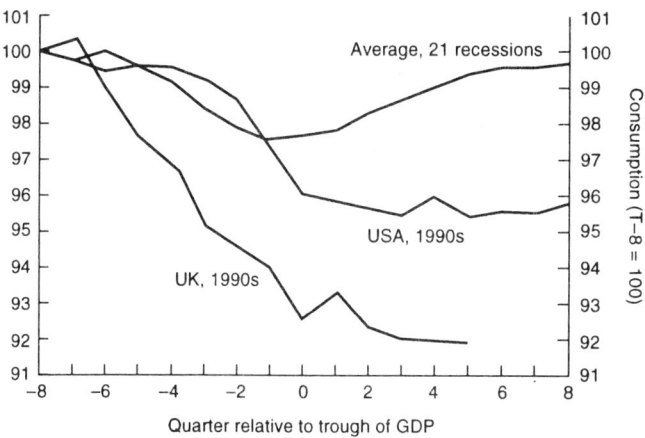

Sources: OECD (1992); own calculations.

Figure 5.2   Consumption over the cycle, relative to trend GDP

the profile of consumption over the cycle for an average of 21 recessions in the G7 countries since 1970, and for the most recent recessions in the USA and UK (consumption eight quarters before the trough in output is normalised to 100). In an 'average' recession consumption relative to trend output follows a shallow saucer-shaped profile. But in the recent recession consumption has fallen much more sharply and been slower to recover, especially in the UK. But why were there large negative shocks to consumption? And were there similar shocks in other countries? I shall return to these questions later.

Debt and Consumption

The first two 'stylised facts' concerned debt and consumption separately. Are they connected? So far I have referred only to aggregate data. But the effect of a given debt ratio depends critically upon its *distribution* among the population of households and companies. Indeed, such variation provides another opportunity to identify the impact of debt burdens on spending. Variations in spending and debt among groups of households can throw light on the relevance of debt because they effectively control for unobservable national shocks, especially monetary policy shocks. Household expenditure surveys rarely contain detailed information on the total indebtedness and net worth of individual

Table 5.2   Average real weekly household expenditure of owner-occupiers
in UK, 1989–91 (1989=100)

	Total expenditure		Expenditure excluding housing	
Year	No mortgage	With a mortgage	No mortgage	With a mortgage
1989	100.0	100.0	100.0	100.0
1990	99.1	99.2	98.5	99.6
1991	103.9	98.2	100.9	95.9

Note: The real figures are obtained by deflating weekly expenditure by RPI and RPI excluding housing, respectively.

Source: *Family Spending*, Table 14, issues of 1989–91 (CSO).

households. But it is possible to compare groups of households with very different levels of debt. Given the importance of mortgages in total household debt, it is instructive to examine the behaviour of consumption in the recent recession for two groups of home-owners – those with a mortgage and those who own their house outright. Table 5.2 shows the levels of average real weekly expenditure (both total and non-housing expenditure) for the two types of home-owner in the UK from 1989 to 1991. The estimates are derived from the Family Expenditure Survey (FES) which each year contains responses from around 3000 home-owners with a mortgage and just under 2000 without a mortgage. These time series of cross-sections are subject to sampling error and care must be exercised when drawing inferences about changes over time. Nevertheless, between 1989 and 1991 total real consumption expenditure of households with a mortgage *fell* by about 2 per cent, whereas for those without a mortgage it *rose* by almost 4 per cent. Non-housing expenditure in real terms fell by over 4 per cent between 1989 and 1991 for home-owners with a mortgage and rose by 1 per cent for those with no mortgage debt (see Figure 5.3).[6]

Given these 'stylised facts' about the relationship between increases in debt and a subsequent fall in consumption, there is, therefore, a *prima facie* case for thinking that high debt burdens, especially the increase during the 1980s, led to a deeper and longer recession than might otherwise have occurred. What is the mechanism by which this came about? It is time to turn to Irving Fisher.

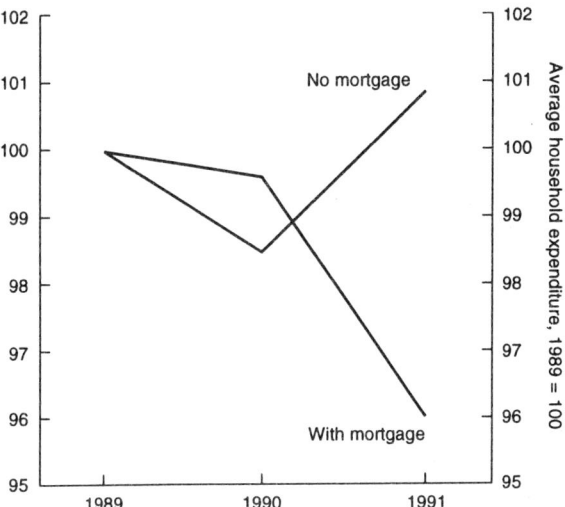

Figure 5.3   Consumption of home-owners, with and without a mortgage,
1989–91

DEBT-DEFLATION, FISHER AND KEYNES

Irving Fisher developed his debt-deflation theory of depressions in his
1932 book *Booms and Depressions*. The book grew out of an invita-
tion to address the American Association for the Advancement of Science. His talk was delivered in New Orleans on 1 January 1932, and
the book was published in November of that year.[7] Fisher repeated,
and to some extent developed, his ideas in his 1933 article in the very
first issue of *Econometrica*.

Fisher identified *nine* factors as characterising the cyclical tendencies associated with the expansion and contraction of debts, and which
can lead to a depression:

1   debts – an exogenous shock (to expectations of future incomes, for
    example) produces a desire to reduce debts;
2   falls in asset prices – change in expectations capitalised in asset prices;
3   real interest rates rise – a negative shock to asset values raises the
    conditional volatility of returns and leads to a higher risk premium;
4   reductions in net worth of businesses and households – follows
    from the above and also leads to:

5 fall in business and consumer confidence;
6 lower profitability;
7 fall in output;
8 contraction in broad money supply and credit;
9 slower velocity of circulation.

These factors reinforce the initial shock and produce a downward spiral. The process stops when the actions of debtors in cutting back on consumption and investment in order to reduce debt are offset by the actions of creditors who are able to increase spending.

Before turning to the analytics of the matter, it is interesting to ask what was the reaction of contemporary economists to these ideas. It has to be said that *Booms and Depressions* was not well received by the critics. It was reviewed in three academic journals and none was favourable. Among the reactions of the reviewers were the following:

> From the pen of Professor Fisher this book cannot but be a disappointment. What little theory it contains is in no way novel. (*Economic Journal*, December 1933)

> In the reviewer's opinion, this book is of little use to the lay reader and of even smaller value to the technical investigator of business cycle phenomena. (*American Economic Review*, March 1933)

> [And even the clarity of the writing was described as] a factor which would in itself be a recommendation, were the reasoning as penetrating as the lucidity of the style. (*Economica*, November 1933)

The economics profession showed little propensity to disagree with the reviewers. There are remarkably few references to the debt-deflation theory of depressions in subsequent literature. Even Keynes, who was an admirer of much of Fisher's work on monetary economics, ignored the book and article. There are no references to Fisher's work on debt-deflation in the *Collected Writings* of Keynes. And the private correspondence between Keynes and Fisher, amounting to 12 letters from Fisher to Keynes and two letters from Keynes to Fisher, contain no mention of debt-deflation.[8] Minsky (1977, 1982) kept the flame alive, although, ironically, his hero was Keynes. In recent years, however, there has been renewed interest in Fisher's ideas, especially in the literature on the cost of financial intermediation.

Why was Fisher's work not well received at the time, and virtually ignored for 60 years? There are three reasons, I think, one personal, one theoretical, and one empirical. First, Fisher was not well-liked by many of his peers. His self-promoting style grated with some – his *Econometrica* article gratuitously stated that two of the best-read authorities in the field had said that the conclusions of his book were 'both new and important' – and he championed some controversial causes, among them prohibition and eugenics. His stock among both professional economists and the general public, whom he liked to lecture at every opportunity, fell after his optimism on the economy and stock prices was undermined by the Great Crash in 1929, and the subsequent depression. Fisher was consistently optimistic. In 1931 he praised Herbert Hoover for 'his calm reassurances to business and Andrew Mellon, Secretary of the Treasury, for asserting that prosperity was "just around the corner"' (Allen, 1993, 235). It is reassuring that arguably the greatest economist America has produced could not forecast the business cycle. And there was worse. His own finances took a tumble. Fisher had massive debts of his own, many of them to his sister-in-law who bailed him out (see Anna Schwartz's Comment). And in the end Yale had to buy his house in New Haven and rent it back to him to save him from eviction.[9]

The second, and important, reason for the lack of attention paid to Fisher's theory of cycles and depressions is, I believe, that it is not a monetary explanation of economic fluctuations but a real business cycle model. This is because Fisher's model is one in which initial shocks to the economy – and Fisher listed many possible types of shock – are magnified by the debt-deflation transmission mechanism. And Fisher proposed his thesis at a time when the attention of Keynes and others was on the incorporation of monetary factors into a theory of the business cycle. Possibly Keynes felt that he himself had anticipated Fisher, because in 1931 he had written an essay entitled 'The Consequences to the Banks of the Collapse of Money Values'. In this, he emphasised the losses to the banks from a fall in asset values and the impact on their willingness to extend further loans to business – a credit crunch in fact. He described the problems of the time as having their 'roots in the slow and steady sapping of the real resources of the banks as a result of the progressive collapse of money values over the past two years' (Keynes, 1931). Keynes was primarily interested in the consequences of a collapse of asset values for the process of financial intermediation by the banking system. In this respect it was Keynes not Fisher who led the way in stressing the role of the cost of financial intermediation in business cycles. In choosing, as I said earlier, to leave this issue to one side, it is because I believe there are other aspects of Fisher's story which merit analysis.

Schumpeter was one of the very few to recognise that Fisher's debt-deflation theory was a real business cycle model rather than a monetary model. Describing the evolution of Fisher's thought on cycles, Schumpeter (1954) wrote:

> But, though he continued to emphasize the monetary aspects of the phenomenon, he so broadened the basis of his analysis so as to end up with the Debt-Deflation Theory, which, contrary to his unduly restricted claim, applies to all recorded business cycles and is in essence not monetary at all. (1954, p. 1122)[10]

The third reason for the lack of attention paid by Keynes to Fisher's concept of debt-deflation is the very different nature of the depressions in the UK and USA in the early 1930s. I have already drawn attention to the large negative consumption shock which both the USA and UK experienced in the 1990s. Was the same true in the 1930s? The answer is, 'yes' in the USA but 'no' in the UK. Following Temin (1976) and Hall (1986), Romer (1993) has pointed out that in the USA, 'consumption accounted for a much larger fraction of the decline in real GNP in 1930 than in most previous or subsequent recessions'. But the experience of Britain was very different. Table 5.3 shows the fall in GDP and consumption (in real terms) during the Great Depression in our group of 10 countries. It is striking that in the UK consumption fell only in 1932 – and then only by about 0.5 per cent – whereas in the USA consumption fell for four successive years and by 20 per cent in total. Indeed, consumption in the UK fell by over five times as much during the recent recession as in the 1930s. Changes in the terms of trade account for much of the variation shown in Table 5.3. In the USA the terms of trade fell by 16 per cent between 1929 and 1932, in Canada by 13 per cent and in Australia by 20 per cent; in the UK, by contrast, the terms of trade improved by 24 per cent over the same period (Liesner, 1989). But another important difference between the USA and UK was the rapid increase in household debt in the USA during the 1920s. Consumer debt more than doubled during the 1920s in the USA, and in the Great Depression repossession of consumer durables bought on credit was common. In 1932 alone over 10 per cent of cars bought on credit were repossessed (Olney, 1992). The experience of the 1930s as well as the 1990s seems to give support to

Table 5.3   The Great Depression, 1929–33

		Percentage change in:	
		GDP/GNP	Consumption
USA	1929–33	−29.7	−19.7
UK	1929–31	−5.5	−0.6
Australia	1929–31	−7.9	−19.2
Canada	1929–33	−30.1	−18.1
France	1929–32	−8.8	N/A
Germany	1929–32	−23.5	−9.5
Italy	1929–31	−7.0	−4.8
Japan	1930–2	+4.5	−0.9
Norway	1930–1	−8.0	·−2.5
Sweden	1930–2	−11.9	−9.1

N/A = Not available.

Sources: Liesner (1989); Mitchell (1981); Central Bureau of Statistics (1965).

the notion that the interaction between prior increases in household debt and negative demand or supply shocks can lead to prolonged downturns in demand and output.

The basic argument is not new. In his 1978 Yrjö Jahnsson Lectures delivered, of course, in Helsinki, James Tobin described Fisher's debt-deflation as a reverse Pigou real balance effect, and pointed to the dangers of ignoring distributional effects:

> Aggregation would not matter if we could be sure that the marginal propensities to spend from wealth were the same for creditors and debtors. But if the spending propensity were systematically greater for debtors, even by a small amount, the Pigou effect would be swamped by this Fisher effect. (Tobin, 1980, p. 10)

A MODEL OF DEBT-DEFLATION

I turn now to the question of how to model debt-deflation. The key insight is that provided by Tobin (1980), namely that the marginal propensity to spend from wealth differs between debtors and creditors. The microeconomic analysis of debt-deflation, therefore, concerns optimal consumption behaviour under uncertainty. The emphasis will be on the role of precautionary saving. I focus on household consumption rather than corporate investment for two reasons. First, the theory of household behaviour under uncertainty is on a surer footing than that of firms, and I wish to avoid the problems of modelling corporate finance when the Modigliani–Miller theorem does not hold. Second, it was a fall in consumption which characterised both the Great Depression in the USA and the 1990s recession in the Anglo–Saxon world.

The macroeconomic analysis is based on the idea that aggregate demand may be a non-monotonic function of the relative price of assets in terms of the numéraire consumption good. Distributional shocks associated with changes in the relative asset price produce a non-monotonic aggregate demand function. Given appropriate assumptions about aggregate supply this leads to multiple equilibria and to the possibility of cyclical behaviour of the kind described by Fisher. Models of credit cycles can, I believe, be described as belonging to a family of this type.

The key features of the model are:

- two types of agent;
- two goods, a consumption good and a capital asset;
- stochastic and uninsurable endowments.

Central to the model is the impact of *distributional* shocks on the aggregate level of consumption. Agents who had borrowed on the expectation of future returns suffer adverse shocks that lead them to consume less and repay debt. Other agents experience offsetting shocks but do not increase consumption by enough to compensate for the reduction of consumption by the first type. In other words, the marginal propensity to consume out of wealth is higher for debtors than for creditors.[11]

Consumption responses of this kind reflect precautionary saving. In the late 1960s Hayne Leland (1968) and a former President of the EEA, Agnar Sandmo (1970), showed how an increase in uncertainty would reduce consumption if preferences exhibited the property of 'prudence'. For this to be the case the third derivative of the utility function defined over instantaneous consumption must be positive. The papers by Leland and Sandmo inspired a number of problem sets which were given to graduate students of my generation, the answers to which always depended upon the third derivative of the utility function. We can now go one better. For, as Kimball (1990a, 1990b) has shown, the marginal propensity to consume out of wealth in a world of uncertainty depends upon the fourth derivative of utility.[12] What matters is how the degree of prudence changes as net worth changes.

The precautionary saving motive means that an increase in uncertainty about future endowments leads households to save more in order to provide for a rainy day. One of the consequences of precautionary saving is that it explains why, in typical life-cycle models, households may choose not to borrow, and hence why consumption may track income. Carroll (1992) and Deaton (1992) have explored this approach as an alternative to the assumption of exogenous borrowing constraints. But a model in which households do not borrow is hardly a useful basis for an analsis of debt-deflation!

I shall construct a model in which households choose to borrow and in which risk is not fully insurable. For some households, at least, I assume that their endowments come toward the end of life. This is similar to modifying a standard overlapping-generations model so that endowments are received in the second rather than the first period of life.[13] The effect of introducing this consideration is that households are now required to borrow to finance consumption, at least in the early part of life. In fact, I shall use a many-period finite lifetime model, but with concurrent rather than overlapping generations. It is now possible to analyse the interaction between prudence and the response of borrowing to shocks to future income and asset values.

The motivation for recognising the importance of deferred endowments is the existence of *illiquid* assets for which use or control is not easy to separate from ownership, and the returns on which are not verifiable. Households will not be able to issue equity in such assets, and the risks will be uninsurable. Such assets may provide consumption services directly (housing, for example), or generate an investment return which cannot be easily realised until late in life (a private business or anticipated inheritance, for example). The illiquid nature of the assets is crucial, because it means that asset price risk is uninsurable. For example, if there is no rental market (because of government interventon to impose rent controls), housing services can be obtained only by buying an asset on which outside equity cannot easily be issued and which must be financed by debt.[14] This means that the risk of the entire asset return falls on the home-owner. If the only source of uncertainty were returns on a tradable asset, then households would face a standard optimal consumption–portfolio decision problem. They could sell part of their claim on these future returns and switch to a diversified portfolio. This would generally imply holding positive quantities of all financial assets, and households would lend not borrow. With isoelastic utility, for example, consumption would be proportional to current wealth where the constant of proportionality would reflect time preference and the distribution of returns (Samuelson, 1969). Agents with identical preferences and equal access to trading opportunities would consume equal proportions of current wealth. Hence redistributions of wealth would have no effect on aggregate consumption. When assets cannot be traded analytical solutions are generally not to be had, but prudence comes into its own.

To investigate the relationship between shocks to future endowments, borrowing and consumption, I turn now to a simple formal model. There are equal numbers of two types of agents, $i = 1,2$. Both types have finite lives and live for T periods. Preferences are defined over consumption in each period and in period t are given by the additively separable form

$$V_t = E_t \sum_{\tau=0}^{T-t} U(c_{t+\tau}) (1 + \rho)^{-\tau} \tag{5.1}$$

where c denotes consumption, ρ the rate of pure time preference, and E_t the expectations operator conditional upon information available in period t.

The two types of agent differ with respect to their endowments. Type 1 agents are endowed with a fixed quantity of an illiquid capital good which does not depreciate and pays off only in period T when the asset can be redeemed as q units of consumption. The value of q is stochastic and 'news' about its expected value in period T arrives each period. The revision in the expected terminal value of the asset, $(E_t - E_{t-1})q$, constitutes the 'news' in period t about wealth. I shall assume that the risk to q is uninsurable, for example because the return in period T is costly or impossible to verify. Type 1 agents, must therefore, borrow to finance consumption before period T. They are the debtors. The time structure of their endowments is shown in Table 5.4. Access to the capital market is limited to the ability to lend or borrow at a fixed non-stochastic interest rate which, for ease of exposition, is assumed to be zero. Optimal consumption behaviour of Type 1 agents in period t is derived by maximising (5.1) subject to the distribution of 'news' about q and the following budget constraint

$$\sum_{\tau=0}^{T-t} c_{t+\tau}^1 + b_{t-1}^1 = q \tag{5.2}$$

where b_{t-1} is the stock of debt brought forward from the previous period and is equal to cumulated past consumption. The simple dynamics of debt for Type 1 agents are:

Table 5.4 Structure of finite horizon model

	Period 1	Period t	Period T
Type 1: debtors			
Endowments	0	0	q
Expected life-time wealth	$E_1 q$	$E_t q$	q
'News'	$E_1 q - 1$	$(E_t - E_{t-1})q$	$q - E_{T-1} q$
Type 2: creditors			
Endowments	$1 + s_1$	s_t	s_T
Expected life-time wealth	$1 + s_1$	$1 + \sum_{\tau=1}^{t} s_\tau$	$1 + \sum_{\tau=1}^{T} s_\tau$
"News"	s_1	s_t	s_T

$$b_t^1 = b_{t-1}^1 + c_t^1 \tag{5.3}$$

At the beginning of each period 'news' arrives about the value of q in period T. By the law of iterated expectations these revisions to the expected value of q are stochastic shocks with zero mean. The unconditional expectation of q – before the arrival of first-period 'news' – is normalised to unity.

Type 2 agents receive a different structure of endowments from Type 1 agents. But they receive the same unconditional expected value of life-time wealth (see Table 5.4). At the beginning of life they receive one unit of the consumption good which may be consumed or invested at a (zero) non-stochastic interest rate. Access to the capital market is limited to this opportunity to lend or borrow at the safe real rate set on the world capital market. In each period Type 2 agents receive a stochastic labour income, denoted by s_t, which is non-diversifiable and has a zero mean.[15] Type 2 agents will typically save part of their initial endowment ($b_t^2 < 0$). They are the creditors. Their consumption in period t is determined by maximising (5.1) subject to the budget constraint:

$$\sum_{\tau=0}^{T-t} c_{t+\tau}^2 + b_{t-1}^2 = \sum_{\tau=0}^{T-t} s_{t+\tau} \tag{5.4}$$

with debts (assets) evolving according to

$$b_t^2 = b_{t-1}^2 + c_t^2 - s_t \tag{5.5}$$

In order to focus on the impact of distributional shocks, I shall assume that the 'news' for the two types of agent is perfectly negatively correlated, that is

$$s_t = - (E_t - E_{t-1}) \qquad \forall t \tag{5.6}$$

With this assumption *aggregate* lifetime wealth per head, denoted by w, is non-stochastic and constant over time. To see this, note that the expected life-time wealth of a Type 1 agent in period t is $w_t^1 = E_t q$, and of a Type 2 agent is

$$w_t^2 = 1 + \sum_{\tau=1}^{t} s_t$$

$$= 1 - \sum_{\tau=1}^{t} (E_t - E_{\tau-1})q \tag{5.7}$$

$$= 2 - E_t q$$

Total life-time wealth per head, $(w_t^1 + w_t^2)/2$, is, therefore, equal to unity in all periods. The distribution of q is assumed to lie within the interval $[0,2]$.

In order to generate interesting differences in the consumption patterns of debtors and creditors, I shall assume that the distribution of q is *skewed*, with a higher probability of very low realisations for q than of high values. Skewness captures the notion that non-tradable assets can turn out to be almost worthless, and even stock market returns are negatively skewed. This means that the risk of very low consumption is greater for debtors than for creditors, even though expected life-time wealth is the same for the two groups.

The difference in the timing and distribution of endowment means that the consumption functions of creditors and debtors differ. Hence shocks to the distribution of wealth, which follow from 'news' about the value of the asset, will lead to changes in aggregate consumption.[16] To examine this, we need to solve explicitly for the consumption function – the level of consumption in period t expressed as a function of the state variable, the level of debt or assets inherited from period $t-1$, and the stochastic shock in period t. The solution to the model can be found by dynamic programming techniques. In the last period

$$c_T^1 = q - b_{T-1}^1$$

$$c_T^2 = s_T - b_{T-1}^2 \tag{5.8}$$

Similarly backward induction gives

$$c_t^i = f_t^i (b_{t-1}^i, s_t) \qquad i = 1, 2, t = 1 \ldots T \tag{5.9}$$

The consumption function $f(.)$ reflects not only preferences but also the distribution function of endowments. In general there are no analytical solutions, and numerical grid-search techniques must be used either by iterating to find the function $f(.)$ for each t (see King and Robson, 1993) or by evaluating the value function (Deaton, 1992, p. 186). Typical consumption profiles for the two types of agent are shown in Figure 5.4. Precautionary saving means that debtors will typically consume less than creditors before the final period. The greater risk faced by debtors means that, provided preferences exhibit a sufficient degree of decreasing absolute prudence, they have a higher marginal propensity to consume out of expected wealth. The location of the curves also depends upon the past history of shocks and consumption.

The expected wealth of an agent in period t is equal to his expected life-time endowment *less* his cumulative consumption to date. Using this relationship we may map the consumption functions shown in Figure 5.4 into functions expressing consumption in terms of the expected

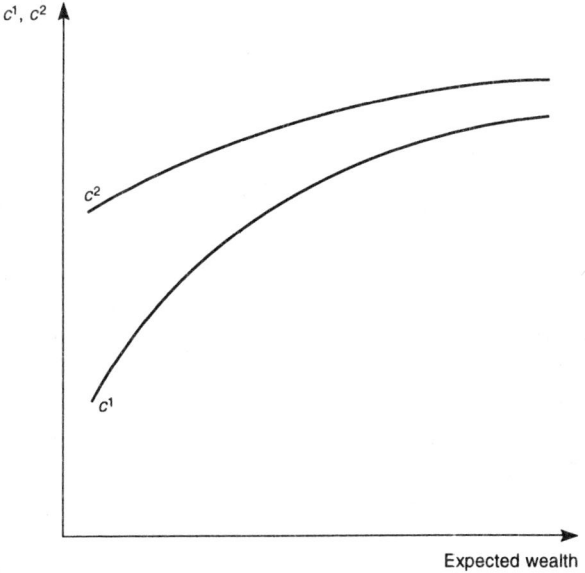

Figure 5.4 Consumption functions

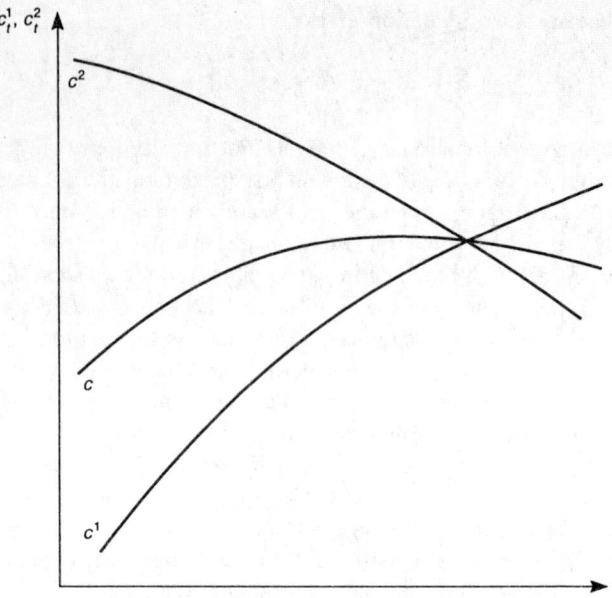

Figure 5.5   Consumption and expected asset values

value of the asset, $E_t q$. These are shown in Figure 5.5, together with aggregate consumption per head, which is the average of the two curves. For debtors consumption is an increasing and for creditors a decreasing function of $E_t q$. At both low and high values for the asset price one or other of the agents has a high marginal propensity to consume out of wealth, and the result is that aggregate consumption is first an increasing and then a decreasing function of the expected asset value.[17]

This non-monotonic relationship provides the basis for some interesting dynamics. In the model described above there was no supply side. Consider now the introduction of a supply response to expected returns.[18] Figure 5.6 plots the aggregate demand function – total consumption as a function of $E_t q$. Aggregate supply is assumed to be (slightly) increasing in the expected asset price to reflect the relative inelasticity of labour supply and the greater responsiveness of entrepreneurial effort to expected returns. It is possible, though by no means either necessary or likely, that there are multiple equilibria, as shown in Figure 5.6. Of the three equilibria shown in Figure 5.6 two are stable and one unstable. Financial instability is clearly possible. Even without any further demand shocks resulting from news about future

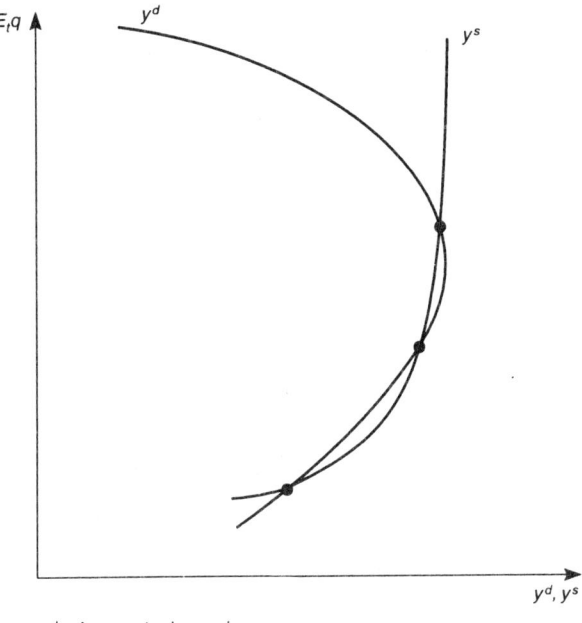

y^d, Aggregate demand
y^s, Aggregate supply

Figure 5.6 Multiple equilibria

endowments, cyclical fluctuations in demand and output can arise as the economy moves over time from one equilibrium to another. Fisher went on to analyse the impact of attempts to reduce debt on the level of asset prices, which in turn exacerbated the initial shock. To analyse this requires an extension of the above model to allow for endogenous asset prices. In a stochastic setting this is by no means straightforward. Kiyotaki and Moore (1993) have produced a very interesting deterministic model of this chain reaction in which falls in asset prices reduce the collateral available to support borrowing. Given the (crucial) assumption that borrowing is necessary not only to finance investment but also some part of current expenditure, they show that falls in asset prices reduce the ability to borrow and hence investment, a process which comes to an end when creditors find assets cheap enough to buy.[19]

EMPIRICAL EVIDENCE

Distributional effects were at the heart of the model that I presented. I want, therefore, to conclude with two pieces of empirical evidence on debt and consumption based on cross-section data.

The first takes us back to the group of 10 countries with which I started this chapter. The correlation between the rise in household debt in the 1980s and the subsequent shortfall in GDP growth between 1989 and 1992 shown in Figure 5.1 is not particularly strong. But the theory relates to the impact of debt on consumption growth. I have repeated the exercise, this time plotting the shortfall in consumption growth (defined as before as the difference between the growth of consumption in 1989–92 and its average growth in 1974–1989) against the change in the ratio of household debt to GDP. The results for ten countries are shown in Figure 5.7 (the solid line denotes the OLS regression). The correlation is much closer than in Figure 5.1 and the significance of the relationship does not depend upon any individual observation. Similar conclusions can be drawn from VAR estimates of consumption and output.

The second piece of evidence exploits regional differences within a country. As before, looking at variations within a country helps to control for differences in national fiscal and monetary policy shocks. Of course if the transmission mechanism of such policies operates via distributional effects then such effects will appear in cross-sectional data within a country. In the UK the recession exhibited an unusual regional pattern, with the normally prosperous south-east region more adversely affected than the manufacturing regions of the north. Unemployment differentials among the regions narrowed very significantly. And house prices fell sharply, even in nominal terms, in the south. The result was that many households found that the nominal value of their mortgage exceeded the market value of their house – a position of 'negative equity'. Of the 11 standard regions in the UK, only seven generate sufficiently large annual samples of households in the FES for estimated changes over time to be reliable. For these seven regions Figure 5.8 shows the relationship between the increase in average real weekly non-housing expenditure from 1988 to 1990 and the new debt acquired by households relative to their income over the same period. The regions fall into two groups, those with low ratios of new debt to income and high consumption growth and those with high new debt ratios and low consumption growth.

These results can be no more than suggestive of the importance of

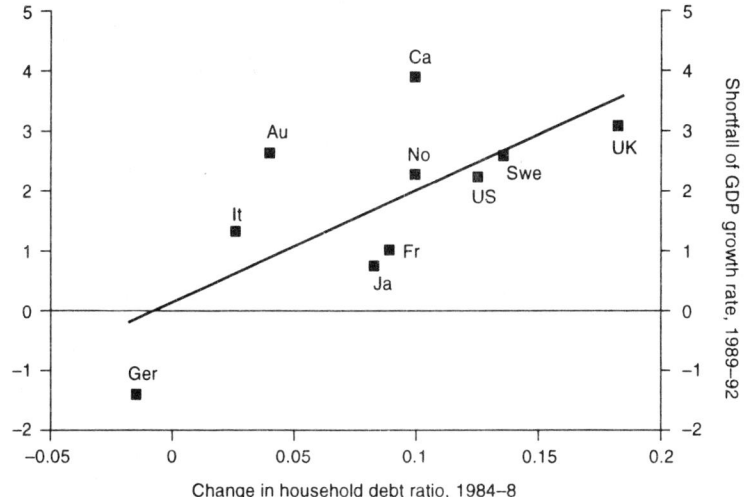

Sources: OECD (1992); own calculations.

Figure 5.7   Consumption and debt, the 1990s: 10 major countries

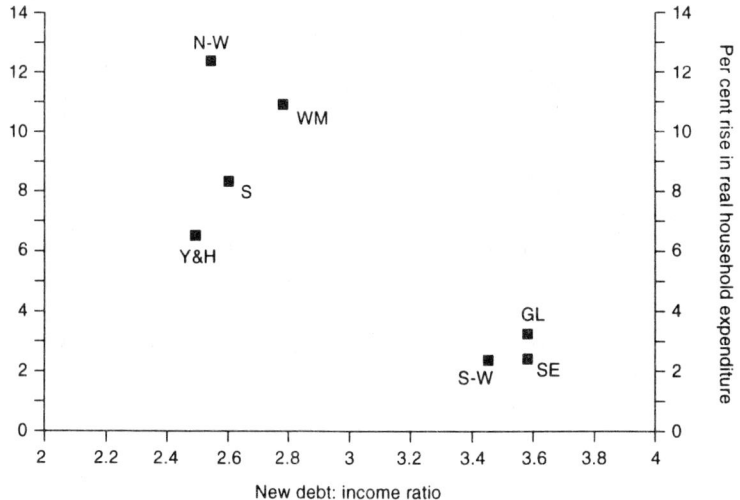

Source: Bank of England.

Figure 5.8   Regional consumption and debt, UK households, 1980–90

precautionary saving in the face of high debt levels. But they illustrate the potential value of microeconomic data for the analysis of those macroeconomic issues where the assumption of a representative agent conceals the essence of the phenomenon of interest. I believe debt-deflation to be a good example of such an issue.

CONCLUSIONS

Debt-deflation has many facets, as shown by Fisher's nine factors. I have examined only one – the impact of distributional shocks between debtors and creditors on aggregate demand. I do not mean to play down the significance of the other aspects of the story, but rather to play up an aspect that is at the heart of Fisher's analysis, namely the real business cycle nature of his model of debt-deflation. To do this I have focused on purely distributional shocks. The observation that distributional shocks can cause changes in aggregate demand which are significant from the macroeconomic perspective may seem a statement of the obvious. As Robert Louis Stevenson put it in his diary of *Travels with a Donkey* after a night in the open air, 'I thought I had rediscovered one of those truths which are revealed to savages and hid from political economists' (Stevenson, 1897). Yet it is worth making the point that the assumption of a representative consumer can sometimes conceal more than it reveals in macroeconomic behaviour.[20]

I have argued that debt-deflation should be seen as a real business cycle rather than a monetary phenomenon. The model I presented was a real model. It is true that unanticipated monetary shocks can exacerbate the problems caused by debt deflation because they lead to instability in the price level and to macroeconomic instability more generally. And it was macroeconomic instability against which both Fisher and Keynes fought so hard. As Keynes wrote in 1937

> I find, looking back, that it was Professor Irving Fisher who was the great-grandparent who first influenced me strongly towards regarding money as a 'real' factor. (Keynes, 1937b).

And Keynes and Fisher were united in their advocacy of price stability.[21] But it is the real structure of the economy which is crucial. A housing market in which many families with low net worth can only obtain housing services by purchasing 100 per cent of an asset worth a multiple of their wealth, exposes such households to great risk.

Debt-deflation is a propagation mechanism which multiplies small shocks into potentially large changes in aggregate demand and output. The existence of multiple equilibria produces the possibility of instability. To understand this requires a real business cycle model, but one in which the representative consumer is replaced by at least two types of agent, debtors and creditors. There is a lesson here for the use of macroeconomic models in policy analysis. There is no single model that can possibly hope to capture all the features of the world that may be relevant in the future. It is the pretence that one model can hope *ex ante* to incorporate all relevant features of the world which is the undoing of large econometric forecasting models. Our aim should be to identify important issues of the day and construct a model which casts light on the problem in question.

Fisher's work on debt-deflation was launched – first in his lecture and subsequently in his book – in 1932. Later that year Fisher also gave a presidential address – to the American Statistical Association. In it, Fisher discussed economics and forecasting. He compared economic forecasting with both astronomy – where accurate predictions of, say, eclipses were possible, and meteorology, where predictions of whether the weather would permit an observation of an eclipse were impossible. He continued,

> Contrast this with our economic predictions. We are now going through an economic eclipse which began in September, 1929. But few if any economists predicted it, or, if so, they failed to make their predictions public . . . It is well that we face these failures and that, when we fail, we confess it with due humility. [Fisher continued] I confess it . . . in September 1929 I publicly stated my belief that . . . there would be a recession . . . Unfortunately I also stated my belief that the recession would be slight and short; and this proved untrue . . . I can now see that my failure was due to insufficient knowledge of both kinds, scientific and historical . . . As to the laws governing depressions, I did not then know . . . the important role of over-indebtedness. (Fisher, 1933b)

Fisher was a poor forecaster but a great economist. We should learn from his experience. Economists should not play the role of fairground fortune tellers. If Oscar Wilde were alive today he would surely describe economic forecasters as the unfathomable in pursuit of the unpredictable. Fisher was sceptical of a purely statistical approach to the discovery of economic relationships – an approach he described as 'the grinding out of correlation coefficients between statistical series whose inner relationships are unknown or possibly non-existent' (1933b). A theoretical framework was essential to the advancement of understanding:

> Theory and fact must go hand in hand. Otherwise the world of observation and statistical data will be almost meaningless for lack of any rational framework to fit into; and conversely our theory will be almost meaningless for lack of any statistical expression or verification. (Fisher, 1933b)

That clarion call of Fisher's could serve as the motto for a research programme into the construction of real business cycle models without a representative consumer, and the use of microeconomic data to throw light on macroeconomic phenomena. There is much to do.

Notes

1. Reprinted from European Economic Review, Vol. 3/4, 1994, Mervyn King, 'Debt Deflation: Theory and Evidence', pp. 419–445, 1994, with kind permission of Elsevier Science B.V., Amsterdam, The Netherlands. I am grateful to Alex Bowen, John Campbell, Andrew Crockett, Oliver Hart, Don Moggridge, John Moore, James Poterba, Agnar Sandmo and Roland Wales for helpful discussions and suggestions, and to the Bank of England for research support.
2. Similar results hold for total private sector debt but there are difficulties in obtaining consistent time series for corporate sector debt in all countries. The model presented in this chapter relates primarily to the behaviour of household consumption.
3. Among the authors who have contributed to this literature are Bernanke, Gertler, Greenwald and Stiglitz. A survey of the relevance of these papers to the causes of the Great Depression may be found in Calomiris (1993).
4. In the USA output fell from peak to trough by 2.2 per cent over three quarters, whereas in the UK non-oil output fell by 3.9 per cent to its trough in 1992:1.
5. In the USA consumption fell for two consecutive quarters and by 1.5 per cent from peak to trough.
6. Expenditure on housing during this period was affected by the switch from rates to the Community Charge. It is, therefore, preferable to look at non-housing expenditure when making comparisons over time. In addition to the effect of the stock of debt relative to expected future incomes, the cash flow burden of servicing debt might also have lowered consumption.

7. The copy in the Bank of England library has a personal inscription from Irving Fisher to the then Governor, Montagu Norman.

8. Keynes also contributed to a *Festschrift* for Fisher in 1936 which made no reference to debt-deflation (Keynes, 1937a). And, in line with the absence of references in the *Collected Writings* of Keynes, there is no reference to Fisher's work on debt-deflation in the two recent biographies of Keynes (Moggridge, 1992; Skidelsy, 1992).

   The correspondence between Keynes and Fisher is in the *Keynes Papers* in the library of King's College, Cambridge. The most interesting item is a letter from Fisher to Keynes dated 5 May 1916:

   > I remember your telling me when I was in England a number of years ago, that you had at one time made a study of the records of the dinner hour in England for several centuries and that you had discovered that the hour of that function had become gradually later, at about a certain rate per century. Can you let me have any definite figures on this point, as to rate of change per century or the times at different century markers? I am gathering material for a book on progress which I hope to write some day.

   Sadly, no record remains of the research results.

9. Tobin (1987, 371) and Allen (1993, Chapter 9). There are two biographies of Fisher, one by his son (Fisher, 1956), and the other by Robert Loring Allen (1993) published after the first draft of this chapter was completed.

10. It is worth quoting Schumpeter in full on the contribution of these ideas:

    > Ostensibly, the burden is chiefly laid upon the fact that in the atmosphere of prosperity debts are accumulated, the inevitable liquidation of which, with the attendant breaks in the price structure, constitutes the core of depression. Behind this surface mechanism there are the really operative factors – new technological and commercial possibilities chiefly – which Fisher does not fail to see but which he banishes to the apparently secondary place of 'debt starters' . . . so that . . . the true dimensions of what is really a great performance are so completely hidden from the reader's view that they have to be dug out laboriously and in fact never impressed the profession as they should have done. (1954, 1122)

11. If shocks were diversifiable through either insurance or asset markets, then they would have no impact on consumption. But the empirical relevance of incomplete consumption insurance has been demonstrated by Acemoglu and Scott (1993), Cochrane (1993), Mace (1993) and Miles (1993). Mace (1993) finds that full insurance cannot be rejected for exponential utility (constant absolute risk aversion) but is rejected for isoelastic utility (constant relative risk aversion).

12. In a two-period model with additively separable preferences, an in-

crease in uncertainty, holding expected wealth constant, will raise the marginal propensity to consume out of wealth, provided that preferences display decreasing absolute prudence, where the degree of prudence may be defined analogously to the degree of risk aversion but in terms of the marginal utility rather than the utility function. Kimball (1990a) has proposed an index of the (absolute) degree of prudence defined as $p(c) = -[u'''(c)/u''(c)]$. This index measures the intensity of the desire for precautionary saving, and reflects the propensity to anticipate future risks by cutting back current consumption. Strictly decreasing absolute prudence is satisfied by isoelastic utility functions (constant relative risk aversion); exponential utility (constant absolute risk aversion) implies a constant degree of absolute prudence. In a multi-period setting with isoelastic utility a sufficient condition for the result to hold is that the degree of risk aversion exceed unity.

13. In an unpublished paper delivered some years ago in Edinburgh, Ragnar Bentzel discussed such a model.

14. I shall assume that marginal utility at zero consumption is infinite. Hence agents will never borrow more than they can repay in period T with certainty. Any claim that there are inadequate resources to repay debt will be known to be false, and can be deterred by a sufficiently large legal penalty on a refusal to repay debt. With no default risk agents are able to borrow at an interest rate free of any default premium – the safe 'world' interest rate.

15. This assumption – that the mean value of labour income is received at the beginning of life – is made for convenience.

16. Differences in the marginal propensity to consume are not imposed exogenously, as in the Cambridge theory of distribution for example, but reflect endogenous optimal behaviour. Hassler (1993) argues that the influence of precautionary saving may be small relative to the impact of income shocks on the demand for goods such as durables for which there are significant transaction costs.

17. Mishkin (1976, 1978) emphasised the role played by household balance sheets as a structural transmission mechanism through which shocks led to a fall in aggregate demand.

18. I am assuming here that non-monotonic aggregate demand functions are generic to precautionary saving in a world without a representative consumer.

19. O'Connell (1987) analyses the investment decision when macroeconomic shocks interfere with the ability of agents to build a reputation with the suppliers of finance. Optimal behaviour then leads to greater fluctuations than would occur if the signals could be disentangled.

20. The importance of heterogeneity has been stressed by Hildenbrand (1983, 1989), Grandmont (1992) and Kirman (1992).

21. See Bank of England (1992).

References

Acemoglu, D. and A. Scott (1993) 'Consumer Confidence and Rational Expectations: Are Agents' Beliefs Consistent with the Theory?' (London: London School of Economics, mimeo.

Allen, R.L. (1993) *Irving Fisher* (Oxford: Basil Blackwell).

Bank of England (1992) 'The Case for Price Stability', *Bank of England Quarterly Bulletin*, 32, 441–8.

Bernanke, B. (1983) 'Non-Monetary Effects of the Financial Crisis in the Propagation of the Great Depression', *American Economic Review*, 73, 257–76.

Bernanke, B. (1993) 'The World on a Cross of Gold', *Journal of Monetary Economics*, 31, 251–67.

Blanchard, O. (1993) 'Consumption and the Recession of 1990–1991', *American Economic Review, Papers and Proceedings*, 83, 270–4.

Calomiris, C.W. (1993) 'Financial Factors in the Great Depression', *Journal of Economic Perspectives*, 7 (Spring), 61–85.

Carroll, C.D. (1992) 'The Buffer-Stock Theory of Saving: Some Macroeconomic Evidence', *Brookings Papers on Economic Activity*, 2, 61–156.

Central Bureau of Statistics (1965) *National Accounts 1865–1960* (Norway: CBS).

Cochrane, J.H. (1993) 'A Simple Test of Consumption Insurance', *Journal of Political Economy*, 99, 957–76.

Deaton, A.S. (1992) *Understanding Consumption* (Oxford: Clarendon Press).

Eichengreen, B. (1992) *Golden Fetters: The Gold Standard and the Great Depression 1919–1939* (Oxford University Press).

Fisher, I. (1932) *Booms and Depressions* (London: George Allen & Unwin).

Fisher, I. (1933a) 'The Debt-Deflation Theory of Great Depressions', *Econometrica*, 1 (October), 337–357.

Fisher, I. (1933b) 'Statistics in the Service of Economics', *Journal of the American Statistical Association*, 28, 1–13.

Fisher, I.N. (1956) *My Father, Irving Fisher* (New York: Comet).

Friedman, M. and A.J. Schwartz (1963) *A Monetary History of the United States, 1867–1960* (Princeton: Princeton University Press).

Grandmonth, J.-M. (1992) 'Aggregation, Learning, and Rationality', CEPREMAP, *Discussion Paper*, 9214, mimeo.

Hall, R.E. (1986) 'The Role of Consumption in Economic Fluctuations', in R.J. Gordon (ed.), *The American Business Cycle: Continuity and Change* (Chicago: The University of Chicago Press).

Hall, R.E. (1993) 'Macro Theory and the Recession of 1990–1991', *American Economic Review, Papers and Proceedings*, 83, 275–9.

Hassler, J. (1993) 'Variations in Risk – A Cause of Fluctuations in Demand?', *Seminar Paper*, (Stockholm: Institute for International Economics).

Hildenbrand, W. (1983) 'On the Law of Demand', *Econometrica*, 51, 997–1019.

Hildenbrand, W. (1989) 'Facts and Ideas in Economic Theory', *European Economic Review*, 33, 251–76.

Keynes, J.M. (1931) 'The Consequences to the Banks of the Collapse of Money Values', in J.M. Keynes *Essays in Persuasion* (London: Macmillan; New York: W.W. Norton, 1963).

Keynes, J.M. (1937a) 'The Theory of the Rate of Interest', in A.D. Gayer (ed.), *The Lessons of Monetary Experience: Essays in Honour of Irving Fisher* (New York: Farrar & Rinehart).

Keynes, J.M. (1937b) 'Alternative Theories of the Rate of Interest', *Economic Journal*, 47, 241–52.

Kimball, M.S. (1990a) 'Precautionary Saving in the Small and in the Large', *Econometrica*, 58, 53–73.

Kimball, M.S. (1990b) 'Precautionary Saving and the Marginal Propensity to Consume', National Bureau of Economic Research, *Working Paper*, 3403.

King, M.A. and M.H. Robson (1993) 'A Dynamic Model of Investment and Growth', *Scandinavian Journal of Economics*, 95, 445–66.

Kirman, A.P. (1992) 'Whom or What Does the Representative Individual Represent?', *Journal of Economic Perspectives*, 6, 117–36.

Kiyotaki, N. and J. Moore (1993) 'Credit Cycles', London School of Economics, mimeo.

Leland, H.E. (1968) 'Saving and Uncertainty: The Precautionary Demand for Saving', *Quarterly Journal of Economics*, 82, 465–73.

Liesner, T. (1989) *One Hundred years of Economic Statistics* (London: *The Economist* Publications).

Mace, B.J. (1993) 'Full Insurance in the Presence of Aggregate Uncertainty', *Journal of Political Economy*, 99, 928–56.

Miles, D. (1993) 'A Household Level Study of the Determinants of Incomes and Consumption' (London: Birkbeck College), mimeo.

Minsky, H.P. (1977) 'A Theory of Systemic Fragility', in E.I. Altman and A.W. Sametz (eds), *Financial Crises* (New York: Wiley).

Minsky, H.P. (1982) 'Debt Deflation Processes in Today's Institutional Environment', *Banca Nazionale del Lavoro Quarterly Review*, 143, 377–93.

Mishkin, F.S. (1976) 'Illiquidity, Consumer Durable Expenditure, and Monetary Policy', *American Economic Review*, 66, 642–54.

Mishkin, F.S. (1978) 'The Household Balance Sheet and the Great Depression', *Journal of Economic History*, 38, 918–37.

Mitchell, B.R. (1981) *European Historical Statistics 1750–1975*, 2nd edn, (London: Macmillan).

Moggridge, D.E. (1992) *Maynard Keynes: An Economist's Biography* (London: Routledge).

O'Connell, S.A. (1987) 'Moral Hazard, Reputation, and Intertemporal Substitution of Bankruptcies', CARESS, *Working Paper*, 87–18, University of Pennsylvania, mimeo.

OECD (1992) *Economic Outlook*, 52 (Paris: OECD).

Olney, M.L. (1992) 'Household Credit, Default Consequences, and Consumption in the 1930s: the Importance of Institutional Characteristics', University of Massachusetts, mimeo.

Perry, G.L. and C.L. Schultze (1993) 'Was this Recession Different? Are They All Different?', *Brookings Papers on Economic Activity*, 1, 145–211.

Romer, C.D. (1993) 'The Nation in Depression', *Journal of Economic Perspectives*, 7, 19–39.

Samuelson, P.A. (1969) 'Lifetime Portfolio Selection by Dynamic Stochastic Programming', *Review of Economics and Statistics*, 51, 239–46.

Sandmo, A. (1970) 'The Effect of Uncertainty on Saving Decisions', *Review of Economic Studies*, 37, 353–60.

Schumpeter, J.A. (1934) 'Depressions', in J.A. Schumpeter, *The Economics of the Recovery Program* (New York: McGraw-Hill).

Schumpeter, J.A. (1954) *History of Economic Analysis* (Oxford: Oxford University Press).

Skidelsky, R. (1992) *John Maynard Keynes, Volume 2: the Economist as Saviour* (London: Macmillan).

Stevenson, R.L. (1897) *Travels with a Donkey* (London: Routledge & Kegan Paul).

Temin, P. (1976) *Did Monetary Forces Cause the Great Depression?* (New York: W.W. Norton).

Temin, P. (1993) 'Transmission of the Great Depression', *Journal of Economic Perspectives*, 7(2), 87–102.

Tobin, J. (1980) *Asset Accumulation and Economic Activity* (Oxford: Basil Blackwell).

Tobin, J. (1987) 'Fisher, Irving', entry in J. Eatwell (ed.), *The New Palgrave Dictionary of Economics* (London: Macmillan), 369–76.

Comment

Allan H. Meltzer

It is a pleasure to discuss King's lucid Chapter 5. King is concerned with two important issues: the current or recent prolonged recession in leading market economies, particularly in Europe and Japan, and the comparatively large fall in consumer spending during the recession.

Irving Fisher emphasised the role of rising real debt values in the depression of the 1930s. Fisher's hypothesis did not attract much support, particularly during the long post-war inflation. Recently, there has been a change. In the 1980s, Latin American debtors had to reduce spending, often including consumer spending, to service their international debts. In this case, however, the debts were denominated in foreign currencies. When the creditor countries reduced expected inflation and raised real interest rates, the burden on debtors was real; wealth and spending declined in many debtor countries.

King explores the debt-deflation hypothesis to see whether disinflation can have an effect in a closed economy where creditors' and debtors' decisions are summed to get the aggregate response. One problem with the debt-deflation hypothesis is that it has a twin – the creditors' gains equal the debtors' losses. Economists do not usually find much that is compelling in stories about large aggregative effects of changes in the wealth or income distribution. To pull the rabbit of an aggregate loss out of a distributional hat requires some kind of hat trick.

King takes the reader in a series of precise steps through one set of logical foundations for the debt-deflation hypothesis in a closed economy. I have a few comments on his model. Then I offer an alternative hypothesis about the effects of assets and debt, discuss the evidence King presents and look at some other evidence.

ISSUES OF THEORY

The central proposition that puts the rabbit *into* the hat is Tobin's (1980) assumption that the marginal propensity to consume with respect to wealth is larger for debtors than for creditors. King does not make this assumption, but he does the closest thing. He makes three assumptions that produce the desired result. First, he fixes the shape of the utility functions so that debtors are averse to large changes. Second, he assumes that the distribution of shocks to consumption is skewed, and there is a non-vanishing probability of very large shocks. These assumptions are made very explicit. Together with the assumption that consumption depends on wealth, they imply that in the event of a large negative shock to the debtors' wealth, debtors' and creditors' changes in consumption are unequal. It does not follow that the redistribution of wealth reduces aggregate consumption. There could be few debtors and a large number of creditors. King assumes that the number of debtors and creditors is equal and that each debtor and creditor is a representative agent. This third assumption is sufficient for the desired result.

This strikes me as a long and odd way to the result, so I next ask why King chose this particular hypothesis. The apparent answer lies in his desire to use the real business cycle as the transmission mechanism for debt-deflation. A key assumption of the real business cycle model is that money is always neutral and King, unlike Irving Fisher, wants to maintain that assumption in the short run.

Fisher's debt-deflation occurs *because* the real value of existing debt – surely a real variable – changes with a nominal variable – the price level or the rate of inflation. In standard real business cycle theories, price-level changes do not matter for aggregate wealth; the losses to debtors balance the real effects of the gains to creditors. But with an aggregate effect resulting from redistribution, this is no longer so. Particularly for the UK, debt-deflation and disinflation were consequences of monetary policy. Creditors and debtors did not wake up and decide to revalue debts; they responded to the policy of the Bank of England and the Treasury. These agencies decided to achieve disinflation by pegging the *nominal* exchange rate to the DM.[1] Hence King violates a main proposition of real business cycle theory; consumption falls because the change in a nominal variable has a real effect.

Let me offer an alternative hypothesis, based on Brunner and Meltzer (1976), in which debt matters but distribution effects within the private sector do not. Let the central bank decide to disinflate. This lowers money growth, raises nominal interest rates and reduces nominal asset prices. If output prices adjust more slowly than asset prices, the decline in nominal asset prices has a real effect. Let the reduction in nominal asset prices be a permanent change reflecting the growing expectation that future inflation will be lower than previously anticipated. Since capital must eventually sell at its replacement cost, output prices are now expected to rise less than anticipated before the policy change. With some price rigidity, output falls.

If the assets include buildings, building prices reflect the lower anticipated rate of inflation. Rental prices are typically fixed in long-term leases. Hence asset prices decline now and predict that rental prices will decline before the disinflation is complete. Asset prices also fall relative to the price of new production, so construction falls.

In Brunner and Meltzer, equilibrium on the output market occurs when output, y, equals aggregate spending, d,

$$y = d(i - \pi, P, p, \ldots, e)$$

where i, π, P, p and e are respectively the nominal rate of interest, the anticipated rate of inflation, the asset price level, the output price level, and the expected real return to real capital per unit of real capital. The presence of e distinguishes changes in asset prices that occur because e changes from other effects on the nominal asset price.

In the recent disinflation, P declined relative to p and $i-\pi$ rose. This depressed output, particularly in countries where disinflationary pressure was most severe. The fall in P also reduced the value of equity in buildings (and other durable assets) relative to the mortgages on these buildings leading to default, renegotiation, and transfers of title.

This hypothesis emphasises the role of changes in asset prices relative to the prices of new production. There is considerable evidence from many countries and over many time periods that prices of assets traded on open markets move in advance of output prices. For buildings and land, whose prices are more difficult to measure accurately, the evidence is of necessity harder to assess. The recent experience of Japan, however, shows that during the inflation and disinflation from 1986 to 1992, land and building prices in Tokyo and other major cities moved up and down much more than output prices.

The implication of this discussion is that the wealth effect on consumption need not be large, and the distributional effects can be unimportant for aggregates, as they typically are. The relative price effect on spending and output of changes in the relation of asset to output prices requires, however, that output prices are not always equal to the asset's replacement cost. If King would take this step, he could dispense with the following six features of his hypothesis that have little empirical support:

1   a substantial aggregative effect of wealth redistribution;
2   debt-deflation as a major cause of the recent recession;
3   the importance assigned to differences in marginal propensities to consume between creditors and debtors;
4   some assets, particularly real property, are not tradable;
5   limitations on household diversification;
6   denial of the monetary causes of the recent recession.

EMPIRICAL ISSUES

Let me turn to some of the evidence on which King relies. Figures 5.1 and 5.7 in Chapter 5 are similar. Figure 5.7 replaces the deviation of output from trend with the deviation of consumption from trend.

Figures 5.1 and 5.7 depend very much on the position of Germany. Germany is the only country with a positive deviation of output or consumption from trend in 1989–92. (A positive deviation is recorded as a negative shortfall.) Without Germany there is very little relation, as shown by comparing the original (p. 219) to the revised Figure 7 (Figure D5.1). The revised figure removes Germany, but all other points remain undisturbed. The positive relation is no longer apparent.

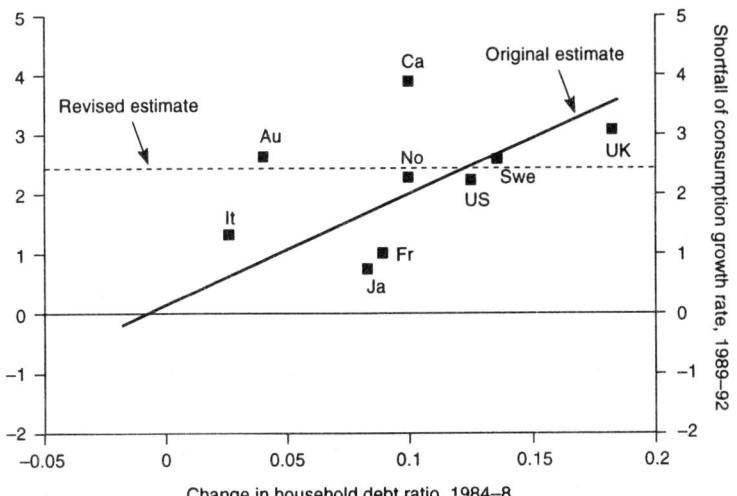

Source: OECD (1992); King's calculations in Chapter 5.

Figure D5.1   Revised Figure 5.7: consumption and debt, 1990s, Germany omitted.

'Germany' means the former West Germany. Western German consumption spending is above trend from 1989 to 1992 principally because of monetary and real factors. The principal real factor is the end of East Germany as a separate state. This alone would not accelerate consumer spending in Western Germany. The monetary factor was critical. The former West German government agreed to a windfall for the former East Germans. The latter spent much of the windfall on goods produced in Western Germany. This is included in West German output along with part of the Eastern German's spending and secondary consumer spending by West German residents. The small decline in the household debt ratio played at most a minor role.

Figure 5.3 of Chapter 5 compares consumption of UK home-owners with and without a mortgage. The two groups differ, and the difference of five percentage points for the change in average expenditure is impressive. I believe a relatively large fraction of UK mortgages are indexed. Rising interest rates would affect discretionary spending by tightening the budget constraint. King should separate the effect of rising interest rates from the effect of debt.

I do not understand the message in King's Figure 5.8. As it stands, it suggests that *non-housing* expenditure increased least where the debt–income ratio was highest. This pattern could occur if the heavier debtors spent proportionally more on housing or borrowed to buy equities or to invest.

King's Figure 5.8 reminds us that there are major differences between the north and the south-east. Inspection suggests that the within-group difference for the change in spending in the north is larger than the differences between the north and the south-east. The within-group difference is unrelated to the debt position.

FINAL REMARKS

Professor King has done a fine job of making a silk purse out of a sow's ear. Stripped of the metaphor, he has offered an explicit hypothesis about how wealth redistribution can affect aggregate spending in an equilibrium model.

Missing from his story are the Bank of England, the Bundesbank, and their colleagues in other European countries. Following the real shock to Germany in 1989, under the policies of the German government, German expansion and borrowing required an appreciation of the German mark. Under the fixed exchange rate system, all members

Table D5.1   Growth and real exchange rates, 1989–92

Country	Change in PPP relative to Germany (per cent)		Growth of real output (per cent)
	Jun. 1990–Jul. 1992	Jun. 1990–Nov. 1993	1989–92
Austria	−2.0	−5.0	8.8
Belgium	+3.3	−3.3	5.7
Denmark	−2.4	−7.3	4.6
Finland	−11.0	−28.7	−10.7
France	+1.1	−4.3	4.6
Italy	+5.8	−16.1	4.4
Netherlands	+9.4	+7.1	7.8
Portugal	+25.4	+10.9	8.1
Spain	+20.0	−4.0	6.7
Sweden	+9.2	−13.3	−1.6
UK	+2.4	−10.8	−2.3

appreciated against the USA, Japan and other non-EMS countries. Appreciation was both nominal and real and imposed disinflation on all Germany's partners in the EMS.

In the UK, the monetary disinflation was severe. Growth of the monetary base fell each year from more than 10 per cent in 1988 to 3 per cent in 1991. For the three-quarters of 1992 before devaluation and floating, the monetary base fell by more than 2 per cent at annual rates.[2]

Table D5.1 suggests how much the appreciation of real exchange rates contributed to the European recession. Real exchange rates are measured as real, purchasing power parities relative to Germany. Output growth is real output at 1985 prices and exchange rates. All data are from the OECD.

Nominal exchange rates remained fixed until September 1992. Prices in the EMS had to fall relative to German prices to adjust real exchange rates within the EMS. Germany chose to disinflate, so all the fixed exchange rate countries had to disinflate relative to Germany to adjust real exchange rates. Since some prices and costs are not fully flexible, output or its growth rate fell during the adjustment.

As expected, column (1) of Table D5.1 shows that in most countries real (PPP) exchange rates appreciated relative to Germany before the realignments of 1992 and 1993. Most depreciated subsequently. The size of the depreciation is a measure of the over-valuation of the real (PPP) exchange rates in these countries.

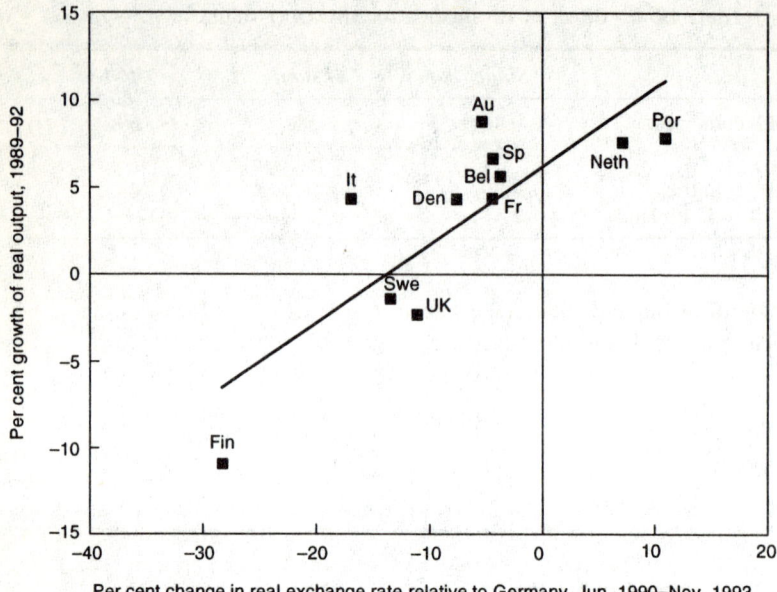

Figure D5.2   Effect of revaluation on growth, Finland omitted

Figure D5.2 suggests that the larger the real over-valuation, the slower was growth (or the larger was the decline) of real output from 1989 to 1992. Note that the exchange rate data extend beyond the period 1989–92 for which growth of real output is shown. Most of the devaluations of nominal and real exchange rates occurred in late 1992 or early 1993. That is why I interpret Figure D5.2 as showing the effect of over-valuation on output and growth. I recognise that an alternative inter-pretation is that countries with the highest growth had the largest appreciation and conversely. The timing of the devaluations, and their magnitude, casts doubt on this interpretation. Also, two countries that devalued real and nominal exchange rates most, Sweden and the UK, have now increased growth.

I ran two regressions of the change in the real exchange rate on the growth of real output using the data underlying Figure D5.2. The first includes 11 countries. The second excludes Finland. The Finnish de-valuation and decline in real output reflect in part the loss of markets in the former Soviet Union. The results are shown in Table D5.2.

The data support the hypothesis that real appreciation depressed output.

Table D5.2   Effect of revaluation on growth (*t*-values in parenthesis)

	Slope	*Constant*	R^2
11 countries	0.46 (4.52)	6.38	.69
10 countries (excl. Finland)	0.30 (2.51)	6.08	.44

Omitting Finland rotates the line in Figure D5.2 and lowers the slope. The principal finding remains.

Notes

1. For the USA and Japan, a principal shock was the change in the expected rate of inflation following central bank decisions to disinflate. In the principal countries of the EU, as in the UK, the principal shock was German disinflation with fixed exchange rates.
2. Growth rates are the annual average of quarterly rates of change. For 1989 and 1990, the growth rates are 9.4 and 4.6 per cent.

Reference

Brunner, K. and A.H. Meltzer (1976) 'An Aggregative Theory for a Closed Economy', in J. Stein (ed.), *Monetarism* (Amsterdam: North Holland), 69–103, reprinted in K. Brunner and A.H. Meltzer (eds), *Monetary Economics* (Oxford and New York: Basil Blackwell, 1989), 159–92.

Comment

Geoffrey E. Wood

Chapter 5 is fascinating. It raises questions in economic history; in the history of economic thought; and in economic analysis. In this Comment these are considered in that order, after some preliminary remarks.

The starting point of the chapter comprises two linked observations. In the recession just past, in Britain, the USA, and some other countries also, the ratio of consumption to income fell much more than it has done in other post-1945 recessions. Further, this ratio also fell sharply in the USA in the Great Depression of the 1930s; but it did not do so in Britain in the same period. Second, all those episodes in which the consumption: income ratio fell were preceded by sharp rises in the ratio of private sector debt to national income. The core of the chapter is a model which suggests that these observations are linked, and that the unusual rise in the debt: income ratio was the cause of the unusual fall in the consumption: income ratio.

Before discussing the historical pedigree claimed for the model, and the model itself, it is worth considering whether there is actually anything to explain. This question arises because the ways in which data are gathered, and series with the same name defined and compiled, can change over time. A well-known example is unemployment in the UK. The coverage and definition of that series has changed greatly since, say, the 1930s, and any analysis of long-term movements in it must be preceded by careful statistical work to ensure consistency of the data, and even then be viewed with caution. Another example is provided by UK monetary statistics. Before the work of Capie and Webber (1982), that series, apparently consistent from 1870 to 1980, had a substantial spurious trend, and a spurious step, in the nineteenth century, simply as a result of how the data had been collected. Happily, the statisticians have been kind on this occasion. The observations which are to be explained are, so far as we can tell, genuine features of the data. They are not statistical artifacts which should be ignored or, preferably, eliminated.

As the model which King uses in Chapter 5 to link the fall in consumption to the prior growth of debt depends on a fall in asset prices, the historical context in which it is placed is that of debt-deflation

236

models – in particular those of Keynes (1936) and Fisher (1922). It is argued that Keynes unjustly neglected the work of Fisher in this area, and further, that the model is derived from Fisher rather than from Keynes. That first point is not considered here, but the second is.

In certain aspects the model actually appears very Keynesian, directly descended from the discussion in Chapter 19 of the *General Theory*. In that chapter, the consequences of a fall in money wages and prices are analysed. It is argued that a major effect of such a fall is to change the distribution of income. Income is shifted away from workers *and entrepreneurs* to rentiers, who have a higher propensity to save. The consequence is, of course, a fall in the consumption: income ratio such as King's Chapter 5 model seeks to explain. Note that this difference in savings ratios is not simply the crude assumption of subsequent 'Cambridge' models that 'workers' and 'capitalists' behave differently. Rather it is argued that entrepreneurs are inclined to save more when prices fall because their previously-incurred debts, fixed in money terms, become more onerous. Although the argument in the *General Theory* is not worked out with such analytical rigour and detail as is that of Chapter 5 here, there is plainly a connection.

A second link comes via the rate of interest. Both Fisher and Keynes had deflation causing a rise in the real rate of interest. But there was a crucial difference between them over *which* real rate.

Fisher (in *Booms and Depressions*) stressed the effect on debtors of the real rate turning out to be higher than they expected, as a result of falls in the price level. (This, according to Hamilton, 1987, is an accurate characterisation of at least one part of the 1930s' experience in the USA; for it appeared from Hamilton's examination both of various data series, and of comment at the time, that the fall in prices was certainly unanticipated in degree, and by a good few not anticipated at all.) Keynes (1936), in contrast, has investment choked off by a rise in the *ex ante* real rate of interest. This rise was produced by expectations of price falls (induced by prior price falls) increasing the demand for real cash balances and thus, give an unchanged or falling nominal money stock, raising the real rate of interest.

Now, the real rate of interest does not figure at all in the formal Chapter 5 model. But if we grant on the basis of that model that a fall in the price of assets will increase the savings rate, then it will affect the equilibrium real rate of interest. It will affect it in the opposite direction to that of Keynes's model, but it is the equilibrium rate, not a disequilibrium rate as in Fisher, that is affected.

All that said, the Chapter 5 model is more in Fisher's tradition than in that of Keynes. The main reason for this conclusion is that both Fisher and Chapter 5 set out models where the existence of debt can, as a result of price falls, produce recession, and with appropriate lags no doubt a cycle. Keynes, in contrast, was concerned in his analysis of deflation to argue in opposition to previous conclusions that a fall in prices would not end a recession.

On the history of thought aspect, a further point should be made. Once a shock has been given to the system to change asset prices, the model of Chapter 5 is, as is claimed, a real model. A change in *relative* prices produces a change in *real* behaviour. Fisher's model was not so pure; a major part of his transmission process was that there was a fall in bank lending as bank loans were paid off (or not, if the borrower defaulted) and new loans not taken out.

All in all the Chapter 5 model is more Fisherien than Keynesian; but not so purely so as its progenitor suggests.

Now to the model itself. The key aspect of the Chapter 5 model is that a distributional shock changes aggregate behaviour. This happens because borrowers have borrowed to buy assets with an uninsurable price risk. The borrowing is fixed in money terms, and the borrowers therefore face all the risks (including risk of gain) arising from changes in the price of what they have bought. Debtors therefore save more than creditors until the debt is paid off because of the risk to the value of their asset. (Note the resemblance to the demonstration, Dynarski and Sheffrin, 1987, that consumption is affected by unemployment because of incomplete insurance against unemployment. There appears to be developing a class of models all of which suggest that incomplete insurance markets exacerbate recessions.)

The Chapter 5 model therefore shows that 'debt-deflation' – defined for present purposes as a fall in the price of assets relative to the general price level – can produce a decline in expenditure without either Fisher's above-noted monetary consequences, or the arbitrary 'Cambridge' assumption of different savings ratios. It also is a quite good description of the actual situation in the UK. Mortgage borrowers bear all the price risk of their houses; and, if their prices fall, they have two reasons for saving more. First, to restore their end-period wealth to what it would have been without the price fall; and second, to make it easier for themselves to buy another house should they wish to move before the full repayment of their mortgage. The model can also, of course, explain why an asset price shock produces a recession; for although it predicts a fall in the real rate of interest, and thus a rise in investment, time must surely elapse to allow the change in the composition of output.

But saying that the Chapter 5 model can do this does not mean that it actually does do so. The model has to be tested against other hypotheses, to see whether more simple explanations also fit the facts, or whether explanations of roughly the same complexity fit a wider range of facts. Is there, in other words, another theory which can do the job better?

At least three hypotheses seem worth examining: permanent income, a prior monetary shock, and liquidity constraints.

The permanent income hypothesis enters because it seems manifestly consistent with at least three very important observations; the consumption: income ratio in the USA in the Great Depression and the UK in the same period, and the consumption: income ratio in the UK in the recently-ended recession. The hypothesis readily explains the contrasting 1930s' experience, for the US recession was extraordinarily severe, while that in the UK was, at the aggregate level, very modest. The severity of the US downturn meant that a fall in measured income fed through to permanent income with abnormal rapidity – hence the fall in consumption relative to income. And the recession Britain has emerged from was, although not the deepest in post-1945 experience, certainly the longest – so here, again, permanent income was affected. Nevertheless, there is one crucial item of evidence which cannot be accounted for by the permanent income hypothesis. This item comprises the cross-section data, which show that it was the consumption of householders with mortgages that fell sharply. That is consistent with the 'debt-deflation' model, so there appears at least something for that model to explain, even if we can get the permanent income model to do a good bit of the work.

What of a prior monetary shock? A monetary expansion occurred in the UK (and in the USA before the Great Depression). This temporarily brought down the real rate of interest, and encouraged asset accumulation. It also, however, produced inflation. That led to a monetary squeeze which led first to recession and then to falling inflation. In other words, on this account the high debt: income ratio and the falling consumption to income ratio *are* linked, but linked by a common cause – prior monetary policy. But again, the cross-section data tell us that this explanation, also, cannot do all the work.

It is clear so far, then, that the cross-section data have to carry a lot of weight, for they play a major part in rejecting two very straightforward and otherwise apparently satisfactory hypotheses. Future work investigating the robustness of these data is plainly desirable.

The third and last competing hypothesis is the existence of a liquidity constraint. When interest rates rise in the process of tightening monetary policy, mortgage rates (which are generally linked to short-term rates in the UK) rise. Most of this rise is passed on to depositors, but they do not spend it, as they see it as transitory. Borrowers, meanwhile, may well also see the situation as temporary, but by the nature of the capital market can not borrow to maintain their consumption during the period of interest rate-induced squeeze on their liquidity.

This explanation fits the UK in the last recession rather well, and is of course consistent with the cross-section data from the UK.

How can we distinguish between this route by which debt influences the economy and that of Chapter 5? Many of their predictions are similar. Both, for example, produce a rise in the savings rate and thus affect the *ex ante* real rate of interest. But there is one difference. In the Chapter 5 model, consumption only recovers when asset prices do. The liquidity constraint model suggests that consumption will recover when interest rates fall, and will not wait for a rise in asset prices. In the recent UK recovery, consumption has risen with lower interest rates, and before any significant rise in house prices. This gives support to the liquidity constraint being the mechanism by which debt affects aggregate activity; but the evidence is far from conclusive, not just because between 1992 and 1994 there is only one observation but also because consumption recovered more slowly than is usual after recessions.

Drawing the above arguments together, three points should be made in conclusion. First, the behaviour of the consumption: income ratio is something to be explained, not just a statistical artifact. Second, there does seem to be a role for debt in explaining the behaviour of that ratio. The third is a general point, relating to the methods of economic analysis. Demonstrating that there is a role for debt required forsaking the usual representative agent model. Generally that model is used automatically, without prior thought. Usually that simplification is well justified by the tremendous analytical and empirical tractability it brings. But now and again something important is lost. Chapter 5 should lead us to think before we use the representative agent model. Most of the time, after thinking, we will go ahead and use it. But now and again we will not. In giving us a straightforward, readily comprehensible, reminder to think about our methods of analysis, Chapter 5 has served a most important role.

References

Capie, F.H. and A. Webber (1982) *A Monetary History of the UK: Volume 1: Data, Sources, and the Methods* (Hemel Hempstead: Allan & Unwin).

Dynarski, M. and S.M. Sheffrin (1987) 'Consumption and Unemployment', *Quarterly Journal of Economics*, 63, 411–28.

Fisher, I. (1932) *Booms and Depression* (London: George Allen & Unwin).

Hamilton, J. (1987) 'Monetary Factors in the Great Depression', *Journal of Monetary Economics*, 19, 145–70.

Keynes, J.M. (1936), *The General Theory of Employment, Interest and Money* (London: Macmillan).

6 Debt-Deflation in Japan

Kagehide Kaku

INTRODUCTION

The current Japanese recession, which started in the spring of 1991, can be characterised by three features.

First, the length and depth of the recession. The Japanese economy was unusually weak in 1992–3: average GDP growth in real terms declined from 4.8 per cent during 1987–91 to 0.6 per cent during 1992–93. In spite of successive stimulative policy measures, including substantial monetary easing and increased public expenditures, the Japanese economy remained sluggish and both the length and depth of the recession have been unexpectedly severe.

Second, the movements of some demand factors have been in sharp contrast with past patterns. Household consumption, which used to be relatively stable and tend to mitigate the overall deflationary impact during past recessions has, on the contrary, led the economic downturn. More specifically, the propensity to consume, which rose during past recessionary periods in accordance with the permanent income hypothesis, declined in FY 1991, the first year of the recession. Also, fixed investment by small and medium-sized non-manufacturers, which accounts for about 40 per cent of total fixed investment in Japan, has shown a different picture this time. In the past, when recession deepened and monetary easing was correspondingly prolonged, it was typically the fixed investment by this sector which first picked up, contributing to the start of overall economic recovery. In the course of the current recession, however, fixed investment by this sector has so far failed to respond to monetary easing, having shown no sign of recovery thus far.

Third, the recent boom and recession have been characterised by the simultaneous volatile movement of asset prices, or so-called 'asset inflation' and 'debt-deflation'.

Obviously there are various explanations found for the first two features. Excessive investment in the previous boom and the subsequent unavoidable stock adjustment, or the prevailing bearish sentiment in the economy as a whole are among others. What we try to do in this chapter is to interpret the first two features in the light of the third

242

observation, the wide fluctuation of asset prices; the discussion focuses on the deflationary effects of the decline in 'net worth' which was brought about by over-indebtedness on the one hand and the collapse of asset prices on the other.

The second section discusses general aspects of these deflationary effects on the real sector, while the third section concentrates on the deflationary outcome of the increased cost of financial intermediation caused by the deterioration of bank assets in particular. Tentative conclusions with respect to the decline in net worth in Japan are give in the fourth section.

DEFLATIONARY EFFECTS OF THE DECLINE IN NET WORTH ON THE REAL SECTOR

First, let us consider the mechanism whereby asset deflation affects the macroeconomy in a deflationary way. Suppose that asset prices had first doubled and then halved, while all firms had held the same volume of assets throughout the period under consideration, then there would have been no decline in net worth. Asset holders would have enjoyed capital gains first then suffered capital losses later, ending up with the same net worth, meaning the absence of a 'balance sheet problem'. For the net worth of firms to decline, two prerequisites must be met. First, there must be active transactions in the asset markets in the course of asset price fluctuations which means asset holders must change. Second, the firms concerned must finance their acquisition of assets through borrowings. When these two conditions are met, the firms that are new purchasers of the assets, finishing up with a fixed nominal value of the borrowings on the one hand and a declined value of the assets on the other, incur a loss in net worth. Behind these net losers, however, there should be net gainers or sellers of the assets who enjoy a corresponding increase in net worth. Thus, for a deflationary impact on the macroeconomy to arise from the fluctuation in asset prices, an asymmetry in the effects of changes in net worth on expenditures between the losers and the gainers should be assumed. In this sense, the swing in asset prices essentially concerns a distribution problem.

Major observations underlying the possible decline in net worth will next be reviewed. First, a huge volume of transactions in land and stocks did take place in the late 1980s when asset prices fluctuated. Since the mid-1980s, asset prices have been very volatile, while general

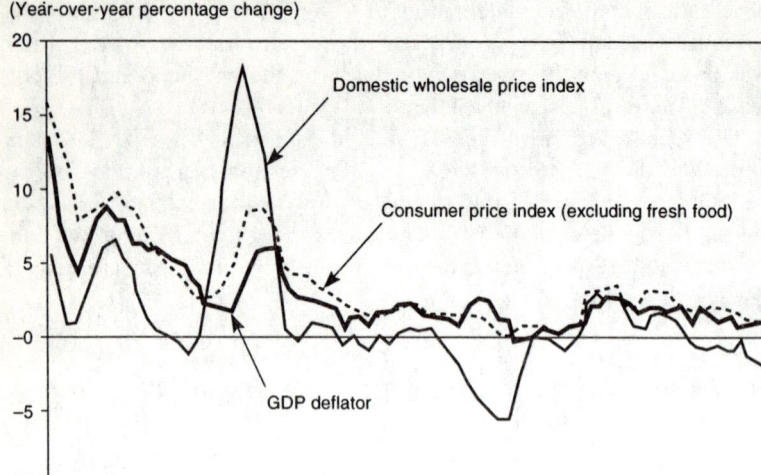

Source: Bank of Japan, *Economic Statistics Monthly*.

Figure 6.1 Inflation rates, 1975–93

prices such as CPI have been stable (Figure 6.1). Land prices in the six major cities soared dramatically in the second half of the 1980s, followed by a sharp decline in the 1990s (Figure 6.2). At the moment, while land prices in residential areas seem to be levelling off, those in commercial areas are still falling. Stock prices have shown a similar trend but have slightly recovered since the end of 1992 (Figure 6.3).

Second, the ratio of corporate debt to nominal GDP in Japan rose rapidly in the second half of the 1980s and has stayed at a high level in the 1990s, while the same ratio for the USA had already come down (Figure 6.4). Notably, a comparison of the ratio of borrowing to GDP by industry shows that ratios for the real-estate industry and other non-manufacturers increased substantially during the second half of the 1980s and have stayed at high levels (Figure 6.5). The real-estate industry aggressively purchased land in the second half of the 1980s and has incurred huge capital losses from the recent drop in land prices, pointing to a likely sharp decline in its net worth due to its large debt financing.

It should be noted, however, that those observations themselves are inconclusive in assessing the balance sheet problem we are looking at

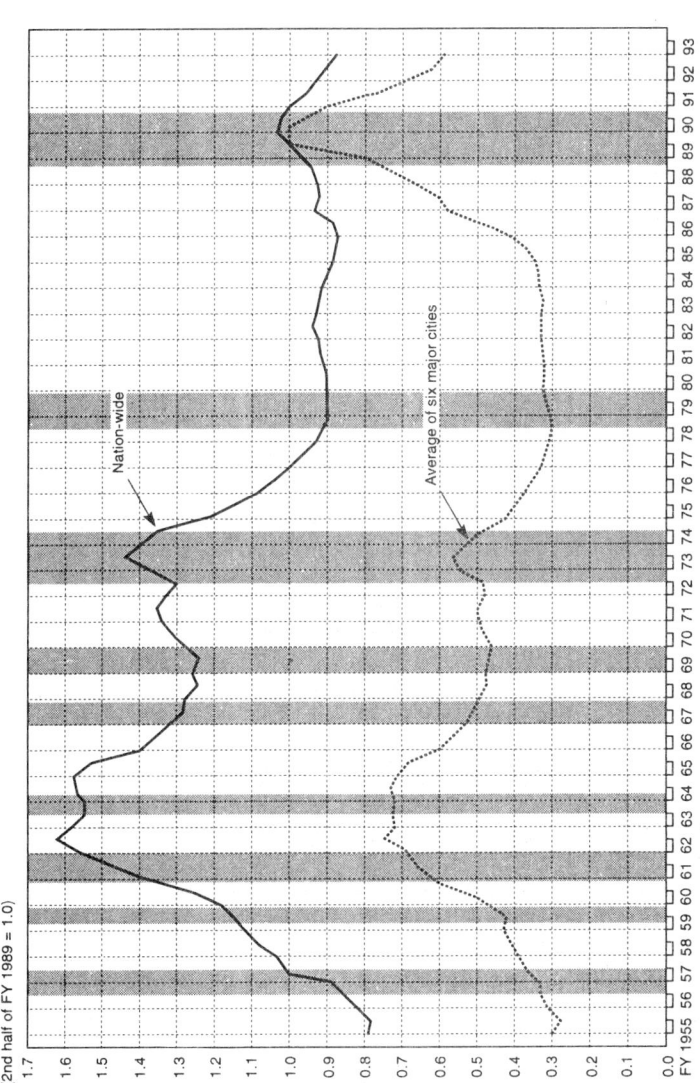

(2nd half of FY 1989 = 1.0)

Nation-wide

Average of six major cities

Notes:
1. Both figures are ratios to nominal GDP index.
2. Shaded areas show periods of increase in the official discount rate.

Source: Japan Research Institute of Real Estate.

Figure 6.2 Land prices in the cities, 1955–93

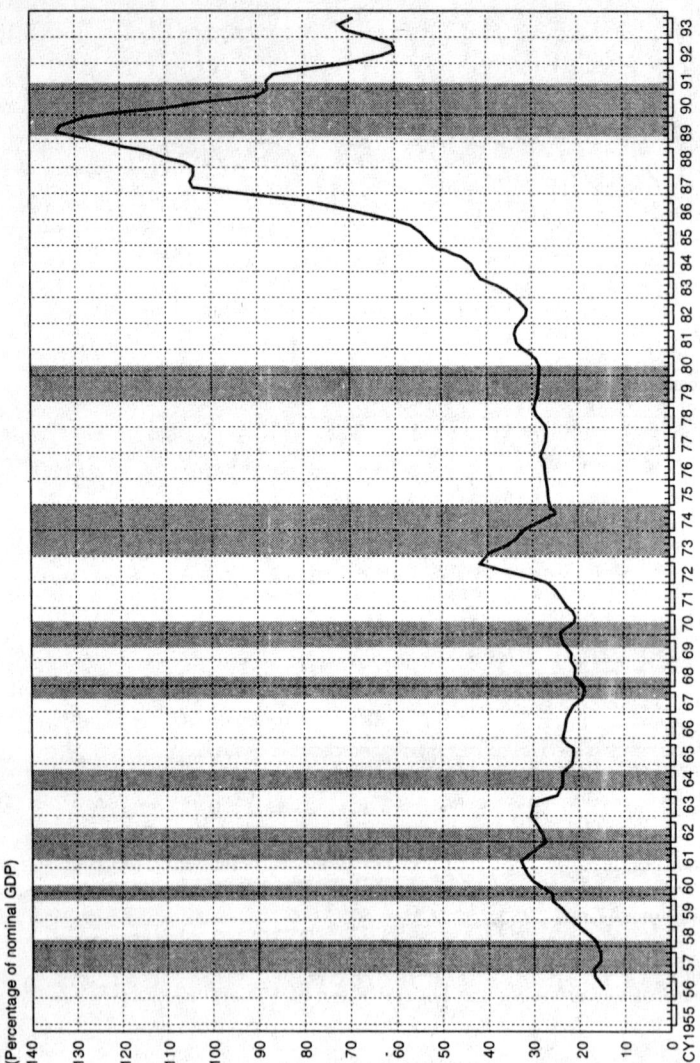

(Percentage of nominal GDP)

Notes:
1. Sum of stocks listed on the 1st section of the Tokyo Stock Exchange.
2. Shaded areas show periods of increase in the official discount rate.

Source: Tokyo Stock Exchange, *Annual Securities Statistics*.

Figure 6.3   Total market value of stocks, 1955–93

(Percentage of nominal GDP)

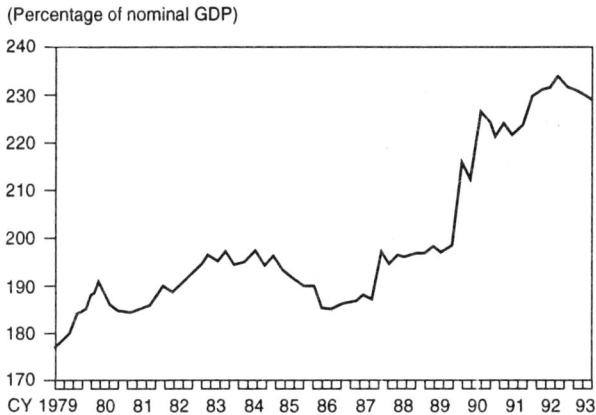

(a)

(Percentage of nominal GDP)

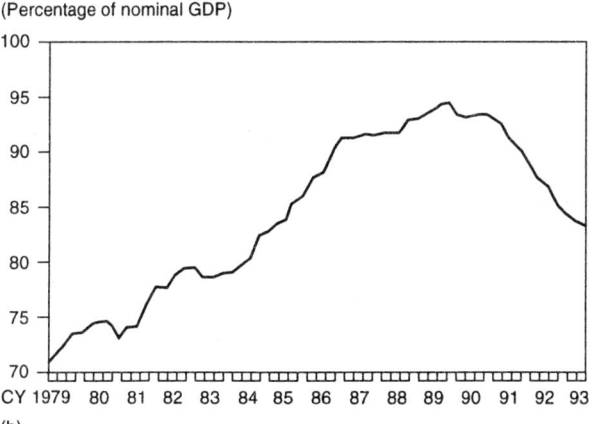

(b)

Note for Japan: Figures for NTT (Nippon Telegraph & Telephone), JR (eight Japan Railway Corporations), and JT (Japan Tobacco) are included even before their privatisation in April 1985.

Sources: Bank of Japan, *Flow of Funds Accounts and Economic Statistics Monthly*; Board of Governors of the Federal Reserve System, *Flow of Funds Account*.

Figure 6.4   Total liabilities of the non-financial private sector: (a) Japan, (b) USA, 1979–93

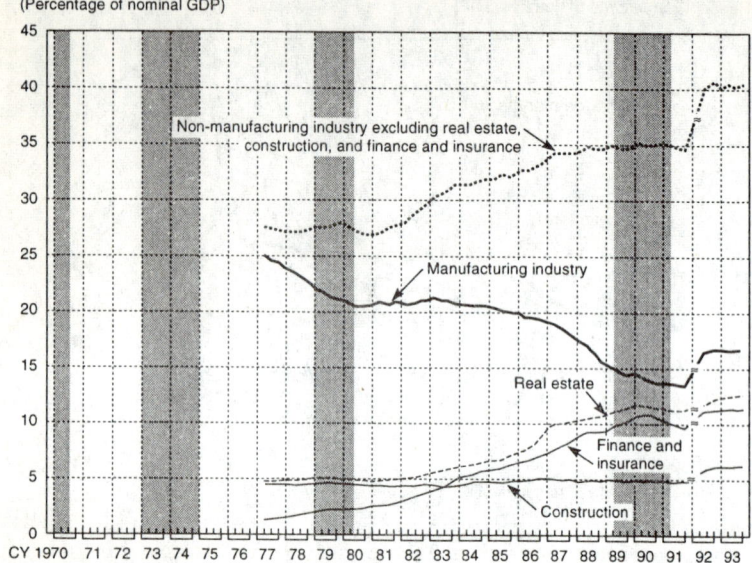

(Percentage of nominal GDP)

Notes:
1. All figures are loans and discounts extended by all banks (*Zengin*), while since 1992:2 overdrafts and cash advanced are also included; data discontinuity between 1992:1 and 1992:2 is indicated by ≈.
2. Shaded areas show periods of increase in the official discount rate.

Source: Bank of Japan, *Economics Statistics Monthly*.

Figure 6.5   Loans and discounts outstanding to major industries, 1970–93

here. For instance, Figure 6.6, showing the estimated capital: asset ratio, which is 'effective' in the sense that the capital incorporates latent reserves (unrealised capital gains on land and securities), of the non-financial sector excluding the real-estate industry, is also informative. This ratio, after rising rapidly in the second half of the 1980s, declined sharply in the 1990s due to the drop in hidden gains on stocks as well as on land reflecting the collapse of asset prices. However, the recent level remains comparable to what it was in the first half of the 1980s, even for non-manufacturers which have a relatively high proportion of land in their assets. These aggregated data should be carefully examined as they are most likely to conceal the serious losses incurred by some specific firms in the course of asset-price fluctuation, with the reasoning above.

(Per cent)

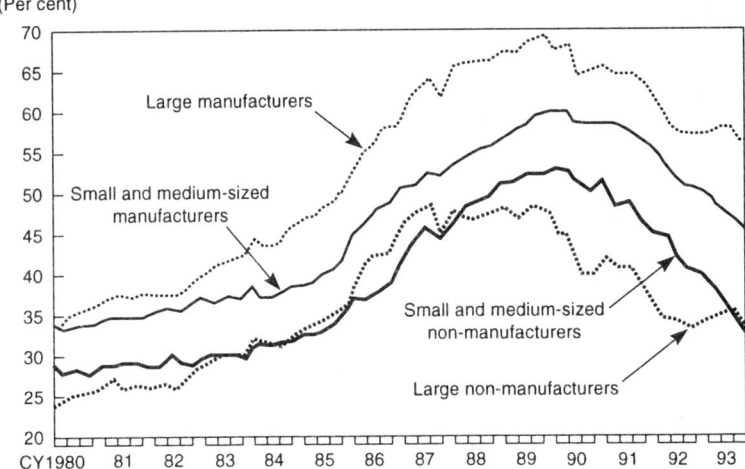

Notes:
1. Large non-manufacturers excluding real estate, electricity, and transportation and communication.
2. Small and medium-sized non-manufacturers excluding real estate.

Sources: Ministry of France, *Corporate Business Statistics Quarterly*.

Figure 6.6 Effective capital:asset ratio, 1980–93

Importantly, under the circumstances of active asset transactions combined with volatile asset price movements, the size of the swing, not the level, of the effective capital: asset ratio should matter. Accordingly, it may be fairly asserted that asset-price swing or asset deflation in this context has exerted some adverse impact on the balance sheet of the business sector. As for the possible deflationary outcome from the deteriorated balance sheet in the macroeconomy, however, the overall quantitative impact is difficult to measure despite abundant anecdotal or qualitative evidence. In addition, our attempts to identify the size of the impact by econometric methods, through estimation of investment functions for example, have so far not been very successful.[1] In spite of the lack of statistical evidence, the sustained weakness of fixed investment by small and medium-sized non-manufacturers, as mentioned, is reasonably understandable in taking account of their declining net worth. One piece of circumstantial evidence is that the swing of the effective capital: asset ratio for small and medium-sized non-manufacturers observed in Figure 6.6 is the largest.

Apart from a possible decline in net worth, the decline in asset prices or the anticipated further decline may have provided more direct adverse impact with the fixed investments of small and medium-sized non-manufacturers, either because a substantial part of such investment involves the purchase of land, or because small and medium-sized non-manufacturers traditionally depend heavily on bank borrowing collateralised by land.

Another possible link between sluggish investment by this sector and asset price declines stems from the weakened capacity of financial intermediation on the part of banks due to a deterioration in their assets. This interpretation is of particular interest because the pick-up in fixed investment by this sector must be dependent, at least partly, on bank lending behaviour. In the past, when recession deepened and monetary conditions eased, demand for credit by big firms remained typically sluggish, which compelled banks to find lending opportunities among small and medium-sized non-manufacturers whose borrowing is more interest rate elastic. Obviously this type of aggressive lending by banks to possibly risky borrowers is inconspicuous at best under the current recession. This point will be examined below.

Let us next turn to the household sector. One of the most conspicuous characteristics of the current recession is the unusual weakness of household consumption. There exist various possible explanations, including the excessive purchase of consumer durables in the preceding boom, the possible downward shift of income or employment expectations for the future, or deferred purchases due to deflationary expectations. How about the effect of debt increase combined with the asset price decline? First, as for the degree of over-indebtedness, the situation in the household sector is not quite the same as that in the corporate sector. Compared with the corporate sector, the household sector is suffering less over-indebtedness even though consumer credit outstanding increased significantly in the second half of the 1980s (Figure 6.7). This is well depicted by the facts that the household sector in Japan holds a sizable amount of interest-bearing assets and that net financial assets as a percentage of disposable income are still increasing, which is not the case in other industrialised countries, for example, the UK (Table 6.1).

It can be argued that changes in the distribution of wealth, which is the driving force behind the balance sheet problem, may affect the overall propensity to consume. However, empirical work suggests that the impact on the household sector in Japan of the increased debt combined with asset-price declines is smaller than in the USA or the UK.

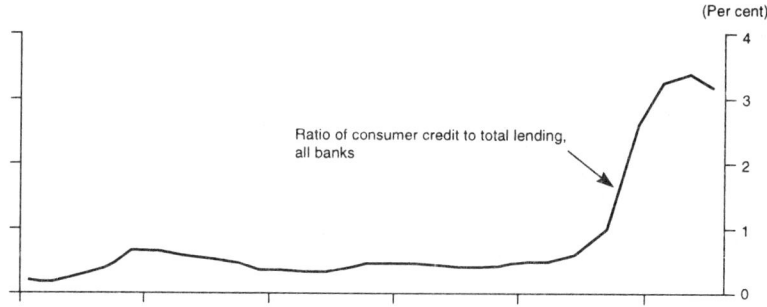

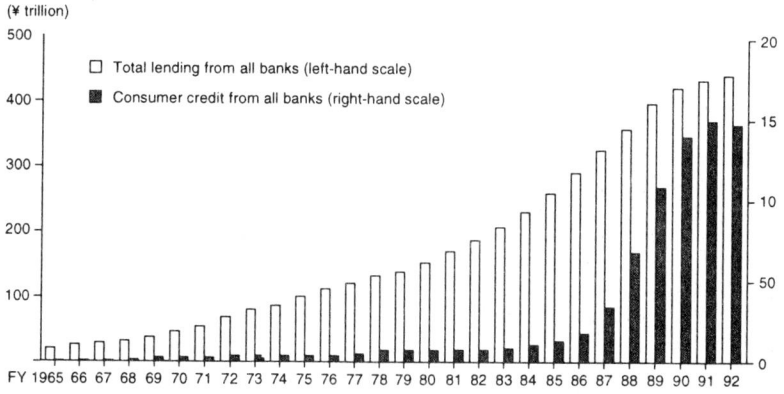

Note: Because of the data constraint, banks belonging to Regional Banks II are excluded.

Source: Bank of Japan, *Economic Statistics Annual*.

Figure 6.7   Ratio of consumer credit to total lending, all banks, 1965–92

For instance, efforts to find some systematic differences in the propensity to consume by class of consumer, such as households having mortgages and those not, or households broken down by income brackets, during the recent boom and bust period failed. While the possible relevance of debt or asset-price changes with respect to consumption is not disregarded and research remains to be done, at this juncture, it may be asserted that those factors play less clear role in Japan than in either the UK or the USA.

Table 6.1   Non-financial sectors, net financial positions, 1984 and 1992

| | Net interest-bearing[1] assets of households[2] | | Net interest-bearing[1] liabilities of enterprises[3] | |
| | As a percentage of disposable income | | As a percentage of GNP | |
	1984[4]	1992[5]	1984[4]	1992[5]
UK	30	−5	10	25
USA	42	21	16	23
Sweden	5	26	45	68
Canada	38	28	39	44
France	62	40	33	38
Germany	110	114	22	23
Italy	N/A	129	N/A	46
Japan	126	136	52	81
Belgium	140	175	23	12

Notes:
1. Net deposits, credits, bonds and money market instruments.
2. For the UK, Canada and Japan, including unincorporated businesses.
3. For the UK, Canada and Japan, non-financial corporate businesses; for the USA, non-farm corporate business.
4. For Sweden, 1985; for Belgium, 1981.
5. For Sweden, Canada, Germany, Japan and Belgium, 1991.
N/A not available.

Sources: Individual countries, flow of funds accounts.

DEFLATIONARY EFFECTS CAUSED BY THE DETERIORATION OF BANK ASSETS

Another striking feature of the current recession in Japan is the extremely weak growth of monetary and credit aggregates under a record low level of interest rates. M_2+CDs has grown very slowly with a period of negative growth between the end of 1992 and the beginning of 1993 (Figure 6.8). In spite of low interest rates, the velocity of M_2+CDs gradually increased from mid-1990 until early last year (Figure 6.9).[2] The question arises as to whether this feature is somehow related to the asset-price decline or balance sheet restructuring of financial institutions. Though the degree varies from bank to bank, their balance sheets have more or less deteriorated due to the increase in real-estate-related non-performing loans which had accumulated in the second half of the 1980s. The extent of the asset deterioration in the

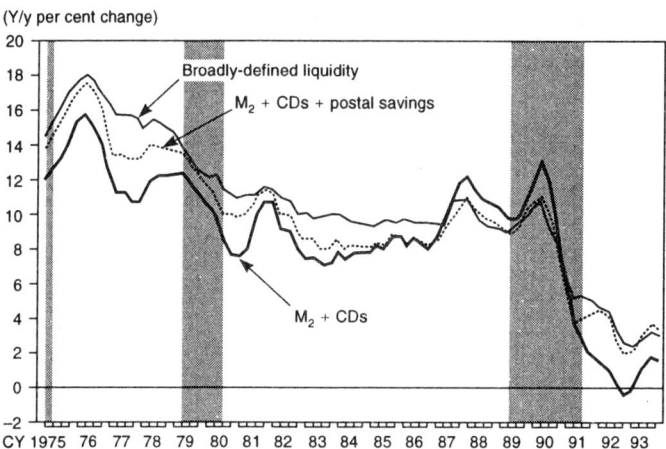

Notes:
1. All growth rates based on average outstanding.
2. Figures before 1979 for broadly-defined liquidity are estimates.
3. Shaded areas show periods of increase in the official discount rate.

Source: Bank of Japan, *Economic Statistics Monthly*.

Figure 6.8 Monetary aggregates, 1975–93

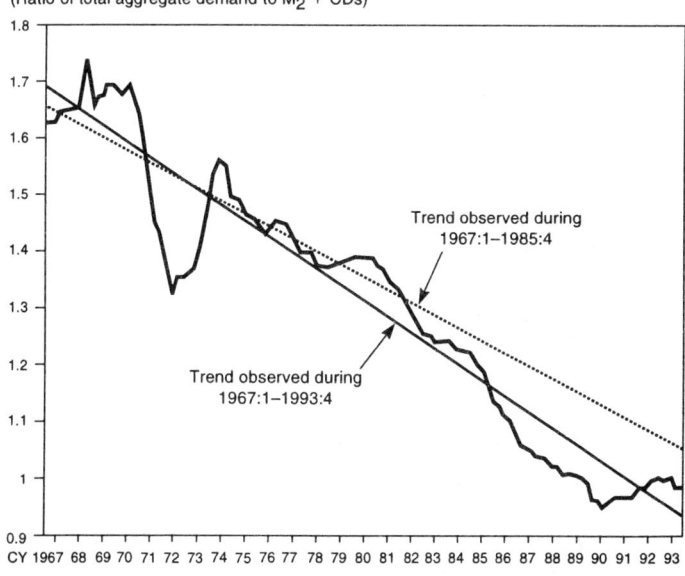

Source: Bank of England.

Figure 6.9 Velocity of M_2 + CDs, 1967–93

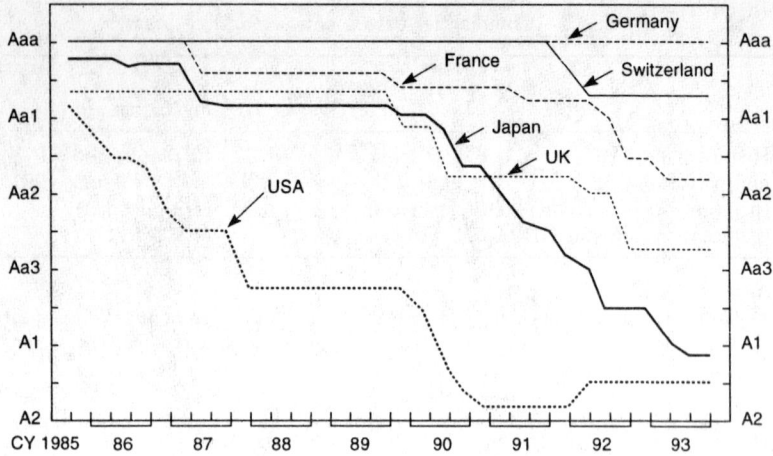

Note: Figures calculated as non-weighted averages of ratings given by Moody's Investors Service to the long-term debits of following major banks.

Japan:	Bank of Tokyo, Dai-ichi Kangyo Bank, Fuji Bank, Industrial Bank of Japan, Long-Term Credit Bank of Japan, Mitsubishi Bank, Mitsubishi Trust Banking Corp, Sanwa Bank, Sumitomo Bank, and Tokai Bank.
USA:	Bankers Trust Company, Bank of America NTSA (also Security Pacific Corp.); Chase Manhattan Bank, NA; Citibank, NA; Morgan Guaranty Trust Co. of New York.
Germany:	Deutsche Bank AG, Dresdner Bank AG.
France:	Banque National de Paris; Crédit Agricole d'le-de-France; Crédit Lyonnais; Société Génerale.
UK:	Barclays Bank plc; Midland Bank plc.; National Westminster Bank plc.
Switzerland:	Credit Suisse; Swiss Bank Corp.; Union Bank of Switzerland.

Source: Moody's Investors Service, *Global Ratings Guide*.

Figure 6.10   Bank ratings, 1985–93

banking sector is nearly comparable to that of the USA (Table 6.2) and reflecting this, the credit ratings of Japanese banks by Moody's have been downgraded significantly (Figure 6.10). Although only a few bank failures have been witnessed in Japan, the possibility cannot be denied that the deterioration of bank assets may have a further depressive impact on monetary and credit aggregates and, in turn, on the real economy to some extent.[3] The questions are two-fold: First, do any factors on the financial institutions' side seriously affect lending

Table 6.2 Commercial banks, non-performing loans

	Japan: 21 largest banks	USA: FDIC insured banks
Historical peak of	¥ 13.7 trillion	$107.8 billion
non-performing loans	at end of September 1993	at end of June 1991
(per cent of total credit)	(3.5 per cent)	(5.2 per cent)
(per cent of nominal GDP)	(2.9 per cent)	(1.8 per cent)

Notes:
1. Non-performing loans are defined as the sum of non-accrual loans past due more than six months and loans to delinquent borrowers for Japan; and the sum of non-accrual loans past due more than 90 days and real estate and other assets acquired in full or partial satisfaction for the USA.
2. Japan's 21 largest banks are 11 city banks, three long-term credit banks, and seven trust banks.

Sources: Individual banks' *Annual Reports*.

growth? Second, to what extent do they have a negative impact on the real economy? Some results concerning the first question are as follows.

First, the lending margin is examined. It is true that the lending margin of Japanese banks has widened remarkably since 1991 (Figure 6.11), an observation which has been often cited as evidence that supply-side factors have adversely affected the lending growth. It must be noted, however, that the lending margin has in the past been rather closely related to the bankruptcy ratio of firms, a proxy for credit risk. While the widening of the margin in the early 1990s can also be largely explained by a higher bankruptcy ratio, it is true that the larger gap between these two variables has been observed since 1992. This is confirmed by a large estimation error of regression of the lending margin on the bankruptcy ratio in recent years (Figure 6.12). This suggests that the lending margin has widened more than what can be explained by increased credit risk.

Second, the diffusion index regarding the lending attitude of banks judged by small and medium-sized companies in The Bank of Japan's quarterly business survey (*TANKAN*) has not improved during the current period of monetary easing. In the past, on the contrary, it improved almost in parallel with the decline in interest rates. The recent movements of the diffusion index, on the other hand, can be better traced with the ratio of long-term debt and land prices added as explanatory varibles (Figure 6.13). It should be borne in mind, however,

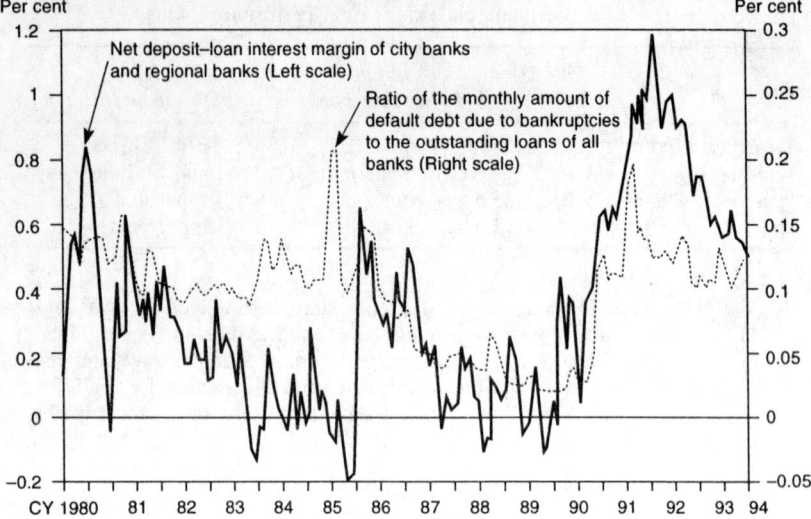

Note: The 'net' deposit–loan interest margin is the difference between the 'gross' deposit-loan interest margin and average banking expense.

Sources: Bank of Japan, *Economic Statistics Monthly*; Federation of Bankers Association of Japan, *Analysis of Financial Statements of All Banks*; Tokyo Business Credit Research, *Bankruptcy Monthly Report*.

Figure 6.11 Deposit–loan interest margin on bankruptcy ratio, 1980–94

that an identification problem is unavoidable in the sense that a drop in land prices and an increase in long-term debt ratio may imply a reduction in net worth on the side of borrowers.

Third, cross-sectional analyses of Japanese banks show that the capital: asset ratio has moderately significant explanatory power in the lending margin and lending growth equations. The higher the capital: asset ratios of banks, the smaller the widening of their lending margins and the larger their lending growth rates (Tables 6.3 and 6.4). In interpreting these results, the effect of the introduction of BIS capital adequacy requirements at the end of FY 1992 may have to be more explicitly considered. Generally speaking, however, we can see the estimation outcome reasonably showing banks' attitude to regard the capital: asset ratio as one of the main guideposts for their loan management. And, if this is the case, the increase in non-performing loans would make banks more cautious towards lending since it might work as a constraint on their capital: asset ratio over the medium-term.

Equation (6.1)

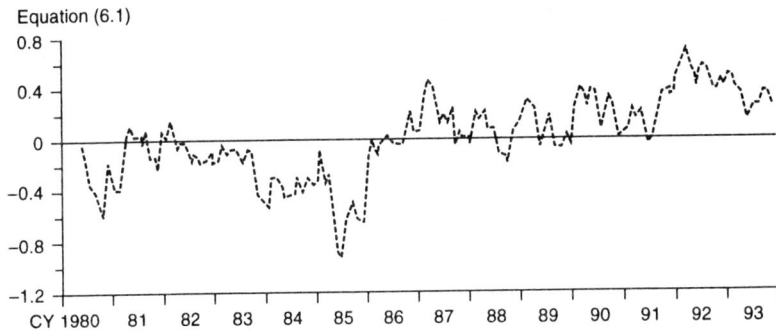

Equation (6.2)

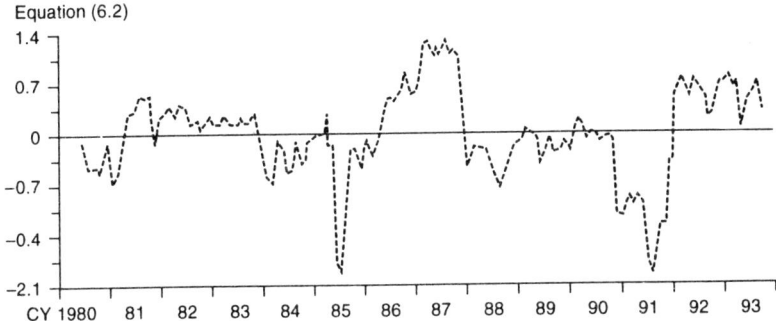

Note: Regression equations:

(6.1) $M = a_1 + b_1B + e_1$
(6.1) $M = a_2 + b_2B + c_2D + e_2$.

Regression period: 1980:1–1993:12

M: Average deposit–loan interest margin of city banks and regional banks.
B: Up to six-month lagged variables of ratio of default debt amount to total lending from all banks.
D: Dummy variable for the period of January 1988–December 1991.
a, b, c: Regression coefficients
e: Estimation error

Source: Author's calculation.

Figure 6.12   Estimation error of deposit–loan interest margin on bankruptcy ratio, 1980–93

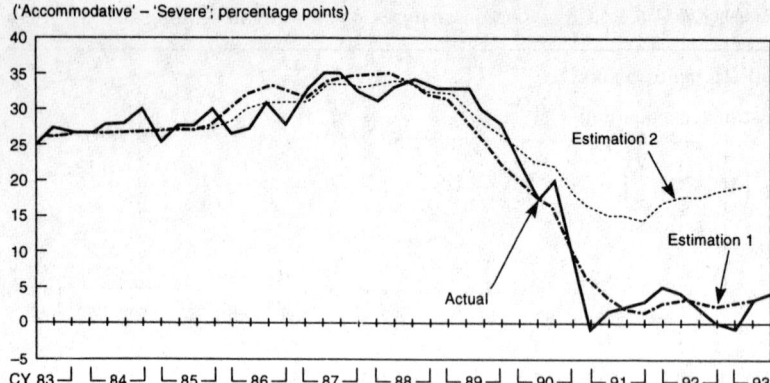

('Accommodative' – 'Severe'; percentage points)

( ): t-value

		Constant	Interest rate	Debt ratio	Land price	$\bar{R}^2$	DW	SE
Estimation 1	Sample 1983:2 ~ 1993:2	76.5 (22.7)	–3.6 (–8.9)	–1.9 (–18.9)	0.7 (4.5)	0.97	1.35	2.2
Estimation 2	Sample 1983:2 ~ 1990:2	67.4 (13.2)	–3.6 (–4.6)	–1.2 (–3.0)	0.4 (0.8)	0.74	1.66	1.8

Notes:
1. Debt ratio is the average ratio of long-term borrowing and bonds to quarterly sales for non-manufacturing corporations.
2. Dotted line of Estimation 2 since 1990:2 plots out-of-sample forecasts.

Sources: Ministry of Finance, *Corporate Business Statistics Quarterly*; Economic Planning Agency, *National Income* Statistics, Capital Stock Statistics of Corporate Business; *National Income Statistics; Capital Stock Statistics of Corporate Business*; Japan Real Estate Institute, *Land Price Indexes of Urban Districts*, Bank of Japan, *Short-term Economic Survey of Enterprises in Japan*.

Figure 6.13   Estimation Diffusion index of lending attitude of financial institutions assessed by the non-manufacturing sector, 1983–93

The results are not decisive. Taking into account the fact that both the decline in interest rates and the lower growth of lending have proceeded simultaneously, the slow growth in bank lending in recent years can basically be understood as reflecting shrinking demand for borrowing and increased credit risk on the part of borrowers. It is highly probable, however, that the deterioration of bank assets has restrained lending growth to some extent.

Table 6.3 Cross-section analyses of changes in lending margin

(a) 21 major banks[1]

Estimated equation:

$$\left(M_t - M_{t-1}\right) = \alpha + \beta \left(\frac{C_{t-1}}{A_{t-1}}\right) + \gamma \left(\frac{C_t}{A_t} - \frac{C_{t-1}}{A_{t-1}}\right) + \delta \left(\frac{W_t}{L_t}\right)$$

$$+ \ \varepsilon \left(\frac{N_{1t}}{L_t}\right) + \zeta \left(\frac{N_{1t} + N_{2t}}{L_t}\right) + \text{error}_t$$

where

M_t : Net deposit-loan interest margin for period t.

$\dfrac{C_{t-1}}{A_{t-1}}$: The capital: asset ratio (BIS standard) at the end of period $t-1$.

L_t : Amount of loans at the end of period t.

W_t : Amount of loan write-offs and provisions for possible credit losses in period t.

N_{1t} : Credits to bankrupt borrowers.

N_{2t} : Non-accrual loans other than N_{1t}.

Regression no.	Coefficients of OLS (t-value in parenthesis)						$\bar{R}^2$ SE	F-value
	α	β	γ	δ	ε	ζ		
(Regressions for FY1992)								
1	10.565 (8.010)² **	−1.294 (−8.720) **	−0.371 (−2.203) **	0.011 (0.026)			0.816 0.279	30.576 **
2	11.566 (10.692) **	−1.354 (−11.816) **	−0.460 (−3.398) **		−0.738 (−3.155) **		0.884 0.221	51.792 **
3	10.556 (8.056) **	−1.295 (−8.709) **	−0.371 (−2.211) **			0.002 (0.033)	0.816 0.279	30.577 **
(Regressions for the 1st half of FY1993)								
4	3.556 (1.206)	−0.450 (−1.445)	0.073 (0.198)	0.209 (0.251)			0.105 0.420	1.784
5	3.930 (1.544)	−0.483 (−1.738)	0.046 (0.127)		−0.015 (−0.035)		0.101 0.420	1.753
6	3.343 (1.236)	−0.396 (−1.228)	−0.054 (−1.131)			−0.053 (−0.501)	0.115 0.417	1.862

Notes:
1. 21 major banks are 11 city banks, three long-term credit banks, and seven trust banks.
2. ** shows that the null hypothesis that each coefficient is (all coefficients are) zero can be rejected in 95 per cent probability t-test (F-test).

Sources: 21 individual banks' *Annual Reports*.

(b) 69 regional banks[1]

Estimated equation:

$$\left(M_t - M_{t-1}\right) = \alpha + \beta \left(\frac{C_{t-1}}{A_{t-1}}\right) + \gamma \left(\frac{C_t}{A_t} - \frac{C_{t-1}}{A_{t-1}}\right)$$

$$+ \delta \left(\frac{W_t}{L_t}\right) + \varepsilon \left(\frac{N_{1t}}{L_t}\right) + error,$$

where

M_t : Net deposit-loan interest margin for period t.

$\dfrac{C_{t-1}}{A_{t-1}}$: The capital: asset ratio (BIS standard) at the end of period $t-1$.

L_t : Amount of loans at the end of period t.

W_t : Amount of loan write-offs and provisions for possible credit losses in period t.

N_{1t} : Credits to bankrupt borrowers.

Regression no.	Coefficients of OLS (t-value in parenthesis)					$\bar{R}^2$ SE	F-value
	α	β	γ	δ	ε		
(Regressions for FY1992)							
7	−0.052 (−0.160)	−0.016 (−0.494)	−0.038 (−0.845)	0.006 (0.040)		−0.032 0.137	0.298
8	−0.344 (−1.023)	0.010 (0.278)	−0.016 (−0.377)		0.113 (1.892)[2] *	0.022 0.133	1.507
(Regressions for the 1st half of FY1993)							
9	−0.747 (−2.497) **	−0.055 (−1.599)	−0.052 (−0.680)	−0.090 (−0.380)		0.001 0.134	1.028
10	−0.722 (−2.208) **	0.052 (1.450)	−0.051 (−0.676)		−0.024 (−0.415)	0.003 0.134	1.071

Notes:
1. Out of 129 regional banks, only 69 which adopt the BIS standard for calculating the capital: asset ratio are included in the sample for regressions 7–10.
2. ** shows that the null hypothesis that each coefficient is (all coefficients are) zero can be rejected in 95 per cent probability t-test (F-test), while * stands for 90 per cent.

Sources: 69 individual banks' *Annual Reports*.

Table 6.4   Cross-section analyses of growth rates of lending

(a) 21 major banks[1]

Estimated equation:

$$\left(\frac{L_{At} - L_{At-1}}{L_{At-1}}\right) = \alpha + \beta \left(\frac{C_{t-1}}{A_{t-1}}\right) + \gamma \left(\frac{C_t}{A_t} - \frac{C_{t-1}}{A_{t-1}}\right) + \delta \left(\frac{W_t}{L_t}\right)$$

$$+ \varepsilon \left(\frac{N_{1t}}{L_t}\right) + \zeta \left(\frac{N_{1t} + N_{2t}}{L_t}\right) + \text{error}_t$$

where

L_{At} :   The average amount of loans for period t.

$\dfrac{C_{t-1}}{A_{t-1}}$:   The capital: asset ratio (BIS standard) at the end of period $t-1$.

L_t :   Amount of loans at the end of period t.

W_t :   Amount of loan write-offs and provisions for possible credit losses in period t.

N_{1t} :   Credits to bankrupt borrowers.

N_{2t} :   Non-accrual loans other than N_{1t}.

Regression no.	Coefficients of OLS (t-value in parenthesis)						$\bar{R}^2$ SE	F-value
	α	β	γ	δ	ε	ζ		
(Regressions for FY1992)								
11	−35.869	4.551	5.105	−8.436			−0.046	0.705
	(−1.078)	(1.216)	(1.203)	(−0.783)			7.028	
12	0.481	−4.039	2.702		3.037		−0.105	0.367
	(0.078)	(−0.750)	(0.727)		(0.403)		7.222	
13	−25.516	2.083	3.894			2.381	0.054	1.377
	(−0.811)	(0.584)	(0.968)			(1.572)	6.684	
(Regressions for the 1st half of FY1993)								
14	−31.883	3.154	7.580	8.511			0.275	3.527^{**}[2]
	(−1.043)	(0.976)	$(1.974)^{*}$[2]	(0.982)			4.352	
15	−15.436	1.660	6.768		−0.154		0.234	3.039^{**}
	(−0.569)	(0.561)	$(1.759)^{*}$		(−0.033)		4.471	
16	−5.446	0.128	8.563			0.962	0.266	3.417^{**}
	(−0.192)	(0.038)	$(1.989)^{*}$			(0.860)	4.377	

Notes:

1. 21 major banks are 11 city banks, three long-term credit banks, and seven trust banks.
2. ** shows that the null hypothesis that each coefficient is (all coefficients are) zero can be rejected in 95 per cent probability *t*-test (*F*-test), while * stands for 90 per cent.

Sources: 21 individual banks' *Annual Reports*.

(b) 69 regional banks[1]

Estimated equation:

$$\left(\frac{L_{At} - L_{At-1}}{L_{At-1}}\right) = \alpha + \beta \left(\frac{C_{t-1}}{A_{t-1}}\right) + \gamma \left(\frac{C_t}{A_t} - \frac{C_{t-1}}{A_{t-1}}\right)$$

$$+ \delta \left(\frac{W_t}{L_t}\right) + \varepsilon \left(\frac{N_{1t}}{L_t}\right) + \text{error},$$

where

L_{At} : The average amount of loans for period t.

$\dfrac{C_{t-1}}{A_{t-1}}$: The capital: asset ratio (BIS standard) at the end of period $t-1$.

L_t : Amount of loans at the end of period t.

W_t : Amount of loan write-offs and provisions for possible credit losses in period t.

N_{1t} : Credits to bankrupt borrowers.

Regression no.	Coefficients of OLS (t-value in parenthesis)					$\bar{R}^2$ SE	F-value
	α	β	γ	δ	ε		
(Regressions for FY1992)							
17	8.610 (1.727)[2]	−0.360 (−0.646)	−1.519 (−2.202)[2]	−4.161 (−2.010)		0.053 2.111	2.260*
18	8.957 (1.657)	−0.397 (−0.671)	−1.335 (−1.941)*		−1.378 (−1.429)	0.024 2.142	1.567
(Regressions for the 1st half of FY1993)							
19	1.166 (0.122)	−0.407 (−0.373)	0.834 (0.341)	−16.492 (−2.186)**		0.026 4.273	1.599
20	14.813 (1.549)	−1.626 (−1.539)	0.499 (0.224)		−7.126 (−4.265)**	0.183 3.914	6.069**

Notes:
1. Out of 129 regional banks, only 69 regional banks which adopt BIS standard for calculating capital: asset ratio are included in the sample for regressions 17–20.
2. ** shows that the null hypothesis that each coefficient is (all coefficients are) zero can be rejected in 95 per cent probability t-test (F-test), while * stands for 90 per cent.

Sources: 69 individual banks' *Annual Reports*.

CONCLUDING REMARKS

Both the decline in the net worth of the corporate sector and the deterioration of bank assets owing to the fall in asset prices have more or less deepened the adjustment of the Japanese economy. But it is extremely difficult to measure the influence of 'debt-deflation', thus defined, quantitatively.

As of April 1994, even the bottoming-out of the Japanese economy had not been well confirmed, and land prices, especially those for commercial sites in major cities, still keep declining. Thus, we have not reached the point from where the whole process of asset inflation and deflation can be reviewed so as to draw a robust conclusion. In this sense, this report is quite tentative. What is clear is that the cost of accommodating the economic boom, which saw tremendous land price hikes in the second half of the 1980s, has been very considerable.

Appendix

Equations were estimated to explain bank loans to manufacturers, non-manufacturers, real-estate companies, and households based on the same specifications use by Lown and Wenninger (1994) for US data. In the case of the USA it was shown that factors relating to borrowers and the macroeconomy could not satisfactorily explain the growth of lending and that adjusted R^2s were low (Table 6A.1). Their results suggests that other factors might have affected lending significantly. In the case of Japan, to the contrary, lending growth rates were almost fully explained by factors relating to borrowers and the macroeconomy and the influence of factors on the financial sector's side could not be detected (Table 6A.2).

Table 6A.1 USA, bank loan equations

Estimation period: 1961:2–1991:4

	(6.1) C&I loans		(6.2) Real estate loans		(6.3) Home mortgage loans		(6.4) Consumer loans	
Explanatory variables								
Constant	0.01	(1.25)	0.005	(1.10)	−0.007	(1.35)	0.002	(0.46)
Lag. dep. var.$_{t-1}$	0.10	(1.1)	0.45	(0.74)	0.45	(4.70)	0.53	(5.52)
Lag. dep. var.$_{t-2}$	0.31	(3.4)	0.36	(3.46)	0.26	(2.47)	0.25	(2.25)
Lag. dep. var.$_{t-3}$	0.04	(0.37)	−0.05	(0.44)	−0.07	(0.68)	0.13	(1.18)
Lag. dep. var.$_{t-4}$	0.05	(0.54)	−0.007	(0.06)	0.01	(0.05)	−0.26	(2.78)
i_{t-1}	−0.003	(1.60)	−0.002	(1.84)	−0.002	(0.88)	−0.005	(1.29)
i_{t-2}	0.002	(1.43)	−0.002	(1.62)	−0.002	(1.26)	−0.003	(0.90)
i_{t-3}	0.001	(0.51)	−0.002	(1.57)	−0.001	(0.49)	−0.004	(1.17)
i_{t-4}	0.000	(0.16)	0.002	(1.75)	−0.000	(0.27)	−0.005	(1.59)
$XGDP_{t-1}$	−0.07	(0.36)	0.09	(0.70)				
$XGDP_{t-2}$	−0.37	(1.80)	−0.09	(0.68)				
$XGDP_{t-3}$	−0.06	(0.28)	−0.06	(0.45)				
$XGDP_{t-4}$	0.07	(0.34)	0.06	(0.47)				
YP_{t-1}					−0.04	(0.27)	−0.02	(0.11)
YP_{t-2}					0.01	(0.08)	0.23	(1.44)
YP_{t-3}					0.07	(0.48)	−0.12	(0.77)
YP_{t-4}					0.13	(0.86)	−0.19	(1.14)
I_{t-1}	0.06	(0.75)	−0.006	(−0.16)				
I_{t-2}	0.02	(0.21)	0.04	(1.00)				
I_{t-3}	0.05	(0.61)	0.04	(0.99)				
I_{t-4}	0.28	(3.89)	0.03	(0.64)				
INV_{t-1}	−1.0	(0.62)						
INV_{t-2}	−0.08	(0.47)						
INV_{t-3}	0.28	(1.64)						
INV_{t-4}	−0.14	(0.73)						
HS_{t-1}					−0.000	(1.23)		
HS_{t-2}					0.000	(0.98)		
HS_{t-3}					−0.000	(0.95)		
HS_{t-4}					0.000	(2.16)		
Adj. R^2	0.39		0.53		0.61			(0.60)

Notes: (absolute) t-statistics are in parentheses. All variables are in nominal terms and are specified in growth rates except where noted. The real–estate loan variable excludes residential mortgages. $XGDP$ = nominal GDP *less* expenditures on producer durables, structures, and inventories. I = expenditures on producer durables in equation (6.1) and expenditures on structures in equation (6.2). YP = personal income. INV = the stock of business inventories. i = the change in the prime rate in equations (6.1) and (6.2), the change in the mortgage rate in equation (6.3) and the change in the consumer loan rate in equation (6.4). The consumer loan rate is a weighted average of four consumer loan rates; actual data was available beginning in 1973:1, extrapolated data was used prior to that. HS = the level of housing starts.

Source: Lown and Wenninger (1994).

Table 6A.2 Japan, bank loan equations (6.1)–(6.4)

Coefficient (absolute t-values in parentheses)
Dependent variable growth rate of:

Explanatory variables	(6.1) Manufacturing loans			(6.2) Non-manufacturing loans		
Estimation period	1967:1–1993:3	1971:1–1980:4	1981:1–1993:3	1964:1–1993:3	1971:1–1980:4	1981:1–1993:3
Constant	−5.90 (3.50)	−11.80 (4.22)	−1.99 (0.59)	−15.58 (2.14)	−0.05 (0.02)	−0.72 (0.75)
Lag. dep. var.$_{t-1}$	0.94 (8.26)	0.98 (5.15)	0.44 (2.32)	0.98 (9.90)	2.05 (10.43)	1.46 (9.34)
Lag. dep. var.$_{t-2}$	−0.17 (1.10)	−0.54 (1.81)	0.11 (0.59)	0.96 (0.96)	−1.30 (2.85)	−0.32 (1.18)
Lag. dep. var.$_{t-3}$	0.10 (0.61)	−0.13 (0.46)	0.57 (2.82)	−0.96 (0.53)	0.13 (0.29)	−0.12 (0.43)
Lag. dep. var.$_{t-4}$	−0.09 (0.90)	0.03 (0.20)	−0.36 (1.95)	0.18 (0.17)	0.12 (0.55)	−0.02 (0.12)
i_{t-1}	0.63 (2.20)	−0.26 (0.72)	0.64 (1.89)	3.81 (1.34)	−0.71 (1.33)	−0.55 (1.77)
i_{t-2} (Long-term price	−0.20 (0.49)	1.09 (1.90)	0.11 (0.24)	−4.46 (1.04)	1.03 (1.25)	−0.13 (0.31)
i_{t-3} lending rate)	0.36 (0.90)	−0.24 (0.41)	−0.25 (0.53)	5.55 (1.28)	−0.43 (0.49)	0.54 (1.28)
i_{t-4}	−0.14 (0.48)	0.70 (1.79)	−0.02 (0.06)	−3.08 (1.06)	−0.17 (0.29)	0.11 (0.36)
$XGDP_{t-1}$	0.00 (0.10)	0.06 (0.88)	0.07 (0.41)	−0.36 (0.65)	−0.07 (0.68)	0.22 (1.70)
$XGDP_{t-2}$	−0.00 (0.10)	−0.05 (0.66)	0.03 (0.16)	0.33 (0.47)	−0.03 (0.29)	−0.12 (0.73)
$XGDP_{t-3}$	0.02 (0.27)	0.01 (0.17)	−0.15 (0.82)	−0.03 (0.04)	−0.02 (0.01)	−0.29 (1.82)
$XGDP_{t-4}$	0.04 (0.78)	−0.05 (0.76)	−0.16 (1.04)	−0.11 (0.22)	0.06 (0.70)	0.33 (0.75)

	(1)	(2)	(3)	(4)	(5)	(6)
I_{t-1}	-0.05 (0.55)	0.20 (2.05)	0.21 (0.82)			
I_{t-2}	0.19 (1.10)	-0.32 (1.91)	0.38 (1.17)			
I_{t-3}	-0.17 (0.99)	0.26 (1.60)	-0.48 (1.52)			
I_{t-4}	-0.00 (0.02)	-0.06 (0.73)	0.28 (1.31)			
INV_{t-1}	0.09 (0.32)	0.20 (0.48)	0.26 (0.59)			
INV_{t-2}	0.47 (0.98)	0.13 (0.24)	-0.41 (0.52)			
INV_{t-3}	-0.51 (1.03)	-0.08 (0.14)	1.27 (1.48)			
INV_{t-4}	0.16 (0.58)	0.55 (1.19)	-1.11 (2.02)			
Adj. R^2	0.98	0.99	0.96	0.65	0.99	0.96
SE	0.85	0.48	0.77	9.54	0.94	0.76

Notes: (absolute) *t*-statistics are in parentheses. All variables are in nominal terms and are specified in growth rates except where noted. The real estate loan variable excludes residential mortgages. *XGDP* = nominal GDP *less* expenditures on producer durables, structures, and inventories. *I* = expenditures on producer durables in equation (6.1) and expenditures on structures in equation (6.2). *YP* = personal income. *INV* = the stock of business inventories. *i* = the change in the long-term prime rate in equations (6.1), (6.2) and (6.3) and the change in the housing loan lending rate in equation (6.4). *HS* = the level of housing starts.

Source: Author's calculation.

(continued on page 268)

Table 6A.2   continued

Explanatory variables	Coefficient (absolute t-values in parentheses) Dependent variable growth rate of:					
	(6.3) Real estate loans					
Estimation period	1966:1–1993:3		1971:1–1980:4		1981:1–1993:3	
Constant	0.50	(0.21)	4.63	(1.02)	–2.31	(0.39)
Lag. dep. var.$_{t-1}$	1.64	(16.21)	1.62	(6.11)	1.65	(8.28)
Lag. dep. var.$_{t-2}$	–0.66	(3.35)	–0.43	(1.00)	–0.80	(2.22)
Lag. dep. var.$_{t-3}$	–0.08	(0.41)	–0.79	(1.83)	–0.04	(0.12)
Lag. dep. var.$_{t-4}$	0.06	(0.56)	0.72	(2.46)	0.10	(0.61)
i_{t-1}	–0.49	(0.64)	–1.85	(1.22)	–0.63	(0.84)
i_{t-2} (Long-term prime	0.44	(0.39)	3.71	(1.89)	0.51	(0.51)
i_{t-3} lending rate)	1.14	(1.00)	–2.77	(1.35)	1.26	(1.27)
i_{t-4}	–1.03	(1.37)	1.47	(0.96)	–0.97	(1.30)
$XGDP_{t-1}$	–0.06	(0.38)	–0.49	(1.60)	0.24	(0.84)
$XGDP_{t-2}$	–0.04	(0.20)	–0.33	(1.22)	0.43	(1.24)
$XGDP_{t-3}$	–0.03	(0.14)	0.19	(0.67)	–0.33	(0.93)
$XGDP_{t-4}$	0.02	(1.52)	–0.12	(0.55)	0.19	(0.56)
Housing I_{t-1}	–0.65	(3.98)	–0.85	(4.26)	–0.83	(2.27)
Housing I_{t-2}	0.11	(0.44)	0.55	(1.52)	0.76	(1.53)
Housing I_{t-3}	0.68	(2.65)	0.03	(0.08)	–0.12	(0.24)
Housing I_{t-4}	–0.66	(3.37)	–0.55	(1.65)	–0.21	(0.64)
I_{t-1}	0.52	(1.67)	0.92	(2.00)	–0.66	(1.10)
I_{t-2}	0.01	(0.03)	–1.22	(1.85)	0.66	(0.97)
I_{t-3}	–0.52	(1.08)	1.35	(2.11)	–1.52	(1.95)
I_{t-4}	0.35	(1.37)	–0.36	(1.06)	1.05	(1.91)
Adj. R^2	0.98		0.99		0.97	
SE	2.41		1.68		1.59	

Table 6A.2 continued

Explanatory variables Estimation period	Coefficient (absolute t-values in parentheses) Dependent variable growth rate of:					
	(6.4) Consumer loans					
	1974:3–1993:3		1974:3–1980:4		1981:1–1993:3	
Constant	6.07	(2.02)	15.42	(0.77)	4.95	(0.93)
Lag. dep. var.$_{t-1}$	1.38	(10.02)	1.09	(2.61)	1.32	(6.56)
Lag. dep. var.$_{t-2}$	−0.20	(0.86)	−0.23	(0.35)	−0.08	(0.24)
Lag. dep. var.$_{t-3}$	−0.05	(0.19)	0.38	(0.54)	−0.17	(0.51)
Lag. dep. var.$_{t-4}$	−0.24	(1.52)	−0.56	(1.36)	−0.16	(0.72)
i_{t-1}	−0.47	(0.65)	−1.12	(0.68)	−0.27	(0.23)
i_{t-2} (Housing loan	0.26	(0.24)	1.14	(0.51)	0.21	(0.13)
i_{t-3} lending rate)	−1.82	(1.72)	−4.13	(1.24)	−1.77	(1.17)
i_{t-4}	1.24	(1.85)	2.17	(1.25)	1.30	(1.07)
HS_{t-1}	−0.08	(3.15)	−0.09	(1.73)	−0.05	(1.13)
HS_{t-2}	0.00	(0.23)	0.04	(0.93)	−0.05	(0.94)
HS_{t-3}	0.02	(0.94)	0.05	(0.55)	0.06	(1.15)
HS_{t-4}	0.03	(1.65)	0.08	(1.63)	0.02	(0.52)
YP_{t-1}	−0.03	(0.31)	0.17	(0.34)	−0.10	(0.67)
YP_{t-2}	0.12	(1.35)	0.21	(1.18)	0.04	(0.26)
YP_{t-3}	0.05	(0.52)	0.08	(0.42)	−0.12	(0.74)
YP_{t-4}	0.20	(2.78)	0.23	(1.76)	0.18	(1.12)
Adj. R^2	0.97		0.95		0.96	
SE	0.91		1.28		1.95	

Notes

1. See the Appendix for our estimation results of some investment functions.
2. For more detailed discussion, see Bank of Japan (1992).
3. As for general discussion on the deflationary effect of weak bank lending, see Bernanke (1983).

References

Bank of Japan (1992) 'Recent Developments in Monetary Aggregates – Analysis and Evaluation', *Special Paper*, 221.

Bernanke, B.S. (1983) 'Nonmonetary Effects of the Financial Crisis in the Propagation of the Great Depression', *American Economic Review*, 73, 257–76.

Lown, C. and J. Wenninger (1994) 'The Role of the Banking System in the Credit Slowdown', in Federal Reserve Bank of New York (ed), *Studies on Causes and Consequences of the 1989–92 Credit Slowdown*, 69–112.

Comment

Alan Davies

Kaku's Chapter 6 well illustrates the problems associated with attempting to assess the importance of debt-deflation as an explanatory factor in accounting for the depth of the current slowdown in Japan compared with other factors.

Regarding the *personal sector*, Kaku finds it difficult to find evidence for debt-deflation as an explanatory factor in the behaviour of household consumption. This is not particularly surprising since the rise in indebtedness of Japanese households in the late 1980s was much more subdued than in the USA or UK. Similarly, the slowdown in personal consumption expenditures has been less exaggerated.

What is more surprising is the failure to find differences in the propensity to consume from disaggregated data; for example, between households having mortgages and those without. The Bank of England has identified such differences in the UK (King 1993; also Smith *et al.*, 1994). The failure to find any association in Japan may be due to the smaller proportion of household liabilities accounted for by mortgages (40 per cent, compared with three quarters of liabilities in the USA and two thirds in the UK), the smaller proportion of households with mortgages and lower interest rates (since interest rates in Japan never reached levels seen in the UK in the recent recession).

The evidence for the restraining influence of high debt levels is even less clear if the net position is examined. In Japan in 1991 capital gearing (financial liabilities as a percentage of net wealth including tangible assets) was lower than it was 10 years earlier, unlike in the USA or UK. It is also worth noting that income gearing is at a much lower level in Japan, rose only slightly in the early 1990s and is now barely above the levels which prevailed throughout the early and mid 1980s (OECD, 1993).

It must also be borne in mind that the Japanese household sector benefits from a much more stable environment with regard to employment than its counterparts in the USA and UK (although this is increasingly less so) and perhaps faces less severe pressures to adjust to short-term fluctuations in income.

Regarding the *corporate sector*, evidence that higher debt levels have

271

inhibited recovery is also difficult to come by. Whereas, in the 1980s US corporates took on large amounts of debt and repaid equity, Japanese companies raised both debt and equity to finance balance sheet expansion. Although Japanese companies started with much higher levels of gearing, there was no change in gearing levels unlike in the USA, suggesting that there was no change in the financing burden on corporates in relation to balance sheet size.

Furthermore, although the debt GDP ratio of the corporate sector rose sharply in the late 1980s, interest payments as a proportion of GDP were lower in 1992 than in the first half of the 1980s (but they did rise sharply in relation to cash flows or profits).

All this suggests there has been no significant increase in the debt burden on corporates which would inhibit investment compared with pressures from lack of demand, low capacity utilisation rates or low profitability, for which there is plenty of evidence.

Regarding the *banking sector*, evidence for a 'credit crunch' is similarly hard to obtain. The banks met the Basle Capital Convergence standards by raising large amounts of subordinated debt and cutting back inter-bank positions. There does not therefore appear to have been a severe capital constraint.

With the benefit of two more *TANKAN* surveys to draw from than Kaku, it is clear now that the banks' lending stance has eased, but this has not been accompanied by any acceleration in the growth of the main money supply measure M2 and CDs. It should be noted that slow growth in lending was also a feature of the recoveries in the USA and UK.

In conclusion, it is difficult to find evidence to support the proposition that high levels of debt have had a depressive influence on the Japanese economy. This is not to argue that debt-deflation has had no impact, only that it has not been a major factor on the behaviour of Japanese economic agents in the recent slowdown.

References

King, M. (1993) 'Debt Deflation: Theory and Evidence', Presidential Lecture delivered to the European Economic Association (*Husinna*) (August). OECD (1993) *Economic Outlook* (December).

Smith, J., A. Sterne, and M. Devereux (1994) 'Personal and Corporate Sector Debt', *Bank of England Quarterly Bulletin*, 34 (Man), 144–55.

Comment

John Whittaker

Kaku in Chapter 6 is concerned with two main issues. The first (which is also the subject of King's Chapter 5 in this volume) is the proposal that an important element of debt-deflation is the redistribution of wealth from debtors to creditors, and that spending reductions by those with greater debt are not fully compensated by increases in spending by others. As relevant descriptive statistics for Japan, Kaku records the marked rise in land and particularly in stock values ahead of the recession and the subsequent decline in these values, and the general rise in indebtedness, notably of the real-estate sector. Significantly, however, he notes that the net worth of the main industrial sectors (as measured by capital:asset ratios, Figure 6.6) has not fallen below the levels of the early 1980s. There has been a redistribution of debt but no net loss of wealth. Thus if these events are to be held responsible for the fall in activity, it must be assumed that reductions in spending by those with reduced worth have not been completely offset by increases in spending by those with greater worth: there must be asymmetric spending behaviour between firms that incurred greater debt and those that did not.

Similarly, for households, whilst the decline in consumption is one of the most obvious features of the recession, he remarks that 'net financial assets as a percentage of disposable income are still increasing'. This suggests that overall household debt levels are not a cause of the diminished spending. The diminished spending can only be a result of debt if there has been redistribution and if spending behaviour is dominated asymmetrically by those whose net debt increased.

This is an useful argument, but no evidence is presented to support this asymmetric behaviour in the case of firms. For households, the author notes that tests designed to identify this different behaviour by different groups of (e.g. those with mortgages vs those without) have proved inconclusive. I suggest that another possible influence which may merit investigation is the *trend* in asset values. For the same aggregate value of assets, spending behaviour of both firms and individuals is surely likely to be more aggressive when the value of their assets is rising than when it is falling.

The other feature of the Japanese recession which Kaku seeks to investigate is the extent to which bank lending behaviour was responsible (a matter also addressed in Eichengreen and Grossman's Chapter 2). Kaku suggests that, in contrast with previous Japanese recessions, erosion of banks' asset bases may have reduced their willingness to lend. Thus the fall in bank intermediation is not wholly due to a fall in demand for loans. As suggestive evidence, he notes that small and medium-sized non-manufacturers have suffered a greater loss in capital: asset ratios than other sectors, whilst it is this sector which relies most heavily on borrowing and this sector which has led the recovery from previous recessions. More formally, he argues that banks' lending margins have been unusually large, and larger than can be explained by increased credit risk alone, implying that banks are showing more prudence as a result of their own weakness. This is a plausible argument, but unfortunately his statistical evidence, relating interest margins to the bankruptcy ratio as a proxy for credit risk, is unconvincing.

As further evidence, from a number of cross-sectional regressions (Tables 6.3 and 6.4) Kaku concludes that 'the higher the capital: asset ratios of banks, the smaller the widening of their lending margins and the larger their lending growth rates'. Again, though these results are indeed what one might expect, this interpretation of his econometric results is hardly justifiable, since most of the 20 reported regressions show insignificant explanatory power and the results are not consistent across the two time periods (1992 and first half of 1993).

Finally, Kaku reports in detail (Tables 6A.1 and 6A.2) the results of estimations of equations explaining bank lending to manufacturers, non-manufacturers, real-estate companies and households. Although these studies are reported in the text as 'investment functions', his interpretation (in the Appendix) of the results seems rather to relate to this question of the degree to which banks themselves were responsible for reduced bank lending. He takes it that the regressions, which have high values of R^2, show that lending growth rates were almost fully explained by 'factors relating to borrowers', a description which presumably applies to the explanatory variables. This is then supposed to show that 'the influence of factors on the supply side [i.e. banks' supply of loans] could not be detected'.

Apart from this comment, however, Kaku offers no analysis of these regressions, and one wonders why the large array of coefficients and associated statistics has been reported. In fact, inspection of the results reveals few individually significant coefficients, and indicates that most of the explanation can be attributed to lagged changes in the dependent variable, so that it is difficult to see how even Kaku's tentative conclusion can be supported. All that can be said from this exercise is that bank lending to the various sectors is best explained by its own persistance.

In conclusion, whilst there is no doubt that the questions which Kaku raises are of interest, his formal investigations shed little light on the mechanisms of Japan's debt-deflation episode. Surely, although it is not his stated objective, if one is to explain Japan's recession, the place to start is with the dramatic rise and fall in consumer spending. As Kaku mentions but passes by, this might well be related to future income and employment expectations. Measurement of these variables is not however straightforward, and it would therefore not be easy to find convincing formal confirmation of this conjecture.

Index

Note: 'n' after a page reference indicates the number of a note on that page.